FLOWER ADORNMENT SUTRA

PURE CONDUCT
CHAPTER 11

Verse Upon Opening A Sutra

The unsurpassed, deep, profound,
Subtle and wonderful Dharma,

In hundreds of millions of kalpas
Is difficult to encounter.

I now see and hear it,
Receive it and maintain it,

And I vow to understand the Thus Come One's
True and actual meaning.

大方廣佛華嚴經華嚴海會佛菩薩

*The Avatamsaka Assembly of Buddhas
and Bodhisattvas as Vast as the Sea*

Universal Worthy

Bodhisattva Mahasattva

Mañjushri

Bodhisattva Mahasattva

The Venerable Master Hua

THE GREAT MEANS EXPANSIVE BUDDHA FLOWER ADORNMENT SUTRA

PURE CONDUCT
CHAPTER 11

COMMENTARY BY

TRIPITAKA MASTER
HSÜAN HUA

Translated into English by
Dharma Realm Buddhist University
Buddhist Text Translation Society
Talmage, California ❀ 1982

FLOWER ADORNMENT SUTRA The Pure Conduct Chapter 11

Translated from the Chinese by the Buddhist Text
Translation Society

Primary Translation: Shramanerika Heng Tsai
Reviewed by: Bhikshuni Heng Tao
Edited by: Bhikshuni Heng Ch'ih
            Upasika Kuo Tsai Rounds
Certified by: Venerable Abbot Hua and
               Bhikshuni Heng Ch'ih

First Printing: 1982

For information and booksales:

    Gold Mountain Monastery,
    1731, 15th street, San Francisco, Ca. 94103
    Tel: (415) 626-4202

    City of Ten Thousand Buddhas,
    Box 217, Talmage, Ca. 95481
    Tel: (707) 462-0939

    Gold Wheel Temple
    1728 West 6th Street,
    Los Angeles, CA 90017
    Tel: (213) 483-7497

ISBN-0-917512-37-5

Acknowledgements:

    Cover and Calligraphy: Shramanerika Heng Liang
    Chinese Calligraphy: Shramanerika Heng Duan
    Proof-reading: Shramanerika Heng Bin
                   Shramanerika Heng Chia
    Index: Bhikshuni Heng Ch'ih

Buddhist Text Translation Society
Eight Regulations

A translator must free himself or herself from the motives of personal fame and reputation.

A translator must cultivate an attitude free from arrogance and conceit.

A translator must refrain from aggrandizing himself or herself and denigrating others.

A translator must not establish himself or herself as the standard of correctness and suppress the work of others with his or her faultfinding.

A translator must take the Buddha-mind as his or her own mind.

A translator must use the wisdom of the Selective Dharma Eye to determine true principles.

A translator must request the Elder Virtuous Ones of the ten directions to certify his or her translations.

A translator must endeavor to propagate the teachings by printing sutras, shastra texts, and vinaya texts when the translations are certified as being correct.

PURE CONDUCT
CHAPTER 11

SUTRA:

SUTRA:

THE GREAT MEANS EXPANSIVE BUDDHA FLOWER ADORNMENT SUTRA, TRANSLATED BY KHOTANESE TRIPITAKA MASTER SHIKSHANANDA. PURE CONDUCT, CHAPTER ELEVEN.

COMMENTARY:

Today we begin to lecture CHAPTER ELEVEN, PURE CONDUCT. "Pure" means clean and clear, which is opposite of "defiled." What is defiled is not pure, and what is pure is not defiled. What is meant by "pure"? It means when the three karmas of body, mouth and mind are clean and clear. What is meant by "undefiled"? When you do not commit any evil deeds with your body, mouth, or mind, then your three karmas are undefiled. If your three karmas of body, mouth and mind are defiled, you are an ordinary person. Those of the Two Vehicles have already attained the state of no outflows, but are they pure? No, they are not. Although they have attained non-outflows, they don't have the virtuous conduct of benefitting others, so they cannot be said to be really clean and pure.

Pure Conduct is the conduct of Bodhisattvas--

what Bodhisattvas cultivate. Great Vehicle Bodhisattvas not only can benefit themselves, but can
also benefit others. Not only can they enlighten
themselves, they can also enlighten others; so they
are cultivating Pure Conduct. This practice-door
of Pure Conduct is what all cultivators should
reverently follow and cultivate. Enumerated in
this chapter are over one hundred vows, all cultivated for the sake of living beings. This is a
practice-door which Great Vehicle Bodhisattvas
cultivate.

　　PURE CONDUCT in Chinese is *Ching Heng* (淨行),
which can also be pronounced *Ching Hsing*, "cultivating purely", actually going ahead and doing it.
The first part of this Sutra, the Door of Belief
and Understanding was discussed. This Chapter belongs
to the section on the Door of Cultivation. If you
only believe or understand the principle, but do
not go ahead and cultivate, it is useless. The
Buddhadharma has to be practiced. One must truly
and actually do the work. By the same token, telling others to cultivate and not doing so yourself.
Every Buddhist should pay particular attention to
this point and be keenly aware that one has to cultivate oneself. You shouldn't demand that others
cultivate but get out of it yourself. If you can
actually do the work and be reliable and true in
your cultivation, then you will not employ any tricks
or put out any false advertising, but instead will
even more genuinely rely on the Dharma to cultivate.

　　If we know one fraction, we should cultivate
that fraction. If we know two, we should cultivate
two. There should be no disharmony between knowledge and practice. In the Ming Dynasty in China,
there was a gentleman called Wang Yang Ming who
promoted the principle of the harmony between
knowledge and practice. He said that the reason
one fails to practice is from not knowing, and that
if one really knew, one would not fail to cultivate.
He felt that if you really knew, you would really
practice; and if you really cultivated, you would
really know. That is the principle of "harmony
between knowledge and practice." Although this
kind of principle belongs to the Confucian School,
we needn't hesitate to adopt it as a Buddhist
doctrine.

　　If you advocate the theories of the Buddhadharma but do not put them into practice, then even if you speak so well that "the heavens rain down fragrant blossoms, and the earth wells forth golden lotuses", it will merely be like talking about food and counting the wealth of others. As it is said,

> *There are those who all day long count the*
> *   wealth of others,*
> *Without owning half a cent of it themselves.*
> *If you do not cultivate the Dharma,*
> *The result will be the same as that.*

It is like tellers in a bank, who count one-does-not-know-how-much money everyday. But all the money they count is not their own, and when they get off work they don't own even half a cent of it. They just count it for others. If you don't cultivate the Buddhadharma, the result will be exactly like that. It's the same as only talking about food but not going ahead and eating it. You say, "This rice tastes good", "That vegetable tastes delicious", or "There is a certain kind of food which can be stored for two weeks and never get rotten, which makes good soup." But if you only talk and don't really go ahead and eat it, that's useless. That is talking about food and counting the wealth of others.

VERSE UPON OPENING A SUTRA:

> THE UNSURPASSED, DEEP, PROFOUND, SUBTLE AND
>   WONDERFUL DHARMA,
> IN HUNDREDS OF MILLIONS OF KALPAS IS
>   DIFFICULT TO ENCOUNTER.
> I NOW SEE AND HEAR IT, RECEIVE AND MAINTAIN
>   IT,
> AND I VOW TO UNDERSTAND THE THUS COME ONES'
>   TRUE AND ACTUAL MEANING.

COMMENTARY:

The principles of the Buddhadharma are the most supreme and unsurpassed, and so it is said, *THE UNSURPASSED, DEEP, PROFOUND, SUBTLE AND WONDERFUL DHARMA, IN HUNDREDS OF MILLIONS OF KALPAS IS DIFFICULT TO ENCOUNTER.* Actually, it is not difficult to meet, it is difficult to practice. Meeting the Dharma is relatively easy, but cultivating the

Dharma is hard. *I NOW SEE AND HEAR IT, RECEIVE AND MAINTAIN IT.* To receive and maintain it means to truly cultivate it. *AND I VOW TO UNDERSTAND THE THUS COME ONES' TRUE AND ACTUAL MEANING.* I wish to understand the Buddhas' true and actual principles. Why do I want to understand the true and actual meaning of the Thus Come Ones? It is because I want to practice honestly and sincerely. If you truly understand, then you can honestly and sincerely go ahead and cultivate.

This *PURE CONDUCT CHAPTER* lays down the rules and regulations which left-home people should reverently follow. It is a standard and guideline that left-home people should never forget. If you reverently follow this method, you can reach the other shore and become a Buddha. Therefore, from the time of leaving home up until the time of becoming a Buddha, one should follow this method to cultivate. In a previous section the Sutra talks about Faith and Understanding. Now, this chapter talks about Cultivation. The intent of this chapter is to rely upon the Dharma to cultivate, to practice according to the methods.

"Conduct" is what you practice, and what you practice should be pure. Not just one, but all kinds of conduct should be pure. There are more than one hundred vows in this chapter. Within those hundred vows, there are twenty major divisions, beginning with the words, *HOW DOES A BODHISATTVA ATTAIN...*, and within those twenty, there are eleven minor divisions, each containing ten statements. Taken together that makes 110 vows (11 minor divisions x 10 statements = 110)--110 virtuous conducts--which fall into three categories. The first is *with the three karmas apart from error one accomplishes virtues.* The "three karmas" are those of body, mouth, and mind. In cultivating we should not look elsewhere to cultivate. We should turn the light within, illuminate ourselves, and be sure we are cultivating purity of the body, which means no killing, no stealing, and no sexual misconduct. We should also cultivate purity of the mouth, which means no loose speech, no lying, no harsh speech, and no double-tongued speech. Cultivating purity of the mind means having no greed, no hatred, and no stupidity. We people who study the Buddhadharma all acknowledge and understand this, yet we still have these faults, and for that

reason we are unable to be pure. We should attain
the purity of the three karmas, which means making
no mistakes with the body, mouth, and mind. That
is the most important thing for cultivators of the
Way.
     There are three evil deeds of the body: kill-
ing, stealing, and sexual misconduct. Why should
we avoid killing and instead liberate living beings?
It's because:

> *One of the virtues of heaven is that it spares
>   the lives of living creatures.*

We should avoid killing because we know that the
universe has the virtue of being concerned for
living beings. Moreover,

> *All living beings have the Buddha Nature.
> All can become Buddhas.*

If we kill one living creature, it is the same as
killing a Buddha. If we can think in this way,
then we will not kill. Also, we see that all
living creatures are fond of living and are afraid
of death. No matter whether the creature is big
or small, each prefers to be alive and does not
want death. Notice how even a tiny creature such
as an ant runs away hurriedly when it sees people.
It's a pity it doesn't have a rocket. If it had
one, it would take the rocket and go as far away
as the moon. Even though they don't have rockets,
they still escape and flee. We human beings get
lice on our bodies if we do not bathe often. In
China, people in the South rarely have body lice,
because they regularly bathe and wash their clothes.
But people in the North during the winter don't
bathe or wash their clothes very often, and so
there are lots of lice hidden in their clothes.
When they take the clothes off, the lice flee and
hide somewhere else. Why is that? It's because
they wish to live and are afraid of dying. So,
even such tiny creatures still prefer to be alive,
and do not want to die. We should ponder this,
and in the future avoid killing but liberate living
beings instead. In ancient times there was a
saying that goes like this:

> *From a hundred thousand years to the present, the
>   stew in the pot*

> *Has brewed resentment as deep as the four seas,*
>   *which is hard to level.*
> *If you want to know the reason for wars and*
>   *calamities in the world,*
> *Then listen to the piteous cries from the*
>   *slaughter-house at midnight.*

It says *from a hundred thousand years* to now, people
have been making pots of stew. Making stew is not
important, but what counts is that the stew in the
pot contains hatred and resentment which is as
deep as the sea. So it says it *has brewed resentment
as deep as the four seas, which is hard to level. If you
want to know the reason for wars and calamities in the
world, then listen to the piteous cries from the slaughter-
house at midnight.* In the slaughter-house, if it
isn't the squealing of pigs, then it's the bleating
of sheep, or the wailing of cows. We can see from
this that those kinds of resentment tie tighter
and tighter knots that bind us up in wars and
calamities in the world. This principle is very
simple, but precisely because it is so simple,
people do not pay attention to it. Because of that
neglect, a lot of calamities of war are created.
This is the problem with killing, so every one of
us should observe the prohibition against taking
life.

Stealing is defined as taking something without others' permission. The Ancients, who were
honest and pure, did not casually give away a
blade of grass to others, nor did they casually
take a blade of grass from others. They practiced
pure conduct. Honest and pure people are like
this: they do not casually ask for things from
other people, nor do they casually give gifts to
others or casually receive others' gifts. That is
the kind of behavior very lofty, pure people should
have. Even if you don't consider yourself to be
lofty and pure, you should still be careful. If
you take something away without telling other
people, you are breaking the precept against
stealing. If you take something without permission
and give it to someone else, you're also breaking
this precept.

In the <u>Analects</u>, Confucious said, "Who said
Wei Sheng Kau was a straight and upright person?
He was not. Why do I say that about him?" Confucius

told his disciples:"Do you know? Once a person
asked Wei Sheng Kau for a little vinegar. At that
time Wei Sheng Kau didn't have any vinegar, but he
wanted to toady up to this person, so he went to
the neighbor's to borrow the vinegar, and then lent
it to this person. This is not a straight mind,
this is a crooked mind," Confucius concluded. So,
although people said Wei Sheng Kau was a straight
and upright person, Confucius criticized him and
said he was not. If you have something, you can
lend it to others, but if you don't, just don't
lend it. Straight people will not steal. Even
though his crookedness wasn't actually a case of
stealing, it was close to it. Stealing even occurs
in one's mind. If you are greedy for others'
things, you are also not in accord with the precept.

The precept against sexual misconduct is even
more difficult to keep. From beginningless kalpas
until now, people have been born from defiled
dharmas. Therefore, it is very difficult to purify
the mind of sexual desire. The most essential
aspect of *pure conduct* is to purify sexual desire.
The <u>Shurangama Sutra</u> makes this clear: *If the
thoughts of sexual desire aren't gotten rid of, one cannot
leave the dust.* If the mind of sexual desire isn't cut
off, and you want to cultivate, it is like *trying
to obtain rice from cooking sand.* It is totally impossible! One should be aware of thoughts of sexual
desire and try to cleanse one's mind. Cultivators
should have a pure mind and few desires; they should
cut off desire and emotional love. If one is that
way, then one can be said to be pure. If you are
not that way, you cannot yet be called *pure*. Therefore, *pure conduct* means one really should be clean
and clear.

The main principle in the chapter of *Pure
Conduct* is this: if one is free from errors with respect to one's three karmas, and increasingly practices the Bodhisattva conduct of great compassion,
one's pure conduct will be enhanced by wisdom.

Previously, we talked about the three evil
deeds of the body: killing, stealing, and sexual
misconduct. The mind also has three evil deeds:
greed , hatred, and stupidity.

Greed. Greed is insatiable; one never tires
even when one is full. No matter how much
one gets, one does not feel content. That's the
meaning of being insatiable. A greedy person is

discontented. Being discontented, your mind is
always distressed. If you're content, you're
happy all the time. Greed for fame is coveting,
greed for authority is coveting, greed for leadership is also coveting. But it should be said that
if you are greedy for benefit for all people
and not for the sake of yourself, then you're not
really being greedy.

Hatred. If you can't obtain what you're
greedy for, then you'll bring forth the mind of
hatred. It is said, "When one thought of hatred
arises, eighty thousand doors leading to obstructions open." It is because one has heavy karmic
obstacles. Therefore one has a big temper and one's
fire of ignorance is also huge. If one's karmic
obstacles were lighter, one would not have such a
big temper.

Stupidity. Stupidity is the foolish mind and
false thinking which just means: whatever one is
not supposed to think about, one wants to think
about; whatever one is not supposed to obtain, one
wants to obtain; whatever one is not supposed to
accomplish, one wants to accomplish; and whatever
one's not supposed to do, one wants to do. I often
tell people: Those who are fond of "wine, form,
wealth, and anger" think in such a way:

*If only the fine flowers would bloom every day,
And why shouldn't the bright moon be full every night?
If only the streams on earth could turn to wine,
And trees in the forest would all grow money!*

Stupid people who are fond of beautiful flowers
will have this kind of false thought, "If only my
flowers could bloom and be beautiful every day,
that would be wonderful. I wish they would never
fade or fall." They long for the impossible.

Stupid people who are fond of the full moon
will think in this way, "If only the moon could be
full every night, then I could enjoy the moonlight
every night, and that would be really wonderful.
Why shouldn't the bright moon be full every night?"
They will think, "The sun is round every day, so
why shouldn't the moon be round every night?"

Stupid people who like to drink wine will
think in this way, "If only the streams on earth
could turn to wine. If all the pools of water on
earth were transformed into fountains of wine, then I

wouldn't have to pay money or go to a bar. I
could just go over to the pool to take a drink."

     Those infatuated with the pursuit of wealth
will have a false thought like this, "*If only the
trees in the forest would all grow money,* then when I
wanted to use money, I would just have to go and
shake the trees, and obtain a lot of money. Wouldn't
that be wonderful?"

     Actually this is stupidity. Also, I can bring
up other examples to illustrate the meaning of
stupidity. For example, one may not be studying
and yet expect to get a Ph.D. from the best university. This person basically didn't even go through
elementary school or learn how to read, but he
expects to get a Ph.D. Isn't that stupid? It is
impossible to get a Ph.D. just by hoping for one.
There's also the case of one who didn't plant the
field, but at the time of harvest when he saw other
people harvesting grain, he also wanted a harvest.
One is supposed to plant in the spring and harvest
in the autumn. If you don't plant during spring,
how can you harvest in the autumn? This is also
an example of sheer stupidity. There is also the
case of one who didn't buy a lottery ticket but
expected to win at the sweepstakes. These are all
examples of stupid thoughts. Stupid thoughts are
easy to talk about, but not easy to get rid of.
Therefore, left-home people should

> *Vigorously cultivate precepts, samadhi and wisdom,*
> *And extinguish greed, hatred, and stupidity.*

     We've discussed the three evil deeds of the
mind: greed, hatred, and stupidity. The evil deeds
of the mouth are those which people err with most.
It is said, "Diseases enter through the mouth, and
calamities come out of the mouth." If you say a
wrong word, you may reap some kind of calamity in
return. If you eat the wrong food, you may get
sick. "Harsh speech", which means scolding people,
is one of the evils of the mouth. People who create
this karma will scold everyone they come in contact
with. I've met a lot of people like this who only
know how to scold others. They even scold others
in the essays they write. They write articles in
order to berate others and to battle with their
pens. This is just another kind of harsh or abusive

speech. They also revile or libel others in conversation. That is also harsh speech. "Double tongue" means to make trouble among people, to gossip. Such a person talks to A about B's fault, and talks to B about A's. He goes back and forth to make mischief and gossip between the two parties. This is called double tongue. "Frivolous speech" means discussing deviant knowledge and deviant views. It is very defiled speech, which causes people to have improper thoughts. "False speech" means to talk falsely; no matter what one says one has to lie. It's almost as if one couldn't live if one did not engage in false speech.

The mouth has four evil deeds, the body has three evil deeds, and the mind has three evil deeds. Together they are referred to as the three karmas of body, mouth, and mind. These three karmas should be pure. If these three karmas are not pure, then one can't cultivate. You have to purify these three karmas in order to cultivate. Therefore, in morning and evening recitation, we recite a four-line verse:

Of all evil deeds which I have committed in the past,
Based on beginningless greed, anger, and stupidity,
And created by body, speech, and mind,
I now completely repent and reform.

The evil deeds we have committed in the past are created from greedy thoughts, hateful thoughts, and stupid thoughts, which extend through limitless kalpas. If there's no longer any greed, hatred, or stupidity, the three karmas will not be defiled. If is only because of greed, hatred, and stupidity that the three karmas are defiled. *I now completely repent and reform* of these. If you can repent and reform, then you can be pure. If you cannot repent and reform, then you can't be pure. If the three karmas aren't pure, you cannot be said to have *Pure Conduct*. *Pure Conduct* means to get rid of all falseness and all bad habits. Bad habits are what we've accumulated for unlimited lives through unlimited kalpas. One such habit is to laugh at others. Why do you want to laugh at others? Why do you want to ridicule or mock them when they make mistakes? Why do you tease others? This is due to bad habits accumulated from the

past. By analogy, as though you've always liked
to wash other people's clothes, or preferred to
take others' pictures. But what about your own
picture? You can't take your own picture, which
means you can't return the light and illuminate
within. You can't recognize yourself. Not being
able to recognize yourself, you've forgotten yourself. Because you've forgotten yourself, your Way-
karma cannot be accomplished.

When we listen to and study the Buddhadharma,
we have to practice it ourselves and apply all our
effort to it. If you don't practice wholeheartedly,
no matter how many years you study the Buddha-
dharma--even to the end of future
time-- it'll be useless. Meanwhile, you just obtain worldly
wisdom along the way. With
worldly wisdom, you say that
you know something when a
question is asked. But you
only understand it, you
can't really do it. Being
unable to do it is being
like the stone-person who
can only talk, but cannot
practice! If all Buddhists
can put their emphasis on
practice--actual cultivation--
they'll be models for
other people. This way
there'll be hope for
the future of Buddhism.
We should each truly
be a disciple of the
Buddha and give every-
thing we've got to
Buddhism. You should
think, "I am a Buddhist
disciple. If Buddhism
doesn't prosper it's
because I have not fulfilled
my responsibilities." Everybody
has to carry the responsibility of practicing
and propagating Buddhism. Then Buddhism will be
brought to light and long flourish in the world.

In this so-called Dharma ending age, in
general people say, "it's not necessary to culti-

vate or to keep the precepts. This is actually spoken by the demon kings. The more it is the Dharma ending age, the more we have to cultivate, the more we have to keep the precepts and the more we have to strive to be true disciples of Shakyamuni Buddha! We should be true cultivators and disciples who "respectfully offer up our conduct in accord with the teaching." If both left-home and laypeople can be this way, if every Buddhist can carry this responsibility, then the Orthodox Dharma age will reappear in this world. If the Orthodox Dharma appears in the world, then sages who certify to the fruition will also appear in the world. If the sages who certify to the fruition appear in this world, then the suffering of living beings will be eliminated and the blessings of living beings will be increased. Therefore, we Buddhists should not say that since it is the Dharma ending age we are not going to pay attention to the Dharma. Ultimately who caused the Dharma ending age? It's people. People created the Dharma ending age. It didn't start out as the Dharma ending age. Therefore, we should make a vow to protect and uphold the Orthodox Dharma, so that the Proper Dharma will stay permanently in this world.

Everybody should think, "I am a human being, I am a Buddhist. I should protect the Proper Dharma." If you are a Buddhist, and yet you continuously say that Buddhism is on the decline, what good are you doing? If Buddhism were to disappear, is that something you would be proud of? If Buddhism is not flourishing, we should feel ashamed. As long as we live we should truly protect and uphold the Buddhadharma, and cause the Proper Dharma to dwell permanently in this world. **Every** one of us should consider this our own responsibility.

The intent of the *Pure Conduct Chapter* is to completely set forth the virtuous conduct of Universal Worthy Bodhisattva. The aim is to describe this truly virtuous conduct. All the vows talked about in the *Pure Conduct Chapter* are ones which every Buddhist should accord with and cultivate by. Everybody who can follow this method to cultivate can quickly become a Buddha.

Those of you present in this Sutra assembly represent the renewal of Buddhism. Despite your busy schedules, you have come to listen to the lecture. This makes me feel apologetic because I cannot offer you the best of the Dharma. What I can offer is the power of my vows. What are my vows?

First, I wish the patrons Layman Ch'ou and his wife will have all their hopes fulfilled. They are protecting the Dharma and helping living beings realize the karma of the Way and for this they deserve to be praised.

Secondly, I wish that everyone in this entire assembly will open wisdom, increase his or her good roots, and quickly accomplish the Buddha Way!

I lecture the Sutra in a very ordinary way. There is nothing magical or magnificent about it. I just lecture honestly and so all of you should listen honestly. Open your heart. If you can do this, there will be no more views of prejudice. Consequently, you can comprehend more about the Buddhadharma. In America at Gold Mountain Monastery I lecture every evening and twice on Saturdays and Sundays. Why do I lecture every night? It is because I eat everyday and wear clothes everyday, and as long as I do those things everyday, I will also lecture the Sutras everyday. When I lecture Sutras I do not ask for any recompense. Therefore, even though I lecture everyday in America, nobody makes any offerings--not a single one. The same applies to my lecture-tours. I always say that as long as I have one single breath left, I will explain the Dharma for the sake of living beings. It makes no difference if my lectures are good or bad. Even if nobody comes to listen, I will still speak! If no people come to listen, I can lecture for the tables and chairs! I don't care whether anybody listens or not. So, I don't want anyone of you to say, "Let's give this Dharma Master a little face by going to protect and uphold the Way-place tomorrow." If you don't want to listen, you can leave. It's up to you. The principles I explain are very ordinary. This has been my style all along.

In America, I pay no attention to how many people attend when I lecture the Sutras. When there are many people, I still lecture; when there are few people, I also lecture. Actually, a lot of Westerners come to listen. Even though they don't understand Chinese, they still come to listen.

CHAPTER ELEVEN: PURE CONDUCT

PURE CONDUCT. "Conduct" refers to one's actions. "Pure" is clean and clear. In order to obtain the sagely fruition, what you do should be pure. If what you do is not pure, you will certainly not obtain the sagely fruition. This is Chapter Eleven of the *Flower Adornment Sutra*.

SUTRA:

AT THAT TIME, FOREMOST WISDOM BODHISATTVA INQUIRED OF MANJUSHRI BODHISATTVA SAYING......

COMMENTARY:

AT THAT TIME. This is the time when the Pure Conduct Chapter is about to be explained. At this time, among the multitudes in the assembly, there is a Bodhisattva called *FOREMOST WISDOM BODHISATTVA.* He is a great Bodhisattva among Bodhisattvas, who has outstanding virtuous conduct. Therefore, it is he who directs his inquiries at Manjushri Bodhisattva. Is it because he does not understand that he asks? No, this is a situation in which great lords of the Dharma body manifest bodies to speak the Dharma. They exchange questions and answers so that living beings might be helped to understand and to respectfully offer their conduct.

This paragraph starts to explain the actual Sutra text. The Bodhisattva asks the meaning of twenty attainments. The Bodhisattva is asking what kind of causes must be planted in order to obtain certain fruitions. For instance, how does one obtain the fruition of the Bodhisattva? How does one obtain the fruition of the Ten Dwellings? Therefore, what transpires is an exchange of questions and answers which illustrates clearly the principle of cause and effect.

These twenty questions have eleven subdivisions, each of which contains ten statements. These ten statements also elucidate the principle of "layer upon layer without end." The doctrines of the Flower Adornment Sutra form endless layer upon layer and are boundless and limitless. The doctrines are inexhaustible and ineffable. Therefore the Sutra uses ten statements to represent the principles. So within each minor division there are ten statements. Taken together that makes 110 vows, 110 virtuous conducts.

The first division of this chapter talks about how the three karmas should be pure. If the three karmas are apart from violations, then there will be no evil karma created. Being without any evil karma, one can accomplish the cultivation of virtue. Therefore, the first division is titled "With the three karmas apart from error one accomplishes virtue." (三業離過成德)

The second division is titled "One who is a worthy vessel can speak the Dharma." (得堪傳法器)

The third division is titled "One accomplishes a multitude of wisdom." (成就眾慧)

The forth division is titled "One is endowed with the causes and conditions for the way." (具道因緣) This concerns the requirements of the conditions for cultivation.

The fifth division is titled "One has wholesome expertise with the Dharma." (於法善巧)

The sixth division is titled "One cultivates the cause of Nirvana." (修涅槃因) When you cultivate the causes, you have to cultivate the cause of Nirvana. *Nirvana* is Sanskrit, and means "not produced and not destroyed."

The seventh division is titled "One fulfills the conduct of a Bodhisattva." (滿菩薩行) You have to accomplish the path that Bodhisattvas cultivate. What do Bodhisattvas cultivate? They cultivate the Six Perfections and the ten thousand conducts. All of you who often listen to the Sutras know perfectly well what the Six Perfections are. You know what they are, but the question is, have you put them into practice? Now I will discuss the Six Perfections. Those who have heard the explanation before can listen again. Those who haven't heard this before, should listen carefully.

The Six Perfections:

1. Giving. Giving is a method to cure stinginess and greed. Greedy people are those who are stingy and who will not give to others. They expect others to give to them. Not only are they stingy, they're also mean and miserly. People who are not greedy will give. Therefore, giving cures stinginess. If you can give, you will obtain. If you can't give, you will not obtain. The Earth Store Sutra says, "Giving but one fraction, one will obtain a myriad portions of reward." If you can give away a penny, you can obtain a many-fold reward. But actually, when you're practicing giving, you should not be expecting to obtain a many-fold reward. You should not think, "I'm giving away a penny now and in the future I'll obtain such-and-such an advantage." If you expect to obtain a reward, then you are still being greedy. If you think, "If I give now, I will reap wonderful rewards in the future."--really, I'm not slandering you, but you'd do better compounding interest on a loan. If you give with that attitude, it's no better than being a loan-holder. So, how should we practice giving? You should think, "It's my duty to give. I'm not supposed to expect any reward from it. Giving is my responsibility. I should not think about what I'll get in return. My duty is to give. I absolutely must not have any seeking within my giving." Just this is *Pure Conduct*. If all of you who are listening to the Sutra can understand this principle, then the value you have obtained is already very inconceivable.

I often say that a left-home person such as myself should not bow to Wei T'ou Bodhisattva. All of you probably think I'm crazy. "Won't you bow to Wei T'ou Bodhisattva?" You no doubt wonder. "He is a Dharma protector. If you don't bow to him, what will happen if he doesn't protect you?" That is the very reason I am so poor! It's because I don't wish him to protect my Dharma--I wish him to protect other people's Dharma. Why? If I'm a true cultivator, he will protect me even if I don't want him to. That's his job. But if I don't cultivate and only bow to Wei T'ou Bodhisattva and expect him to protect my Dharma, and if he comes

to   protect my Dharma just because I bowed to him,
then I say he is not qualified to be Wei T'ou
Bodhisattva. Why? Because he is greedy and takes
bribes. He is selling the Dharma. If someone bows
to him a few times, he'll protect that person; if
someone doesn't bow to him, he won't carry out his
job of protection. Isn't that just taking bribes?
What do you think? Therefore, if I'm a cultivator,
then even if I don't bow to him, he'll still have
to protect my Dharma. But if I don't cultivate,
then even if I bowed to him, he still should not
protect my Dharma. This is the way I think. All
of you who study the Buddhadharma should genuinely
understand its true meaning. Don't be muddled all
day long, bowing confusedly to the Buddhas. Even
the Bodhisattvas will have a good laugh. Why?
They'll think, "You're really confused. You
say you don't have a greedy mind, but you bow to
me all day just wishing to get some wealth,to get
promoted, and to have everything be successful, to
be calm and peaceful. If your mind were already
calm and peaceful, why would you have to ask me?
If your mind did not have greed, hatred, and
stupidity, then everything would naturally be
successful. Why do you have to bow to me? This
is really pitiful!" Actually, the Bodhisattvas
are all absorbed in Samadhi, but once they see you
bow and hear you beseeching them, they'll break out
laughing.
        Well, what is the proper attitude? When we
bow to the Buddha, we should not seek anything.
Is it the case that some people bow to the Buddha
when they want something and don't bow to the
Buddha when they don't want anything? If so, this
kind of thinking about the Buddhadharma should be
changed. All of you should use your wisdom to
consider the principle I've just talked about. If
you don't agree, you can object and we'll discuss
it together. I certainly will accept it if any
one of you comes up to me and says, "What you've
just said is wrong. It should not be that way."
If your opinion is superior or more accurate than
mine, I certainly will accept your way of thinking.
Therefore, with regard to giving, one should not
have the mind of seeking any reward. The ancients
had a matched couplet that sums it up very wonderfully:

> *Although one has not achieved fame through one's studies,*
> *Ultimately one's character is lofty and one's personality is refined.*

The ancients also said:

> *For ten years one studies under the window,*
> *And no one comes to visit.*
> *But upon accomplishment,*
> *One is renowned throughout the nation.*

You may not be renowned, but nonetheless learned. Because you are well-read, your character is lofty and your personality is refined.

Therefore, in doing wholesome deeds, do not expect a reward. Actually, if you don't wait for a good reward and do not care whether you get a good return, then naturally you will have no nightmares and your spirit will be clear. That is because after you've done good deeds, your mind will naturally be kind and compassionate and without any violence. Being without any violence, you'll not have bad dreams--like dreams of someone holding a gun and shooting at you. If you don't use a gun to kill others, other people will not kill you. In that case, your mind is very peaceful. So you will "have no nightmares and your spirit will be clear." "Clear" means understanding. When you sleep, you will naturally have good and peaceful dreams, and your spirit will be very happy. Being happy, you'll be very clear, and your brains will not be muddled. Therefore, we should consider giving to be our responsibility. You can think about what I've just said. I've just brought up a theory, but not one which says you will reap measureless merit and virtue when you practice giving. Measureless can also mean "nothing". So,

don't listen to that. If you listen to that, I'm
most certain you will not understand the Buddhadharma. You shouldn't think this person is a
Great Knowing Advisor who's done a lot of good
deeds. What's meant by "a lot" anyway? How many
pounds of it? Can you weigh it? No! So why
bother with such things? If one does good deeds,
does he obtain any merit and virtue? Yes, he does
obtain merit and virtue, but he shouldn't have
that expectation in mind. So it is said,

> *If you are mindful of doing good,*
> *Then the good that follows is not little.*
> *If you have no intention to do evil,*
> *Then the evil that follows will not be significant.*

Also,

> *Good that you want others to know about is not true*
> *   good;*
> *Evil that you're afraid others will discover is great*
> *   evil.*

You should understand these two sayings. If you
can fathom these two sayings, then you've not
listened to the Sutra in vain. Someone says, "We
already understand these principles, Dharma Master,
you don't have to repeat them. We don't want to
listen." It's because you don't want to listen
that I am speaking to you! If you want to listen,
then I won't speak. That's strange--this Dharma
Master always likes to say things that people don't
want to hear. Just a few minutes ago, my disciples
were complaining that I always pick on their
faults. Some people can't endure it and have to
run away. If you want to run away, go ahead. If
you run away, I won't keep you. Even if you stay
here, I won't force you to stay. This is the way
I do things.
     There are three kinds of Giving:

     a. Giving of wealth.

     b. Giving of Dharma.

     c. Giving of fearlessness.

a. <u>Giving of wealth</u>. It's not that you donate several billion dollars to build a temple and call that merit and virtue. Look at the giving the Buddhas and Bodhisattvas cultivate. They are able to practice what is difficult to practice; they're able to give what is difficult to give. That's real giving!

Wealth includes outer wealth and inner wealth. Outer wealth refers to household, country, city, wife, and children. One is able to give all these away. Is there anybody who's willing to give away his own household? And if there is, can he do it without retaining the mark of giving? If you can do it as if you hadn't done it, then that is real giving. So it is said,

> *Do what is difficult to do,*
> *Give what is difficult to give.*

This person can even give away his kingdom; he doesn't want it any more. But who can be this way? Shakyamuni Buddha gave away his throne and country. He didn't want the throne of the country and he went to the Ice Mountain for six years, eating only one sesame seed and one grain of wheat everyday. He starved to the point that he was all skin-and-bones. In this way he gave away his own country. He also didn't want his wife. He gave away his wife and did not bother with her. He let her do what she wanted to do. He also gave away his son, Rahula. You see, a person with behavior such as this is called a Great Man, a Great hero, a super-man! So it is said,

> *One is far above the average,*
> *One is outstanding among one's peers.*

In this way, he accomplished his Way-karma and established the greatness of Buddhism. This is giving of outer wealth.

As for inner wealth--one can give away one's body, mind, life, and nature; and one's head, eyes, brains, and marrow. In cultivating the Bodhisattva Way, one sees through all things as empty and false. "If anyone needs my head, I'll cut it off and give it to him!" What do you think--is this difficult or not? He can cut off his head if someone needs it.

Therefore, this kind of Bodhisattva path is not
easy to cultivate. For instance, Shariputra heard
the Buddha extol the cultivation of the Bodhisattva
Way, and he decided to practice the Bodhisattva Way.
He wanted to go from the Small toward the Great.

He went out on the road,
intending to practice the
Bodhisattva Way. He found
a person who was crying
by the roadside and
Shariputra brought forth
his Bodhisattva-mind and
reflected, "This crying
person must be suffering,
I should help him. No
matter what kind of difficulty he has, I will help
him to solve it."

And so in a very
friendly, kind, and com-
passionate manner he asked
this person, "Are you
having a difficult problem?
Can you tell me? I'd like
to help you. No matter
what kind of problem you've got, I will help you.
Don't cry any more!"

This person opened his eyes, looked at
him, and said, "You really want to help me?"

Shariputra said, "I want to cultivate the
Bodhisattva Way. I certainly want to help you out.
Just tell me your difficulty. No need to be polite.
You can speak frankly!"

This person said, "Why am I crying? Because
my mother is sick and she went to see the doctor.
The doctor said this illness requires a certain
kind of medicine. I couldn't find this kind of
medicine in any drug store, and so my mother's
illness will probably not be cured."

After hearing this Shariputra asked, "What
kind of medicine do you want to buy? You
can tell me, and I'll help you find this medicine."

This person answered, "The medicine I need
is the eye of a human being. The doctor said if
I could find the eye of a human being, then it
would cure my mother's sickness. But I went to
all the drugstores asking for a person's eye and
none of them sell such a thing."

This was in ancient times and not like our modern age. In this day and age we have the Eye Banks which can store eyes for transplants and operations, but at that time science was not as finely developed, and they could not make transplants of human eyes.

Shariputra said, "This is not a big problem, if you want to use an eye, I can give you one of my eyes. You can take it home to cure your mother's sickness."

The person said, "Okay, you really can give up an eye? You are not lying?"

Shariputra answered, "Ha! I'm not lying." And thereupon he used his hand to gouge out his pupil. After gouging out his eye, he endured the pain and handed the pupil to the crying person.

This person took a look at it and said, "You made a mistake!"

Shariputra said, "What mistake?"

The person said, "What my mother needs is the left eye, but you gave me a right eye--that's wrong! Your right eye can't cure my mother's sickness." After saying that, he threw the pupil on the ground and smashed it.

Shariputra saw the pupil get smashed, thought the Bodhisattva Way was indeed difficult to cultivate, and retreated. Shariputra didn't pass the test that time. I always say this,

> Everything is a test,
> To see what you'll do.
> If you don't recognize the state,
> You'll have to start anew.

Shariputra gave away his right eye, but what the person needed was a left eye, and Shariputra couldn't bear to give that one away too. Because he couldn't give it away, he retreated and thought, "The Bodhisattva Way is too difficult to practice; I'd better just be a Bhikshu." Therefore, he retreated from the position of a Bodhisattva back to that of a Bhikshu. You see, someone with wisdom as great as Shariputra's tried to cultivate the Bodhisattva Way but still could not "give what is difficult to give." How much the less we ordinary people! We don't have to talk about giving away our entire heads, we can't even give away one eye!

Therefore, "Acting as if not acting" is difficult
to do. And inner giving is more difficult to do
than outer giving.

Inner giving includes giving away one's head,
eyes, brains, marrow, even one's entire body. All
of you think about it, can you reach this level of
the Bodhisattva Way? Even if you can't reach it,
you should not be too self-confident and say, "I'm
such a great cultivator; I've already brought forth
the Bodhi mind." Your Bodhi mind must go through
tests, then it will count.

On this trip I went to Vietnam and there was
a refuge disciple of Dharma Master Ch'au. He was
clever at speech and debating. He said, "We laypeople don't commit killing, stealing, sexual misconduct, lying, and the taking of intoxicants, and
this is exactly like having taken the precepts.
So why should we have to take the precepts?" He
always debated with his teacher about this and his
teacher had nothing to say. This time, he also
brought up this topic before me. He said, "We
laypeople do not have to take any precepts. As
long as we don't commit any killing, stealing,
sexual misconduct, lying, and taking of intoxicants--
just this is like taking the five precepts. Then
why should we have to take the precepts?"

I said to him, "What you said is very logical,
as if for instance, studying at home is just the
same as studying at school. But if you study at
school, you will get a diploma; if you study at
home, is there anybody who can give you a diploma?"
He heard what I said and thought it was very
reasonable, and decided that it would be better to
take the five precepts after all. Therefore everything has to be put through a test and proven. I
said to him, "Since you've understood, it's the
same as if I hadn't even spoken."

Some people may think, "We laypeople have
more cultivation than some left-home people. We
don't need to bow to a teacher or take any precepts.
We're all right the way we are. We are Great
Knowing Advisors ourselves. We have more cultivation than some left-home people." Why do you
want to think like that? Why don't you think,
"I'm very ashamed of myself because I'm so slow in
understanding the Buddhadharma, and the cultivation
of my merit and virtue is far behind other people's."

Why don't you think like that instead? Why do you
always think that you are superior to everybody?
Such is the habit of human beings! Originally you
are not as good as other people, but you always
think you're better than others. In any kind of
career and profession there's always this kind of
trouble--somebody always thinks himself better than
others. Once you have this arrogant thought or
attitude, it will not be easy to develop the Bodhi
mind. You shouldn't be arrogant and think, "I'm
the only Honored One!" Don't think, "In the heaven
above, in all that is below, I'm the only Honored
One." Only Shakyamuni Buddha can say that. We
are but the Buddha's disciples and we shouldn't be
that proud. We shouldn't feel we are higher than
everybody. Actually, what's the use of being
higher than everybody? It's better to be equal
with other people. That will not cause people to
be annoyed. If you're higher than others--for
example, the average height is five feet, but your
height is ten feet, then when people see you they
will think you're a weird creature! They'll most
certainly want to put you on display, but this is
pretty futile.

Cultivators have to smash Sumeru Mountain.
What is Sumeru Mountain? It's our arrogance which
makes us think we're better than anyone else, and
that no one is as good as ourselves. With that
one thought of arrogance, your Way-karma will be
obstructed.

b. <u>Giving of Dharma</u>. Giving of Dharma is to
speak the Dharma for others and giving to them in
accord with Dharma. As it is said,

> Among all kinds of offerings,
> The offering of Dharma is the most supreme.

This is because if as a result of your speaking
Dharma someone can understand the Buddhadharma,
cultivate according to the Dharma, and become a
Buddha in the future, then you have helped that
person become a Buddha. If you help others become
Buddhas, other people also will help you become a
Buddha. This is what is meant by *"helping oneself
and helping others,"* a very important concept.

On the other hand, we shouldn't think, "Oh, I've helped people and in the future if they become Buddhas, I also will become a Buddha." If you make a vow to help all other beings become Buddhas, except yourself, then that is truly practicing the Bodhisattva Way.

I like to help other people to become Buddhas. If anyone of you want to become a Buddha, I'll help you. Let me tell you about my crazy style in America. What crazy style? I tell everybody that I am an engineer. What kind of engineer? An engineer that makes living Buddhas, living Bodhisattvas, and living Patriarchs. Whoever wishes to be a living Buddha can come to Gold Mountain Monastery. Gold Mountain Monastery is not mine, however I'm stationed there temporarily as an engineer. Anyone who wants to be a living Bodhisattva can come, anyone who wants to be a living Patriarch can also come, because I "don't reject those who come and I do not chase after those who leave." If you wish to be the raw material for a Patriarch, I'll make you a Patriarch. If you want to be the raw material for a Bodhisattva, I'll make you a Bodhisattva. If you want to be the raw material for a Buddha, I'll make you a Buddha. The Buddhas I make are not of wood, iron, gold, or silver; I make living Buddhas which have blood and flesh. For this reason I don't suggest building temples; instead I suggest building Buddhas. How does one build? By not being afraid of suffering, not being afraid of difficulty, and not being afraid of having no money. Truly cultivate with your feet firmly planted on the ground. No matter how much suffering, you still have to endure it; no matter how difficult, you still have to bear it. Many young Americans, most of them under thirty, all want to try it out to see what's happening! Because of this, there are a score of Westerners who have left home.

In the past, although there were Westerners who left the home life, their number was very few. At this point, Westerners have a bit more understanding of Buddhism. In the past, even if they wanted to study Buddhism, Sutras were not available. Now, people can study and investigate together. There are about forty to fifty Bhikshus, Bhikshunis, Upasakas, and Upasikas who are involved in translating the Sutras. This is a kind of giving

of Dharma. It is also the turning of the Proper
Dharma Wheel in the West. We want the Orthodox
Dharma to prevail. We don't want the Dharma ending
age to happen. We want to cultivate the Way and
certify to the fruition. In the future there will
be sages who have certified to the fruition. All
of this is a part of the giving of Dharma.

   c. <u>Giving of Fearlessness</u>. Sometimes something terrifying happens to people. Some kind of
horror presents itself and scares them out of their
wits. They are as if tottering on the edge of a
deep river or treading on thin ice--they are distraught and uneasy. The two Chinese characters
for distraught (志, 忑) have the character 'heart'--
one on top, and one on the bottom. This means the
heart is palpitating--the mind is jumping up and
down, without any peace. This describes the state
of being scared. Therefore, in the <u>Four Classics</u>
of the Confucian School, it is said,

> *Once there is terror,*
> *One cannot attain the proper.*

Once you are terrified, proper mindfulness will
not prevail. If proper mindfulness cannot prevail,
you will unwittingly take a side track or wrong
road. At such a time, you need a Good Knowing
Advisor to comfort you, to help you out. The Good
Knowing Advisor will tell you, "Don't be scared.
Just sincerely be mindful of Kuan Yin Bodhisattva.
Recite 'Namo Kuan Shih Yin Bodhisattva' and he
will help you out. Kuan Yin Bodhisattva is one
who bestows fearlessness. He helps dispel people's
terror. Just be earnest and mindful in reciting
Kuan Yin Bodhisattva, and everything will be Okay."
Or he will tell you, "Don't be scared, the world
has truth and principle, it will not trouble you.
Don't be terrified anymore. Just calm down. Then
everything will be fine!" After you hear him say
this, you won't feel scared anymore. So this is
called the giving of fearlessness. The perfection
of Giving transforms stinginess.

   2. Morality. The second perfection is holding
the precepts. Some say, "Why do we have to keep precepts? Isn't this ridiculous? In Buddhism one talks
about keeping precepts, such as the five precepts, the

eight precepts, the ten Shramanera precepts, the
ten major and forty-eight minor Bodhisattva precepts,
the 250 precepts of a Bhikshu, and 348 precepts of
a Bhikshuni--that's too much bother and has no
meaning at all." This is the criticism that comes
from those who don't understand the Buddhadharma.

What is morality? Morality is to "stop evil
and prevent transgressions." To stop evil is to
end all of your bad deeds; to prevent transgressions is to be cautious about your faults. If your
evil doesn't stop, then the good will not develop;
if good can't develop, you will not bring forth
the Bodhi mind; if you don't bring forth the Bodhi
mind, you will not reap the fruit of Bodhi. These
are very important connections. Therefore, you
have to "stop evil and prevent transgressions."
This also means to "do no evil, and practice all
good deeds."

To "do no evil" is just to "practice all good
deeds", and to "practice all good deeds" is just
to "do no evil." So it is said,

Affliction is Bodhi.

If you turn over affliction, just that is Bodhi!
To "do no evil" is the same idea as *Affliction is
Bodhi.* If you know how to use it, then it's Bodhi;
if you don't know how to use it, then it's affliction. You shouldn't seek Bodhi outside of affliction. Just turn over the affliction, and right
there is Bodhi. So all of you should not pile a
head upon a head and say, "I want to cut off my
afflictions." Don't cut off your afflictions but
turn them around instead. This is the way I think.
Other Dharma Masters would not talk like this.
Affliction is Bodhi. If you cut off affliction,
you also cut off Bodhi. Cut what off? What
can be cut off? Basically, you can't seek outside.
One turn of the head is the other shore. Your getting
enlightened is just Bodhi. But if you're confused,
then you have affliction.

Know that the one who does good is you, the
one who does evil is you, the one who brings forth
the Bodhi mind is you, and the one who brings
forth affliction is also you! Don't go looking
for somebody else. The one who becomes a Buddha is

"If one desires to know
All the Buddhas of the three periods of time
One should contemplate the Dharma Realm:
Everything is made from mind alone.

you, the one who becomes a ghost is also you. So
it is said,

> *If one desires to know*
> *All the Buddhas of the three periods of time.*
> *One should contemplate the nature of the*
>   *Dharma Realm--*
> *Everything is made from the mind alone.*

If you want to understand all the Buddhas of the
three periods of time --the past, present, and
future--you should contemplate the nature of the
Dharma Realm: all conditions are made from one's
own mind. One's own mind can become a Buddha, a
Bodhisattva, a sound hearer, one enlightened to
conditions, a god, an asura, a human being, an
animal, a ghost, or a hell-being. Someone who
believes in Buddhism said to me, "Dharma Master,
I really believe in the Buddhadharma, but I don't
believe in ghosts." He didn't believe that ghosts
exist.

   Then I asked him, "Do you believe that Buddhas
exist ?"

   He said, "Yes, I believe that Buddhas exist."

   I said, "Since you believe there are Buddhas,
I'll tell you that Buddhas are just ghosts. That
is, the Buddha's cultivation started from the
status of ghosts. Why don't you understand such
an easy principle?"

   This can be illustrated in the Chinese character for *heart* (心), which is very clever.

> *Three dots spread over above like stars,*
> *And below a hook, like the crescent moon.*
> *Animals arise from it,*
> *And Buddhahood comes from it, too.*

The three dots in this character are like stars
that spread above in the sky. The hook below the
heart is like the crescent moon. Being born with
fur and horns that is, being an animal--arises from
it; becoming a Buddha, also comes from it. That's
why we say *Everything is made from the mind alone.*
Also, there's another verse that says,

> *The Buddha spoke all dharmas,*
> *For the minds of living beings.*

> *If there were no minds,*
> *What use would dharmas be?*

When you get to the point where there is no mind--
just that is the Way. Also,

> *Inwardly contemplate the mind, there is no mind.*
> *Outwardly contemplate appearances, there are no*
>   *appearances.*
> *Contemplate objects from afar, there are no*
>   *objects.*
> *All three are null, one only sees emptiness.*
> *Contemplate emptiness which has been emptied,*
> *Emptiness has nothing that can be emptied.*
> *Stillness has nothing that can be stilled--*
> *How can desire be produced?*

*Inwardly contemplate the mind, there is no mind. Outwardly
contemplate appearances, there are no appearances.* Inside
there is no mind and outside are no shapes and
appearances.

Contemplate objects from afar, there are no objects.
You look at objects from afar, and there are no
objects.

All three are null, one only sees emptiness. These
three refer to inwardly contemplating of the mind,
outwardly contemplating appearances, and contemplating objects from afar. Since these three are
void, you can only see emptiness.

Contemplate emptiness which has been emptied. You
contemplate emptiness and even that is gone.

Emptiness has nothing that can be emptied. It means
even the emptiness itself is gone and there is nothing that can be emptied. At this time, a profound, lucid quietness prevails and one enters
samadhi.

Stillness has nothing that can be stilled. Even the
stillness is gone.

How can desire be produced? Desire means craving.
If you do not give rise to desire then you experience stillness and real purity.

This is only a small state in cultivation.
It's not the great functioning of the entire substance. But you have to go through this kind of
small state in order to obtain the state of the
perfect penetration of the ear organ and *interpenetrating*

function of the six sense organs.

When you hear me talk about the interpenetration function of the six sense organs, none of you will believe me. For example, the eyes can eat food, they can hear sounds, and they can speak, too. Someone says, "I don't believe this!" I knew you wouldn't believe it, but I still have to talk about it. The interpenetrating function of the six organs means that each one of the sense organs possesses six kinds of spiritual penetrations and six kinds of abilities. To obtain the perfect function of light ease in the interpenetrating function of the six organs is not easy. It's not that I just have to talk about it and you will naturally obtain such a state. If it were that easy, then I wouldn't have to speak the Sutras anymore! If you immediately understand when I speak, then what's the use of speaking?

Morality is to "*do no evil, and practice all good deeds.*" If you can really practice to the state of "doing no evil, and practicing all good deeds," then that is the state the Six Patriarch talked about,

> *Not thinking of good,*
> *Nor thinking of evil—-*
> *Right at this time, what is the original*
> *face of the Senior Ming?*

Do you know? Just this question startled Dharma Master Huei Ming into enlightment. Now although my voice is also very loud, I don't know whether any of you got enlightened.

"*Not thinking of good, nor thinking of evil,*"-- this kind of state is true morality. Therefore, precepts are most important and we must maintain them. If one doesn't keep precepts in cultivating the Way, one cannot accomplish one's Way-karma. Therefore, left-home people have to take precepts, and lay-people also have to take precepts. After you take precepts, you can be certified. If you don't take precepts, you will not get the diploma. You see, there are a lot of people who study by themselves and also read a lot of books, but they cannot attain Ph.D's. That's because they didn't go to college. Morality is like this, too. Basically,

the topic of precepts in itself is vast and inexhaustible, but because of the limits of time I'll
just speak about it in general.

If you can be in a state of *"not thinking of
good, nor thinking of evil,"* then that is true morality.
Morality is for transforming transgressions. If you
are always transgressing, then you have to keep
precepts. But human beings are very strange--if
you tell them to follow rules, they will certainly
want to break some rules. But if you tell them
not to follow rules, then they won't break the rules!
If you tell them to keep precepts, they will want
to break the precepts just to try it out, to see
what kind of flavor it has. After breaking the
precepts, they recognize the flavor--but it turns
out not to taste so good--they only fall into the
hells!

3. Patience. The Chinese character for patience (忍) is depicted by a knife on top of the
heart. It means that it is very painful and very
hard to bear, like gouging the heart with a sharp
blade. Although it's very painful, you still have
to endure it. Therefore, it is said,

Patience is like a blade on top of the heart.

The pain caused by this sharp blade is not easy to
bear. If you're able to bear it, then you have
some accomplishment. The Buddha taught us to
practice patience. We also have to endure suffering, endure happiness, endure hunger, endure the
cold, endure the heat, endure the wind, endure the
pain, endure all kinds of things, and also endure
the Dharma. Bear what you cannot bear, endure what
you cannot endure. Therefore, I often use a very
simple set of verses to describe "patience".

> *Patience is a priceless treasure,*
> *But people cannot handle it very well.*
> *If you know how to master it,*
> *Then everything will be okay!*

Although patience is a priceless treasure, people
don't know how to use it. After being patient
once, patient twice, patient thrice--then you cannot be patient anymore, and go up in smoke. Where

there's smoke, there's fire, and being unable to
endure anymore, you explode like a string of fire-
crackers! That's why the verse says, *"people cannot
handle it very well."*

    "If you know how to master it"--if you know how to
use this patience--then *"everything will be okay"*, you
will have absolutely no afflictions.

    We also have to endure the Dharma. People who
study the Buddhadharma should have a certain kind
of patience. It is said,

> *The profundity of the Buddhadharma is as deep as
> the great sea.*

Upon seeing this one heaves a great sigh and says,
"Ai! The sea of Dharma is so broad, when can I ever
completely understand all the Sutras? How could I
ever even read them all?" You shouldn't have such
thoughts. If you have such thoughts, you don't
have patience with Dharma. There are three kinds
of patience :

        a. patience with production.

        b. patience with Dharma.

        c. patience with non-production.

    All of you should return the light and illu-
minate within. Having studied the Buddhadharma
for several years, has your temper changed, or not?
You should pay particular attention to this and
not be sloppy about it. I know that not only laypeople find it difficult to cultivate the perfection of patience, even left-home people find it
difficult. Sometimes, even patient immortals cannot endure anymore and blow their tops! Patience
is used to transform hatred and vexation. Those
who like to blow up in anger should practice the
conduct of patience. If you cultivate patience,
then you will cross over the sea of hatred and
vexation.

    4. Vigor. If every day we talk about the Six
Perfections and every day we are lazy, then this is
a willful offense. You already understand that
being vigorous is good, but you don't respectfully

follow along and practice. You insist on being lax.
When I say this, none of you take it to heart.
After lunch, you have to take a nap and rest for a
while. If you don't rest for a while, then you
feel uncomfortable for the rest of the day. Maybe it's
because of the hot weather. Also it's the custom
of the people who live in the tropics. But at Gold
Mountain of San Francisco, not a single person is
allowed to take a nap. So, when they travel, they
don't need to take naps.

Being vigorous means not letting a single
minute, a single second, pass in vain. The ancients
said,

> *One moment of time is worth an ounce of gold,*
> *One ounce of gold cannot buy back a moment of*
> * time.*
> *An ounce of gold lost is easy to get back,*
> *But time lost is hard to retrieve!*

Taking to heart these words spoken by the ancients,
we should wipe clean our minds and our laziness.
We should renounce our lazy habits. The ancients
also said,

> *One moment of time is worth an inch of life.*

See how important this sentence is! One moment of
time is exactly like one inch of your life. If we
let one second of time pass, it's the same as
losing one inch of our lives. Did you hear that?

> *Don't wait until you're old to study the Way;*
> *Most lonely graves are full of young people.*

Just because you see someone elderly studying the
Buddhadharma, don't suppose that you can also wait
until you are eighty and then start to recite the
Buddha's name. Ha! You can wait, but is there
any guarantee you will live to be eighty? If you
can, then that's good, but maybe you'll die before
you are twenty. That's why you shouldn't wait.
If today you recognize the goodness of the Buddhadharma, then today you should be vigorous. Don't
wait until tomorrow thinking there will always be
another tomorrow. On which tomorrow will you begin
to cultivate the Way? On which tomorrow will you get

enlightened to the Way? On which tomorrow will you
become a Buddha? All of you think about it. Right
at this point you should painfully resolve to not
wait anymore! Don't "wait a minute, wait a minute
..." You wait for a minute, two minutes, three
minutes..., and how many minutes have you waited?
"Wait a minute, wait a minute...", and how many
minutes have you let pass in vain?

Vigor includes vigor of the body and vigor of
the mind. Cultivators in ancient times would stand
before an image of the Buddha for seven days and
seven nights. They didn't close their eyes once
or even turn their gaze, but singlemindedly looked
up at the Buddha, for seven days and seven nights!
This is true vigor and true cultivation. They
stood there for seven days and seven nights but
didn't feel tired at all. Wouldn't you say this
is vigor? You think about it--can you stand for
just seven hours in front of Buddha Image without
closing your eyes once, without turning your gaze,
but respectfully look up at the Buddhas? If you
cannot, then you still don't have enough skill.
Don't be so self-confident and suppose yourself to
be so wonderful. How wonderful are you anyway?
what superior points do you have over other people
anyway? Lots of people don't like to listen to
what I say!

Another example of vigor is Medicine King
Bodhisattva who burned his entire body as an offering to the Buddha. He wrapped his body with cotton,
saturated it with fragrant oils, then lit it up,
and offered his body to the Buddha. He was not
like us who feel we are going to die of pain when
we just burn a little finger. Some of us feel
excrutiating suffering and bitterness when we burn
a piece of incense on our arm, not to speak of
burning our entire bodies. That would be absolutely impossible! "I certainly will retreat--I just
cannot do it!" You see, you should be realistic
about what kind of potential you possess. All the
Buddhas and Bodhisattvas of the past gave up their
bodies, minds, and lives for the sake of seeking
their Way-karma. Somebody says, "Ha! That is
really stupid!" Then you're very smart, right?
For ever so long you never wanted to practice
giving--yes, you have great wisdom but you're not
that vigorous!

Vigor is to transform laxness. Laxness is laziness--not being vigorous in studying the Buddha-dharma and not working hard in cultivation. Consider the person who, when he goes dancing, has limitless energy and spirit. But tell him to bow to the Buddha, and he complains that bowing to the Buddha makes his head dizzy. If he goes dancing he jumps back and forth in the dance hall and he doesn't feel dizzy at all. He'd say, "Today I had a great time!" So you can compare these two situations and you'll understand whether people are vigorous in cultivation or vigorous in playing. You be the judge.

5. Dhyana Concentration. Dhyana concentration transforms scatteredness. It is said,

> *Sitting for a long time,*
> *one attains Samadhi.*
> *Dwelling for a long time,*
> *one develops affinities.*

Indeed, Wherever you dwell for a long period, you will develop affinities with the place and the people. Sitting in meditation for a certain period of time also brings forth Samadhi. *Dhyana* is Sanskrit, and translates as "the cultivation of ponderance (思惟修)", or "reflection in silence (靜慮)." "Reflection in silence" is for emptying our false thoughts and purifying our minds. Therefore, in the Chapter of *Pure Conduct* it is pointed out that if you don't purify your mind, you will not have pure conduct. If your mind is unclean, certainly your conduct will be unclean. Your mind must be pure, and then the manifestations of your conduct will also be pure. So it is said,

> *One conduct, one matter,*
> *But it depends on the doer.*

In all events, your conduct expresses your thoughts; just that is the appearance of your pure mind. If you don't have a pure mind, you won't have pure conduct. Therefore, Dhyana Concentration is very important. There are four levels of Dhyana Samadhi. The four levels of Dhyana and nine sequential Samadhis are explained in detail in the <u>Shurangama Sutra</u>.

If any of you want to investigate the perfection of Dhyana meditation, you should be vigorous in sitting in meditation, and also study the <u>Shurangama Sutra</u>, which is a great aid to investigating Dhyana meditation. If any of you truly want to study the skill of Dhyana meditation, you should recite the <u>Shurangama Sutra</u>. Dhyana Samadhi transforms scatteredness. If you have too much distraction or too many false thoughts, you should sit in Dhyana meditation.

6. Prajna. *Prajna* is Sanskrit, and translates as "wisdom." Why is it not translated? Because it contains "multiple meanings and is not translated （多含不翻）." Wisdom only has one meaning, but Prajna has three meanings:

a. Literary Prajna.   （文字般若）
This means using literature to explain True Principle, such as the Tripitaka and twelve divisions of Sutras.

b. Contemplative Prajna.（觀行般若）

This means to contemplate, investigate, and illuminate all the Sutras in order to understand True Principle. It's the same as using a candle to illuminate darkness.

c. Real Mark Prajna.   （實相般若）

Real mark is no mark. It is said, *"Prajna can break through all marks."* No matter what kind of thing, or what kind of state it is, all are seen through as devoid of marks. What is no mark? It is one's own wisdom, one's own mind. If one's own mind is pure, then one is a Bodhisattva. If one's own mind is confused, then one is a living being.

Because Prajna contains these three kinds of meanings, it is not translated. Wisdom, or Prajna,

A Bodhisattva is one who enlightens sentients,
one who is enlightened among sentients.

transforms stupidity. This is explained very
clearly in the <u>Maha Prajna Sutra</u>.

   In the T'ang Dynasty when Dharma Master Hsuan
Chuang translated the 600 volumes of the <u>Maha
Prajna Sutra</u>, the peach trees blossomed <u>six times</u>
within that year. This auspicious portent was
displayed by the Dharma protecting spirits to call
attention to the importance of the <u>Maha Prajna Sutra</u>.

   At that time, Foremost Wisdom Bodhisattva
INQUIRED OF MANJUSHRI BODHISATTVA SAYING... At the
beginning of this Chapter, the Bodhisattvas carry
on a dialogue of questions and answers. Foremost
Wisdom Bodhisattva asks the initial question.
"Foremost Wisdom" means number one in wisdom, for
he is a Bodhisattva with great wisdom.

   What is a Bodhisattva? People may be accus-
tomed to going to temples to bow to the Bodhisattvas,
but if you ask them the meaning of the term "Bodhisattva", they may be hard put to tell you. They
may stare at you wide-eyed and have nothing to say.
"A Bodhisattva is just a Bodhisattva--what other
meaning is there to 'Bodhisattva'," they may say
lamely. This is a situation akin to Piggy eating
the ginseng fruit without knowing its taste. You
say, we have no idea, because it is not in the
English language. Since we haven't any idea, do
we just count on not knowing it forever? No. Instead, we should become familiar with these terms
when we listen to the Sutras. For example, we
talk about bowing to the Bodhisattva, but if you
don't even understand the meaning of "Bodhisattva",
it will be no different than if you bowed to a
ghost.

   "Bodhisattva" is a Sanskrit word. It means
"one who enlightens sentients (覺有情)"; also
"one enlightened among sentients (有情覺)." A
Bodhisattva also means a "living being with a great
mind for the Way (大道心者)." He is also "one who
opens the Way (開士)"; also a "great knight
(大士)." These are the meanings of the term
"Bodhisattva".

   A Buddha is called "an unsurpassed knight
(無上士)", a Bodhisattva is called "a surpassed
knight (有上士)."

   Because he has wisdom, Foremost Wisdom Bodhisattva knows how to inquire Manjushri about the
Buddhadharma. At this point, he questions Manjushri

Bodhisattva. *Manjushri* also is Sanskrit, and translates as "Wonderfully Auspicious." He is the Bodhisattva of Great Wisdom, because he has "wisdom within wisdom; wisdom on top of wisdom."

Foremost Wisdom Bodhisattva and Manjushri Bodhisattva of Wisdom recognize and understand each other. They can be said to "know each other's sounds." There is a saying that describes the benefits of knowing oneself and knowing others,

> *Knowing one's own situation and that of the enemy,*
> *Guarantees victory in every battle.*

Here they employ the method of mutual question and answer. That's why at this point Foremost Wisdom Bodhisattva questions   Manjushri Bodhisattva.

Previously, we discussed the first seven divisions of this Chapter. Now we go on to discuss the rest.

The eighth division is titled "One gains the ten powers of wisdom. (得十力智)"

The ninth division is titled "One is respected and protected by Ten Kings. (十王救護)"

The tenth division is titled "One can benefit. (能為饒益)"

The eleventh division is titled "Transcendent, sublime, honored, and noble. (超勝尊貴)"

SUTRA:

   *DISCIPLES OF THE BUDDHA, HOW DOES A BODHI-
SATTVA ATTAIN FAULTLESS KARMA OF BODY, SPEECH, AND
MIND?*

COMMENTARY:

   Foremost Wisdom Bodhisattva addresses Manjushri
Bodhisattva and says, "DISCIPLES OF THE BUDDHA,"
because the Buddha is the Dharma King and the Bodhisattva is the disciple of the Dharma King. Someone may think that "Buddha's disciple (佛子)"
literally means the Buddha's son; but actually,
Fo Tzu (佛子) refers to the Buddha's disciple.
Manjushri Bodhisattva is the highest Bodhisattva
among Bodhisattvas. HOW DOES A BODHISATTVA ATTAIN
FAULTLESS KARMA OF BODY, SPEECH, AND MIND? asks
Foremost Wisdom Bodhisattva. "Bodhisattva," here
doesn't refer to any one Bodhisattva, but rather
applies to all the people who resolve their minds
on Bodhi and cultivate Bodhisattva Conduct. This
includes Bodhisattvas of the past, Bodhisattvas of
the present, and Bodhisattvas of the future. It
does not indicate any name, but says "Bodhisattva"
in general.
   How does a Bodhisattva fulfill his resolve to
obtain pure karma in body, speech, and mind which
is without any faults? How should he cultivate
so as to attain purity of the three karmas? It
requires diligent cultivation of precepts, samadhi,
and wisdom, and casting out of greed, hatred, and
stupidity. If you diligently cultivate precepts,
samadhi, and wisdom, then your karma of body,
speech, and mind will not have errors. Not only
will greed, hatred, and stupidity be extinguished,
but even faults will not arise. Therefore, this
is the method by which Bodhisattvas attain three
karmas without faults.

SUTRA:

   *HOW DOES HE ATTAIN NON-HARMING KARMA OF BODY,
SPEECH, AND MIND?*

COMMENTARY:

HOW DOES HE ATTAIN NON-HARMING KARMA OF BODY, SPEECH, AND MIND? "Non-harming" means no hindrance, that is, the karma of body, speech, and mind is so pure that no devices can defile it. How can that come to be? It can be achieved by being "solid, sincere, and constant." The Bodhisattva who cultivates the Way should have a solid mind, a sincere mind, and a constant mind, and not let defiled dharmas sully the karma of his body, speech, and mind. When a Bodhisattva cultivates, he should be particularly careful at all times. He should be watchful of the three karma of body, speech, and mind, and not commit any evil deeds, but just cultivate all good deeds.

SUTRA:

HOW DOES HE ATTAIN UNRUINABLE KARMA OF BODY, SPEECH, AND MIND?

COMMENTARY:

"Ruined" refers to transgressions as a result of carelessness, or violations of the precepts, which result in the defilement of the pure karma of body, speech, and mind. What must one do? One has to keep the precepts at all times, then one will not transgress in the karma of body, speech, and mind.

SUTRA:

HOW DOES HE ATTAIN INDESTRUCTIBLE KARMA OF BODY, SPEECH, AND MIND?

COMMENTARY:

HOW DOES HE ATTAIN INDESTRUCTIBLE KARMA OF BODY, SPEECH, AND MIND? It is by cultivating so that one becomes solid like vajra. Then no matter what state appears, it cannot destroy one's karma of body, speech, and mind.

SUTRA:

HOW DOES HE ATTAIN NON-RETREATING KARMA OF BODY, SPEECH, AND MIND?

COMMENTARY:

Sometimes people make a resolve, but it only lasts for a few days and then they retreat. For example, they resolve to cultivate the Way, or more specifically resolve to practice the Dharma Door of sleeping sitting up and never lying down. But it is not easy to practice never lying down; it's very bitter. No matter how one sits, it never feels as comfortable as lying down. For example, one of my disciples said those who practice sitting sleeping up should move the bed out of their rooms. If there is a bed, then they'll lie down when they want to. If there's no bed, even if they want to lie down, there's no place to do so, so they have to sit up. Therefore, if you want to lie down, that's retreating. However, if there is a bed, but you won't lie down, then that's not retreating. Originally, the karma of body, speech, and mind are pure, but as soon as you don't pay attention or become careless, then you'll transgress and commit errors. The easiest error to commit is false speech. It is very easy for any one of us to utter false speech unconsciously. After uttering false speech, one further tries to be a defense attorney for oneself and says, "I'm not lying, I'm just speaking expediently." He just defends his own case. This is a habit one is born with wherein one doesn't confess one's own mistakes--and this also counts as retreating.

SUTRA:

HOW DOES HE ATTAIN IMMOVABLE KARMA OF BODY, SPEECH, AND MIND?

COMMENTARY:

HOW DOES HE ATTAIN IMMOVABLE KARMA OF BODY, SPEECH, AND MIND? IMMOVABLE means unshakable--to cultivate the karma of body, speech, and mind so they are as firm and resolute as vajra. No matter what kinds of states arrive, they won't be able to move your karma of body, speech, and mind. As a result you won't create evil offenses.

SUTRA:

HOW DOES HE ATTAIN THE MOST SUPREME KARMA OF BODY, SPEECH, AND MIND? HOW DOES HE ATTAIN PURITY OF THE KARMA OF BODY, SPEECH, AND MIND?

COMMENTARY:

Foremost Wisdom Bodhisattva also asks, "HOW DOES THE BODHISATTVA ATTAIN THE MOST SUPREME KARMA OF BODY, SPEECH, AND MIND?" Not only doesn't he commit evil deeds, but also he accomplishes good merit and virtue. *HOW DOES HE ATTAIN PURITY OF THE KARMA OF BODY, SPEECH, AND MIND?* It is by getting rid of defiled thoughts, that one naturally attains the purity of the karma of body, speech, and mind.

SUTRA:

HOW DOES HE ATTAIN UNDEFILED KARMA OF BODY, SPEECH, AND MIND?

COMMENTARY:

HOW DOES a Bodhisattva *ATTAIN UNDEFILED KARMA OF BODY, SPEECH, AND MIND?* From unlimited kalpas until now, people have been harmed by defilement. Our bodies are not clean, our minds are also impure. We are muddled and upside-down, living as if in a dream all day long. There is not an instant when we're pure. If we can eradicate all improper thoughts, then our minds will attain purity. Once our minds are pure, then our three karmas of body, speech, and mind will not be defiled.

SUTRA:

HOW DOES HE ATTAIN THE KARMA OF BODY, SPEECH, AND MIND WHICH TAKES WISDOM AS ITS FOREMOST GUIDE?

COMMENTARY:

When a Bodhisattva brings forth the resolve how does he come to have wisdom which guides the karma of body, speech, and mind so they can be pure? Why do we always commit evil deeds? It is because our Prajna Wisdom doesn't manifest. Since our Prajna Wisdom doesn't manifest, our stupid mind is in command, and we have no wisdom. Because of a lack of wisdom, the karmas of body, speech, and mind are not pure. If one has wisdom, one can use this wisdom to guide the karmas of body, speech, and mind so one naturally becomes pure, intelligent, and wise.

SUTRA:

HOW DOES HE ATTAIN THE PERFECTION OF A PLACE OF BIRTH? THE COMPLETION OF A LINEAGE? THE COMPLETION OF A HOUSEHOLD? THE COMPLETION OF FORM? THE COMPLETION OF MARKS? THE COMPLETION OF MINDFULNESS? THE COMPLETION OF WISDOM? THE COMPLETION OF ACTIVITY? THE COMPLETION OF FEARLESSNESS? THE COMPLETION OF ENLIGHTENMENT?

COMMENTARY:

How does a cultivating Bodhisattva attain *THE PERFECTION OF A PLACE OF BIRTH?* The Bodhisattva vows to be born life after life in places where the Buddhadharma is--in places where he can make offerings to the Triple Jewel--the Buddha Jewel, Dharma Jewel, and Sangha Jewel.

THE COMPLETION OF LINEAGE means to be born in a respected and honorable family. For example, in India, the populace is divided into the four castes of Kashatriyas, Brahmans, Businessmen, and Beggars. The beggars are those whose caste is so poor and low that they aren't even allowed to enter temples to bow to the Buddha. They're considered too dirty, too inferior. In India,

the considerations of caste are very weighty.
They discriminate even to the point that the poor
cannot walk together with the respectable castes--
they make such distinctions. To have perfection of
lineage is to be born in an honorable and lofty
family, and not be born in a poor and lowly
family, or in a beggar's household. The completion of lineage means not to be born in a poor and
lowly family, but to be born in a respectful and
honorable family. How does one achieve the
completion of lineage? You have to cultivate all
kinds of respectful and superior Dharma doors.

THE COMPLETION OF HOUSEHOLD, THE COMPLETION
OF FORM. "Household" here refers to a family
endowed with kind, good, and proper mindfulness
in the Buddhadharma. "Form" refers to one's
appearance being complete, perfect, and dignified.
It can refer to the color of one's complexion.

The following sentence also says THE COMPLET-
ION OF MARKS. "Mark" refers to the thirty-two
characteristics. In the Buddha's past lives, he
cultivated the thirty-two marks and eighty subtle
characteristics. As a result he obtained the
completion of form in which his appearance became
full and perfect.

THE COMPLETION OF MINDFULNESS. This means
to be replete with proper knowledge and proper
views, and not to bring forth deviant knowledge
and deviant views.

THE COMPLETION OF WISDOM. Wisdom can help
you cultivate. If you want to cultivate, you
should have wisdom. Possessing wisdom, you can
truly recognize the Dharma Door of cultivation.
After truly recognizing the Dharma Door of cultivation, then you can follow the Dharma to cultivate. If you don't have wisdom, you'll not
recognize it. Not being able to recognize it,
you will not cultivate. So THE COMPLETION OF
WISDOM is very important. But how does one
achieve completion of wisdom? One should maintain
superior, clear knowledge and views. One should
be skillful in understanding worldly dharmas.

SUTRA:

HOW DOES A BODHISATTVA ATTAIN SUPREME WISDOM?
FOREMOST WISDOM? MOST SUPERIOR WISDOM? MOST
SUPREME WISDOM? BOUNDLESS WISDOM? LIMITLESS
WISDOM? INCONCEIVABLE WISDOM? UNEQUALLED WISDOM?
IMMEASURABLE WISDOM? INEFFABLE WISDOM?

COMMENTARY:

Foremost Wisdom Bodhisattva also asks
Manjushri Bodhisattva about ten kinds of wisdom.
Wisdom includes true wisdom and false wisdom
True wisdom is Prajna wisdom which enables one to
do only good things but not to do evil things.
False wisdom is worldly wisdom. It is different
from true wisdom in that although one may be
really smart, he can do good things and bad things
with this kind of wisdom.
These ten kinds of wisdom are as follows:

1.   How does a cultivating Bodhisattva
     attain Supreme Wisdom?

2.   How does a cultivating Bodhisattva
     attain Foremost Wisdom?

3.   How does a cultivating Bodhisattva
     attain Most Superior Wisdom?

4.   How does a cultivating Bodhisattva
     attain Most Supreme Wisdom?

5.   How does a cultivating Bodhisattva
     attain Boundless Wisdom?

6.   How does a cultivating Bodhisattva
     attain Limitless Wisdom?

7.   How does a cultivating Bodhisattva
     attain Inconceivable Wisdom?

8.   How does a cultivating Bodhisattva
     attain Unequalled Wisdom?

9.   How does a cultivating Bodhisattva attain Immeasurable Wisdom?

10.   How does a cultivating Bodhisattva attain Ineffable Wisdom?

We will hear a detailed explanation when we get into the Sutra.

SUTRA:

HOW DOES HE ATTAIN THE POWER OF CAUSES? THE POWER OF ZEAL? THE POWER OF EXPEDIENTS? THE POWER OF CONDITIONS? THE POWER OF THAT WHICH IS CONDITIONED? THE POWER OF HIS FACULTIES? THE POWER OF INVESTIGATION? THE POWER OF SHAMATTA? THE POWER OF VIPASHYANA? THE POWER OF REFLECTION?

COMMENTARY:

Foremost Wisdom Bodhisattva also asks Manjushri Bodhisattva about ten kinds of power for perfecting the Way. These ten kinds of power are as follows:

1.   How does a Bodhisattva attain the causes of perfecting the Way? In the <u>Gathering</u> <u>Treatise</u> <u>of the Liang</u> (梁攝論), it is said: "Being extensively learned and permeated with practice, one can come to understand the nature of conjoining within the Alaya consciousness." Therefore, all the Sages use this kind of wisdom seed as causes for their cultivation.

2.   How does a Bodhisattva attain the happiness of supreme Zeal? This means the desire for great Bodhi, the causal condition of embarking upon one's cultivation.

3.   How does a Bodhisattva attain the power of expedients? One has to employ six kinds of expedients so

as to accomplish one's wisdom. It is said,

> *"Cultivate both compassion and wisdom."*

This is the basic method in cultivation. The six expedients are as follows:

慈悲顧念 a. Kind and compassionate regard.

了知諸行 b. Understanding and knowledge of all conducts.

欣佛妙智 c. Appreciation of the Buddha's wonderful wisdom.

不捨生死 d. No renunciation of birth and death.

輪迴不染 e. No defilement by the cycle of rebirth.

熾然精進 f. Fervent vigor.

4. How does a Bodhisattva attain the power of Conditions? "Conditions" here refers to encouragement and exhortation by a good knowing advisor.

5. How does a Bodhisattva attain the power of Contemplating the state of compassionate Wisdom?

6. How does a Bodhisattva attain the five faculties of faith, vigor, mindfulness, samadhi, and wisdom?

7. How does a Bodhisattva attain the power of investigating himself and others, and the power of discriminating phenomena?

8. How does a cultivating Bodhisattva attain the power of Shamatta (stopping)?

9. How does a cultivating Bodhisattva attain the power of Vipashyana (contemplating)?

10. How does a cultivating Bodhisattva attain the power of reflection? Reflection--that is, the power to think about which things should be done, and which should not.

"Shamatta" is Sanskrit, and translates as "stopping (止)." "Vipashyana" also is Sanskrit, and translates as "contemplation (觀)."--"Stopping and contemplation." What is meant by stopping? Stopping what? How can it be stopped? This stopping means to cease, it also means being quiet. Contemplation means investigation. These two terms combined are called "stopping and contemplation." There are many terms in Buddhism which refer to stopping and contemplation. The Samadhi of Extinction of Feeling and Thought is one. What is meant by stopping? What is meant by contemplation? Stopping what? Contemplating what? All of these are explained very clearly.

Stopping means to cease your false thoughts, to cease your sexual desire, to cease your ignorance. You should bring forth a kind of wisdom to contemplate--do you still have ignorance? Do you still have false thoughts? Do you still have sexual desire? We can illustrate this contemplation with two ancient verses.

> *"Contemplate the myriad things in stillness;*
> *all are self-contained.*
> *The four seasons are wonderful and joyous;*
> *share them with others."*

To *"contemplate the myriad things in stillness"* is stopping and contemplation. If you can stop and contemplate, then you will understand the principle of the myriad creation and myriad objects. This is the same principle as "to pursue

to the very nature of things (格物)" in Confucianism. What is meant by "to pursue to the very
nature of things"? It means to abandon your desire
for material objects and return to your own nature.
If you can get rid of the desire for material
objects, return to the source and go back to the
origin, understand the mind and see the nature,
then you can arrive at wisdom. Your wisdom will
come forth. After your wisdom comes forth, you
will know how to cultivate. Therefore, the technique of stopping and contemplation is very important. Stopping means to be quiet. There is not
a bit of noise around; everything comes to a stop.
You practice stopping and contemplation to the
point that even your breath can be stopped.
Doesn't this mean one dies? No. Your pulse will
also stop--this is a certain level of accomplishment derived from this practice. In Confucianism
it is said,

> *After one understands stopping, one can obtain*
> *   Samadhi.*
> *After one attains Samadhi, one can be still.*
> *After one is still, one can be at peace.*
> *After one is at peace, one can ponder.*
> *After one has pondered, one can attain.*

What can be attained? One can attain understanding. Understanding comes about through the power
of investigation.
     To go back to the first saying:
*"The four seasons are wonderful and joyous; share them with
others."* The four seasons are spring, summer,
autumn, and winter. *"Wonderful and joyous"* refers to
the best of times when things are good. Such
occasions should not be enjoyed only by oneself.
You should share them with other people. To share
with others is true happiness! If you are
only happy yourself that is not ultimate. You
should be able to share happiness with other
people.
     Stopping and contemplation means to stop all
of your false thoughts and bad habits and to
bring forth all good dharmas, wisdom, and investigation. The ancients also said:

> *Knowing how to be content, one will not be subject to insult.*
> *Knowing how to be still, one will not be endangered.*

If you can be content, you will not be subject to insult. If you're not satisfied, you'll have a greedy mind. If you have a greedy mind, you will be open to abuse. You're greedy, other people also are greedy, and because of that greed among you, you will explode in fighting and struggle. In situations of contention, fighting and struggle break out and then it becomes a case of "survival of the fittest." The superior party is victorious, while the inferior party is defeated. The one with the greater power will oppress the one with lesser power, thus the latter will be abused and insulted. If you can be content at all times and not be greedy for anything, then you'll not be subject to insult.

Knowing how to be still, one will not be endangered. this means not being greedy. If you follow the rules in everything, you will not be subject to insult or be endangered. We who practice stopping and contemplation should first stop being greedy. Once you stop being greedy, then you can contemplate: "Is there a trace of greed remaining in my mind?" So the next sentence says THE POWER OF REFLECTION. After one attains the power of stopping and contemplation, one should make a reflection. Reflection refers to Dhyana. Dhyana is Sanskrit, and translates as "reflection in silence." It is also called the "cultivation of ponderance." In the cultivation of ponderance, you bring forth the power of concentration through the process of reflection.

There are a lot of principles involved in stopping and contemplation, but at present we can explain it simply as "precepts." Stopping means to "do no evil"; Contemplation means to "practice all good deeds." If you do no evil, that's just stopping. If you practice all good deeds, just that is contemplation. We people who cultivate do not need to know too much. If you know too much but don't go ahead to cultivate, it will have an adverse effect and spoil the whole affair. You may become engaged in empty talk and enter into the Samadhi of bantering. What you say is

really wonderful, but what you practice is not so
wonderful--that's useless! That's a case where
"the flower blossoms but does not bear fruit."
The flower is very beautiful, but it does not
bear fruit. Ultimately what use is it?

SUTRA:

> *HOW DOES HE ATTAIN SKILLFULNESS WITH THE
SKANDHAS? SKILLFULNESS WITH THE REALMS?*

COMMENTARY:

"Skandhas" means the five skandhas--form,
feeling, congnition, formation, and consciousness.
In the Heart Sutra it says,

> *"When Bodhisattva Avalokiteshvara was practicing
> the profound Prajna Paramita, he illuminated the
> five skandhas and saw that they are all empty,
> and he crossed beyond all suffering and diffi-
> culty."*

Avalokiteshvara Bodhisattva is another name for
Kuan Shr Yin Bodhisattva. Although Kuan Shr Yin
Bodhisattva is called "the Bodhisattva who contemplates at ease", or "one who contemplates
self-presence (觀見自在)." He is aware that each
one of us is also a transformation body of Avalokiteshvara Bodhisattva. We also can return the
light, illuminate within and contemplate to see
whether we are at ease or not. If you're self-
present but not at ease, then you haven't attained
self-mastery; you've run away. Being without
ease, you haven't attained reception and function.
How does one contemplate at ease? You should see
through everything and put down all your attachments.
Being without any attachments means to put down
all your greed, hatred, and stupidity. Once you
put down greed, hatred, and stupidity, you'll
attain self-mastery and be at ease. If you can't
put them down, you'll not attain ease and you'll
run away. But where will you run to? Well, that
place is really far--suddenly you ascend to the
heavens, suddenly you descend to the hells,
suddenly you become a hungry ghost, suddenly you
become an animal. You run all over the place and

When Bodhisattva Avalokiteshvara was practicing
the profound Prajna Paramita, he illuminated
the five skandhas and saw that they are all
empty, and he crossed beyond all suffering and
difficulty.

revolve in the wheel of the six paths of rebirth, back and forth in a crazy merry-go-round! And you can't get out of the six destinies. Why? Just because you're not at ease! You can't see through it or put it down and you're not comfortable. It means you are not your own master. You cannot practice what you say. You're controlled by the six sense organs and the six sense objects. If you can contemplate at ease, you're the Bodhisattva who contemplates at ease. If you cannot contemplate at ease, then perhaps you are a ghost, a human being, an animal, an Asura , a god--there is no fixed name for you. Since you run all over the place, you'll be named according to the destiny you run off to, but you cannot become the Bodhisattva who contemplates at ease. Because you can't contemplate at ease, you can't be called a Bodhisattva.

Even Avalokiteshvara Bodhisattva had to cultivate. If you don't cultivate, you will fall behind. What should we cultivate? Cultivate the profound Prajna Paramita--the profound great wisdom that takes you to the other shore! If you can reach the other shore, you can illuminate the five Skandhas and *see that they are all empty.* The Five Skandhas are form, feeling, thought, formation, and consciousness. The <u>Heart</u> <u>Sutra</u> also says,

> *Form does not differ from emptiness;*
> *Emptiness does not differ from form.*
> *Form itself is emptiness;*
> *Emptiness itself is form.*

It also can be said that feeling itself is emptiness; emptiness itself is feeling. So too are thought, formation, and consciousness. Now the Sutra talks about the *SKILLFULNESS WITH THE SKANDHAS,* which means to be skillful in explaining the dharma of the five skandhas and to help living beings understand the five skandhas. It means to use clever and expedient methods to explain the five Skandhas clearly.

SKILLFULNESS WITH THE REALMS. The realms refer to the eighteen realms. They are the six sense organs--the eyes, ears, nose, tongue, body, and mind; the six sense objects--sight, sound, smell, taste, object of touch, and dharma; and add to that the six consciousnesses--the eye consciousness, ear consciousness, nose consciousness, body consciousness, and mind consciousness. The combination of the six sense organs, six sense objects, and six consciousnesses are together called the eighteen realms. Between the six sense organs and the six sense objects, the six consciousnesses arise. Combined together they make up the eighteen realms.

The six sense organs are the roots of our false thoughts. The eyes see things, the ears hear sounds, the nose smells fragrances, the tongue tastes flavors, the body craves sensations of touch, and the mind is attracted to dharmas. The eyes see the dust of form and are turned by the dust of form, but cannot turn the dust of form.

If you can be so that "*the eyes see forms, but inside there is nothing; the ears hear defiling sounds, but the mind does not know,*" then you are not turned by form and sound. Somebody says, "It's impossible to do such a thing! If one sees form but inside there's nothing; and if the ears hear defiling sounds but the mind does not know--how is one different from earth, wood, metal, and stone?" The earth, wood, metal, and stone don't have this kind of discriminating mind, but they also haven't accomplished their Way karma. You ask, "How can a person be like that?" It's just because you can't become that way that you have a great many impediments. If you can become that way, then you will attain self-mastery. The eyes aren't turned by the dust of form, therefore they will not be greedy for or attached to beautiful form. This is the same as "not entering into sights, sounds, smells, tastes, objects of touch, or dharmas." After you're certified to the first fruit of Ahartship, then you will not enter into sights, sounds, smells, tastes, objects of touch, or dharmas. This is called the fruition of "entering into the current" (入流) --entering into the current of the Dharma-nature of sages, and going against the current of the six sense objects of common people. Toward sights, sounds, smells, tastes, objects of touch, and dharmas, one remains unmoving. Therefore, the ancients said,

> *Eating all day, but not eating even one grain of rice.*
> *Wearing clothes all day, but not wearing a single thread.*

Somebody says, "This is really lying! Eating all day, but not eating even one grain of rice--then ultimately what did he eat? Haaaaah------? He didn't eat even a grain of rice--isn't he telling a big lie?" If you reach this level, you can also tell big lies. But since you haven't reached this state, you can't pretend you're eating all day but not even eating one grain of rice. If you do, you're lying. If one attains the fruition of not entering into sights, sounds, smells, tastes, objects of touch, or dharmas, then he can be said to be "eating all day, but not eating even one grain of rice." Of course, he hasn't eaten one grain of rice--I can guarantee he's not lying; because he ate a lot of grains of rice, and for sure it's not only one grain. So it says, *"not eating even one grain of rice."* It's not a lie. This is true speech, honest speech, speech about the way it is, and not false speech.

Wearing clothes all day, but not wearing a single thread. He wears clothes everyday. He does not wear only one thread, he wears a lot of threads--this is not a lie either. It is useless if one wears only one thread on one's body. To say that one wears a lot of threads is honest. But yet, although he wears a lot, he is absent-minded. In eating he is absent-minded, in wearing clothes he is also absent-minded. He doesn't become attached to eating and wearing clothes. He's not like us common people who can't go without eating or wearing clothes.

In the beginning, the size of the Buddhist Lecture Hall was only about half the size of this room. How did the monks live? They lived together with the Buddha in one room. They slept in front of the Buddha image. But there was still not enough space. A lot of people at Gold Mountain Monastery practice sleeping sitting up. This custom has its beginning from that time.

Some people used wooden boxes. None of you should
mistake this wooden box for a coffin! In Vietnam
when I talked about the wooden box, the translator
translated it as a coffin. Why do I say it's not
a coffin? Because this box is 3 cubic square
feet, whereas a coffin is 2 by 5 or 2 by 6 feet. The
monks sat in such boxes to meditate and even if
they wanted to stretch their legs there was no
space to do so. They also couldn't lie down.
Because they could neither stretch out their legs
nor lie down, their situation was a bit similar
to the women who had their feet bound in ancient
China. The monks packed themselves into wooden
boxes which were originally used for packing apples.
At that time there were nearly ten people who
lived in such wooden boxes, so I say American monks
had no houses to live in--they only lived in wooden
boxes. And it was bitter in the extreme, not
comfortable at all! It's not like sleeping on a
spring mattress on which you can bounce up and
down, like playing with an electric toy.

American monks also don't have much food to
eat. Why is this? Because they eat only one
meal a day. They eat neither breakfast nor dinner.
But in this way they are practicing as true disciples of Buddha--"not being afraid of bitterness,
not being afraid of suffering, and not being
afraid of having no money." With difficult
practice you strike up your spirits. All of the
Americans who leave the home-life with me eat only
one meal a day. They like to cultivate the Dharma
of having no clothes to wear, having no food to
eat, and having no houses to live in. Some
Chinese youths expressed the wish to leave the
home-life with me, and I said to them: "If you
can practice eating only one meal a day, not be
afraid that your clothes will be ragged, and not
be afraid that the food will not be tasty, then
your wish will be granted."

Right now Buddhism has just started in
America and everybody has to endure suffering and
bitterness. When Buddhism began in China, everybody could endure suffering and do without comfort.
After a while, people felt it was meaningless to
suffer all their lives, and they didn't want to
take any more suffering. Right now Buddhism is a

very new, fresh,and modern thing in America. Therefore, they want to try it out, to taste its flavor.
Actually there's no other flavor--just bitterness!

If you don't enter into forms, sounds, smells,
tastes, objects of touch and dharmas, then your
mind will not be turned by food or clothes. They
will not bother your mind and nature. So, anyone
among you who feel you have some cultivation
behind you should ask yourself: "Do I like to
eat good food or not?" If you like to eat good
food, then you are still far from having reached
the ultimate level. If you like to wear beautiful
clothes, then you're still behind in your accomplishment. You should learn to be:

Eating all day, but not eating one grain of rice,
Wearing clothes all day, but not wearing a single
*   thread.*

If you reach this kind of state, you are "pro-
ducing the mind that does not dwell anywhere."
If you can produce the mind that does not dwell
anywhere, and also not enter forms, sounds, smells,
tastes, objects of touch , and dharmas, then you
will attain the fruition of a Shrotaapanna.

Shrotaapanna is Sanskrit, and translates as
"entering into the flow"(入流).   It means
entering into the current of the Dharma Nature of
sages. The eighteen realms are the six sense
organs, six sense objects, and six consciousnesses.
They vex and bother the nature of our mind and
prevent it from accomplishing its Way karma. But
in the <u>Shurangama</u> <u>Sutra</u> it also says, "The things
that help you to accomplish your Way karma--to
attain the proper fruition and become a Buddha--
are those very same six sense organs, six sense
objects, and six consciousnesses." If you can
master these six sense organs so that they listen
to your orders, then you have some skill. The
eighteen realms are the combination of the six
sense organs, six sense objects, and six consciousnesses. THE SKILLFULNESS OF THE REALMS means you
can **skillfully** employ the eighteen realmsto help
you attain the unsurpassed way.

The Sutra continues. Foremost Wisdom Bodhisattva asks Manjushri Bodhisattva...

SUTRA:

> HOW DOES A BODHISATTVA ATTAIN SKILLFULNESS WITH THE PLACES? SKILLFULNESS WITH THE ARISAL OF CONDITIONS? SKILLFULNESS WITH THE DESIRE REALM? SKILLFULNESS WITH THE FORM REALM? SKILLFULNESS WITH THE FORMLESS REALM? SKILLFULNESS WITH THE PAST? SKILLFULNESS WITH THE FUTURE? SKILLFULNESS WITH THE PRESENT?

COMMENTARY:

HOW DOES A BODHISATTVA ATTAIN SKILLFULNESS WITH THE PLACES? The "places" are no different from the six sense organs and six sense objects. The combination of the six sense organs and six sense objects is called the "twelve places." You also have to know how to apply effort at these twelve places. No matter what--if you know how to use it, then it is in accord with the Buddhadharma; if you don't know how to use it, then it will give rise to obstructions. If you are not turned by the six sense organs and six sense objects, then they become very useful for your cultivation. If you always run after the six sense organs and six sense objects, then they become big obstructions for your cultivation. Therefore, whether it's the five Skandhas, eighteen realms, or twelve places--if you know how to use them, they will help you. If you don't know how to use them, they will destroy you. By way of analogy, if you know how to master the troops, you will be victorious in battle everywhere. So it is said,

> *With ready strategy within one's grasp,*
> *One can most certainly excel beyond 10,000 miles.*

If you don't know how to master the troops, you'll be defeated in every battle.

Our eyes, ears, nose, tongue, body, and mind, together with sights, sounds, smells, tastes, touches, and dharmas, are all helping us to cultivate. If we don't know how to use them, they will become obstructions to our Way karma. Why do we have to eat food? Because we have to survive in order to cultivate. If we die, there will

be no way for us to cultivate. Food helps us to
survive, but one's purpose for living in the world
is absolutely not for the sake of eating! Somebody says survival is for the sake of eating and
wearing clothes--that's being too mean and low.
Eating food is for the sake of survival. But it's
absolutely not for the sake of eating that we live
in the world. Then what's the purpose of living?
We have to create merit in the world and virtue
among people, and benefit all living beings. If
we can do this, then our lives will have some
meaning. Otherwise, we've come to this world in
vain.
     We who first realize this principle should
teach it to those who don't understand it in the
world. The ancients said,

> One must use the knowledge one has already
>   understood to enlighten those who do not yet
>   understand,
> And together with those who have already enlightened,
>   speak of this path to enlighten all people.

Also, there's another saying,

> I take the world as my own responsibility.

In Ancient China, there was a sage called Yi Yen
who said,

> As long as there's a person who suffers starvation,
> It is because I haven't give him food to eat.
> As long as there's a person who suffers from the
>   cold,
> It is because I haven't given him clothes to wear.

Previously I spoke about why the monks at Gold
Mountain Monastery choose to eat one meal a day;
this is because their teacher eats one meal a
day. But why does their teacher want to eat one
meal a day? You might say, he must be a very
stupid person, a very dull person who doesn't know
how to calculate. Why do I say this? If he is a
person who knows how to calculate, then why doesn't
he eat breakfast and dinner? Why does he mistreat
his own stomach? Actually it is not this way. I

don't agree that I am a very stupid person. I
also disagree that I don't know how to calculate.
I don't have to use an abacus, I just have to
take a look at people to know the exact number in
the hall. When I was in Vietnam, I had my little
disciple count how many people. It turned out
that each time, he counted over and over again
and couldn't get the right numbers. Later, I told
him how many people and we settled for that number.
Because of this, I don't agree that I don't know
how to calculate mathematics. But why do I eat
one meal a day?

Today, I might as well tell you the conditions
that brought about this resolve. In Manchuria,
when Japan invaded China, I was mourning beside
my mother's grave. Meanwhile, somebody told me
that the Japanese had seized a lot of Chinese
people and put them into labor camps. They
didn't have enough food to eat or clothes to wear
and so a lot of people starved to death and froze
to death. It was extremely bitter. I pondered
this situation and the severity of their plight,
and then I made a vow to eat one meal a day. I
wished to save my breakfast and dinner for those
who didn't have food to eat. Somebody might say
this kind of attitude is very stupid. Well, you
can say it's very stupid because those hungry
people might not directly receive the food which
I saved. But all of you should know it's the
principle of material without extinction. The
food I didn't eat will remain in the world. Since
it remains in the world, somebody will get to eat
it. So I made this vow to eat one meal a day.
Somebody will say eating one meal a day is not the
system taught by the Buddha. Then what is it?
The system of ghosts? You don't understand the
Buddhadharma, how can you critize it as not the
system taught by the Buddha? You can open the
Sutra of the Forty-Two Sections. In it it says,

> *Bhikshus! Take only one meal a day at noon.*
> *Pass the night beneath trees,*
> *And be careful not to acquire worldly things.*

If this is not the system taught by the Buddha,
then what is it? You don't understand any Buddhadharma, and what's more you casually critize it.

This kind of attitude is exactly what the Buddha
was referring to when he said, "Those people are
to be pitied!"

   Not only did I vow to eat one meal a day, but
from that time on I also vowed not to wear padded
cotton clothing no matter how cold the weather was.
During the winters in Manchuria, the temperature
always dropped to 33 or 34 degrees below zero.
When the temperature dropped to 38 degrees below
zero it would freeze people to death. But even
in such cold weather, I wore only three layers of
clothing. Whether in winter or summer it was the
same, I did not even put on an extra sweater.
By my vow I saved the cotton for those who didn't
have clothes to wear. I transferred it to them.
Did they obtain benefit from it? This again is a
case of material without extinction. Somebody
will use it for sure. Ever since I made that vow
not to wear padded clothes, I didn't feel
cold even in very chilly weather. Later on, I
even went without socks and shoes, and I could
walk with bare feet on icy ground at any time.
My feet didn't get frozen.

   That reminds me of a funny thing that
happened. I had an eighteen-year old disciple
who was a very energetic young man. He saw me
walking on the icy ground without wearing socks
and shoes, and he wanted to try it out. But he
hadn't taken more than 100 steps when his two
feet completely froze and then swelled up fiercely.
He couldn't endure any more and hurriedly ran into
the temple. It took six months before he was able
to walk again. At that time, I was twenty years
old, and I could bear the cold, but even though he
was younger, he couldn't. How could I bear it? It
had to do with my vow not to wear padded clothes.
Since I didn't wear padded clothes, I didn't feel
cold at all. Since I didn't eat so much food, I
didn't feel hungry. Before when I wasn't eating
one meal a day, I had to eat five small bowls of
food at each meal, which means a total of 15 bowls
a day. But after I vowed to eat one meal a day,
I could manage with three bowls of rice at most.
If the bowl was a big one, I ate two bowlsful. If
the bowl was a small one, I ate three bowlsful.

   It is not that I put myself on a diet. Actually I feel uncomfortable when I eat too much.

Even if I didn't eat, I didn't feel hungry at all.
From this, people should recognize the power of
vows. If you make vows, they will fulfill your
wishes. This is the story behind why I eat one
meal a day. Most of my disciples in America also
eat one meal a day. Not only do the left-home
people eat one meal a day, but a lot of the laypeople also eat one meal a day. They like to
learn my stupid method. In this scientific age,
they want to use this stupid method to cultivate.
You can say that they don't know how to calculate.
But viewed from another point, they can be said
to be calculating in great detail.

They give away the food which they don't eat
and save it for other people. This is creating
food-affinities with other people. So, I believe
they will never starve to death through limitless
future time. It is because we're afraid that we'll
starve that we save some food for future use.
The ancients also had a saying,

> *If one decreases the clothes he wears,*
> *One's blessings will grow.*
> *If one decreases the food he eats,*
> *One's lifespan will increase.*

Because I think that my lifespan will probably not
be too long, I want to decrease my intake of food
in order to increase my lifespan. Actually this
is not true, I'm just making a joke with you! But
in fact, eating one meal a day is in accord with
the system taught by the Buddha.

We have to follow the Buddha's system to
cultivate. The Buddha said,

> *Bhikshus should eat one meal a day,*
> *And sleep each night under a different tree.*

Wherever they dwell they should not stay over
three days. Because if they stay over three days,
people may come to make offerings. But shouldn't
they receive any offerings? They are allowed to
accept offerings, but they should not have a
greedy mind when receiving the offerings. Once
you live in a place for a long period, dharma
conditions will arise. It is said,

Sitting for a long time, one attains Samadhi,
Dwelling for a long time, one develops
affinities.

Therefore, unless a Bhikshu has some important
matter to attend to, it is better that he travel
around. So in China left-home people travelled
around everywhere and paid respects at every
famous temple. This is called "hiding one's light."
Not wanting to show off or sell their cultivation,
wherever bhikshus dwelled, they would not stay
over three nights.

There are also a lot of events at Gold Mountain Monastery which I will gradually share with
you, because many people are eager to know why
Americans believe in Buddhism. "They eat one meal
a day and sleep sitting up! Do you recite some
kind of mantra to control them?" I'm often asked.
"Or do you use some type of drug to oppress them?"
There are some people in Taiwan who created that
rumor. They said, "Why are there so many Americans
who left the home life with him? That's because
he smokes dope and uses drugs with them. He
took L.S.D. Those Americans can only take one
tablet, but he could take ten of them and nothing
happened to him. Therefore, they left the home
life with him." This is not true! This is a
rumor. I cannot endure even one tablet of L.S.D.
I don't know what L.S.D. is or what Marijuana is,
but in Taiwan people created the rumor that I took
L.S.D. When I heard this I felt it was very funny.
Think about it. Actually there's no such thing
but people go ahead and make rumors anyway. What
is the principle behind this?

Now, I am a Chinese but I don't have racial
discrimination or a concept of nationality. I am
a man of the world. Therefore, the Buddhism I
teach does not belong to Chinese Buddhism--actually
China doesn't have any Buddhism. The same applies
to India, Japan, Thailand, Cambodia...or any other
country. Buddhism is a world-wide religion. It
does not belong to a particular country. Before,
people's views were narrow and they separated it
into Chinese Buddhism, Indian Buddhism, Japanese
Buddhism, Thai Buddhism, Cambodian Buddhism, and
so forth. This is a mistake. Buddhism belongs to

every living being. The Buddha said,

> *Every living being has the Buddha nature,*
> *All can become Buddhas.*

Since every living being has the Buddha nature
and all can become Buddhas, then every living being is naturally a member of Buddhism. Therefore
my principle of Buddhism extends to the ends of
empty space and pervades the Dharma Realm. There's
no concept of countries, no concept of household,
no concept of race, no concept of people and self.
This is the age of science; human beings have
reached the moon. As it is said,

> *The uttermost end of the earth has become*
> *a neighborhood.*

The prime minister Ye Lu Ch'u T'sai （耶律楚材）
in the Yuan （元） Dynasty said,

> *The Western heaven is three steps away,*
> *The eastern sea is as deep as a cup.*

The entire world has become one community. Within
one day, you can reach any place in the world.
Therefore our thoughts should expand correspondingly.
Again we should not harbor prejudice between sects,
or maintain the view of a self and others. We
should take the Dharma Realm as our mind. The
doctrine of Buddhism includes every living being
in the world. Therefore, in America, why do some
Catholics, Christians, and those of Jewish faith
believe in Buddhism? Let me tell you honestly that
it's because the principle of Buddhism is very
broad.
    Right now you don't believe in Buddhism and
you do not regard yourself as a Buddhist. But I
regard you as a Buddhist. Why? Because you are
a living being and the Buddha said, "All living
beings have the Buddha nature, all can become
Buddhas." Since you are a living being, you've
got an opportunity to become a Buddha in the
future. Of course, if you don't admit you are a
living being, then there's no share for you in
Buddhism. Since you say you're not a living

being, let me ask you, "What kind of creature are
you? What is your name, can you name it?" If
you can't name yourself, then you are a living
being and you possess the Buddha nature. Temporarily, you do not believe in Buddhism, but you
will believe in the future. If you don't believe
in the near future, you will believe in the far future.
If you don't believe in this life, you will believe
next life. If you don't believe today, you will
believe tomorrow. Although you don't believe
right now, I still include you as one who believes.
Therefore, I treat all living beings throughout
empty space and the entire Dharma Realm as
Buddhists. This is the meaning of *"the entire
substance and great function."*

Some Christians hear this and say, "Oh! We
cannot run out of the Dharma Realm!" And so they
return. Therefore, there are a lot of Catholics,
Christians, priests, and so forth who are coming
around and saying, "When I think about the principles of Buddhism, there seems to be a bit of
reason behind them." This is not only a case of
"there seems to be." Investigate deeply
and ask yourself, "Can I run out of the Dharma Realm?"
No, you cannot! The Dharma Realm is not mine, it
belongs to Buddhism. If you cannot run out of the
Dharma Realm, this means you don't have any way to
jump out of the Buddha's palm. Although this is
just a story, there's also a saying that goes,

*Although the incident cited is small,
It can be used as an analogy for the great.*

The principle of the Buddhism which I believe in has
no limits or   boundaries. There's no place
which is not within the region of Buddhism.
To the ends of empty space or the Dharma
Realm, there is not a single dust mote where all
the Buddhas in the past did not sacrifice their
lives. So how can a living being escape the Dharma
Realm? Therefore my principle of Buddhism is not
old-fashioned. I don't say, "Great Vehicle
Buddhism belongs to China." If you think this way,
then your view is very narrow and small. It is
all right to say that Buddhism came from India.
It is all right to say that Buddhism was tran-

smitted from India into China. But you can't say
that Buddhism belongs to China. Buddhism has no
boundaries, no racial discriminations. Actually,
there's nothing at all. Why? Because my principle
is a general doctrine on Buddhism. There's no
prejudice of self within it. It comes from everybody's wisdom. I am just representing Buddhism
in voicing this doctrine.

SKILLFULNESS WITH THE ARISAL OF CONDITIONS.
This may apply to conditions in general, or to
conditions that aid the Way. It means to use
skillful and expedient Dharma doors to teach and
transform all living beings.

"Skillfulness" is to be skillful in knowing
all dharmas: that originally everything is empty;
that there is no need to destroy the false name of
dharmas,or to distinguish the marks of all dharmas.
There is no need to discriminate the real mark of
all dharmas. This is called "skillfulness." No
matter what conditions arise, you should use skillful, expedient methods to speak the Dharma. This
is called the "skillfulness with the arisal of
conditions."

SKILLFULNESS WITH THE DESIRE REALM. The
Desire Realm includes the six desire heavens. The
place that we human beings dwell in is the Desire
realm. That is why living beings have a lot of
impure desires which turn them. They turn back
and forth in the revolving wheel of birth and
death. As it is said,

> *Born of desire,*
> *They die from desire as well.*

There is another saying,

> *The vegetable worm will die in the*
> *vegetable.*

We who are the worms of desire will also die in
desire. Living beings are like big worms. The
difference between big worms and   small worms is
the size of their bodies. Only the nature of
their bodies is different. But their desires are
the same; they all have thoughts of desire. If
you can stop your thoughts of desire--"Cut off
desire, cast away love -- then you can transcend

the three realms, those of desire, form, and formlessness. Although this is not easy, it is just
because it is not easy that we have to cultivate.
You have to cultivate the very things which are
not easy. Somebody says, "I'm an ordinary person."
Well, although you are an ordinary person, isn't
everyone else an ordinary person? Not only are you
an ordinary person, all Buddhas and Arhats in the
past were ordinary people. And because when they
were ordinary people, they cut off desire and
cast away love, they were able to go against the
trend and not be turned by desire. As it is said,

> According with the environment will beget a person,
> Going against the current will bring about
>   Buddhahood.

"According with the environment" means going along
with circumstances that please the desires of
sentient beings. This can only lead to future
human existence. "Going against the current"
means to turn the tide around and not accord with
the desires of sentient beings and not be turned
by them. Buddhas are accomplished by this method.
Buddhas are accomplished from ordinary people.
Therefore all common people are qualified to
become Buddhas. All have the opportunity to
become Buddhas. The only thing to be feared is
that you don't cultivate. If you don't follow
desire and just go ahead to cultivate, you will
have the opportunity to become a Buddha. Therefore, you should not say, "I'm a common person,
and I only can do ordinary things." If a common
person can do the things that sages do, so much
the better! For example, a child cannot insist
on being a child forever. After twenty years,
he is grown up and if he still insists he is a
child, that's just being ridiculous.

   Therefore, anyone has the opportunity to
become a Buddha if he cultivates. He can transcend the three realms--the desire realm, form
realm, and formless realm. There is a saying,

> In the six desire heavens there are the five
>   signs of decay.
> The third dhyana heaven suffers the disaster
>   of wind.

> *No matter how you cultivate, even up to the*
> *heaven of neither thought nor non-thought,*
> *It's still better to be born in the Western land*
> *and then come back again.*

People in the heavens still have limited life-
spans. In the heaven of the Four Kings, their
life-span is 500 years. They take 50 years of
human time as one of their days and nights. Why

is it that their one day and night amount to 50
years in our time? Because they're very happy in
that heaven and so time flies. So their one day and
night is equal to 50 years of worldly time. Their
life-span is 500 years. Above this heaven, the
life span of each subsequent heaven increases
by another 500 years. Therefore the minimum life-
span of heavenly beings is 500 years, but their
life-spans have an end. When the end comes, they

will experience five signs of decay:

1.   The flowers on their crowns start to
wilt. Heavenly people wear hats which are made
of very beautiful, very adorned flowers. But
when their life-spans draw to an end, the flowers
start to fade and their crowns will fall. This
is one of the five signs of decay. Once this
kind of phenomenon appears, they know their life
is going to end soon.
2.   Heavenly people's clothes are very pure,
without any defilement. They are not like the
clothes of worldly people which get dirty and
need to be washed. No, the gods don't need
washing machines. Their clothes are always clean,
and spotless, without a speck of dust. But when the
five signs of decay appear, their clothes start to
accumulate dust, and then get dirty.
3.   Worldly people always sweat, but heavenly
people don't perspire. But when the five signs
of decay appear, their armpits start to sweat.
4.   The bodies of heavenly people always
emit fragrance, a rare kind of perfume. It's not
like worldly people who spray themselves with
perfumes like "Evening in Paris" in order to smell
good. It is a natural fragrance. Why do their
bodies emit such fragrance? It is because they
kept and upheld the five precepts and practiced
the ten good deeds in the past. Let me tell you
a secret. There are some people who have body
odor. They stay far away from others because the
odor from their body repels others. Why do they
have such an odor? It's because in their past
lives they received the precepts but failed to
uphold them. Since they didn't make too many
mistakes, they are still reborn as human beings,
but they carry around with them this odor. Most
Western people have this kind of odor. You may
say that they didn't hold the precepts in their
past lives. Some of them don't keep precepts in
this life, either. They are very casual or sloppy
with their sexual desire. Western people, unlike
those of more conservative cultures, are very
casual. This comes from their fondness for what
they call freedom. It turns out that everything
gets lumped under freedom. Therefore, in western
countries they can marry freely as they wish.

They can get married today, and get divorced
tomorrow, and get married again the day after.
Some of them don't care whether they get married
or not! This type of behavior is impermissible
from the traditional Chinese viewpoint. Therefore,
when you sit beside western people, their "foxy"
odor, onion odor, and dirty-socks odor will
come out. It might be because they eat too much
cheese.

     5.   Heavenly people always sit in meditation,
in an upright position. But when the signs of
decay appear, their karmic retribution will manifest, and they cannot sit still any more. They
want to jump around. After they jump around, they
feel it's not right and they sit down again. When
they sit down, they want to get up. They are just
like a monkey jumping up and down. After they
jump around several times, they die. They do not
die from a stroke or a heart attack, but they do
die. After they die, they will undergo the effects
of whatever karmic retribution is then mature.

     From this you can see that to be reborn in
the heavens is still not ultimate. Buddhists who
really understand the Buddhadharma do not wish to
be born in the heavens, because the realm of
heavens still lies within the revolving wheel of
the six paths.

SKILLFULNESS WITH THE FORM REALM. In the
form realm, beings have less desire than in the
desire realm, but they're still attached to the
mark of form. There still remains the appearance of form--that which one can see.

SKILLFULNESS WITH FORMLESS REALM. They are
no longer attached to visible forms. But they
still have desire for the formless state which
they harbor in their consciousness. Since they
are still afflicted with this kind of trouble,
they remain within the three realms.

     If you can transcend the three realms of
desire, form, and formlessness, then you can end
your birth and death and not have to revolve in
the six paths anymore. If you cannot transcend
the three realms but revolve around and around
within them, then it's like staying in a burning
house. The house is already on fire, but you
still don't realize you should escape. Someday,
you will be burned to death. Therefore, the three

realms are described this way:

> *There is no peace in the three realms,*
> *They are like a burning house.*

So we have to cultivate to transcend the three realms. This refers to using skillful, expedient Dharma doors to teach living beings in the three realms and show them the path of escape.

SKILLFULNESS WITH THE PAST. All Buddhas in the past also used skillful and expedient Dharma doors to teach and transform all living beings.

SKILLFULNESS WITH THE FUTURE. All Buddhas in the future also will use skillful and expedient Dharma doors to teach and transform all living beings. They will cause all living beings to turn back from confusion and go toward enlightenment, give up evil and return to the proper.

SKILLFULNESS WITH THE PRESENT. All Buddhas in the present also use skillful and expedient Dharma doors to teach and transform all living beings. They cause all living beings to transcend the three realms and end birth and death.

SUTRA:

HOW DOES A BODHISATTVA SKILLFULLY CULTIVATE THE ENLIGHTENMENT-SHARE OF MINDFULNESS?   THE ENLIGHTEN-MENT-SHARE OF SELECTING A DHARMA?   THE ENLIGHTEN-MENT-SHARE OF VIGOR?   THE ENLIGHTENMENT-SHARE OF JOY?   THE ENLIGHTENMENT-SHARE OF LIGHT EASE?   THE ENLIGHTENMENT-SHARE OF SAMADHI?   THE ENLIGHTENMENT-SHARE OF RENUNCIATION?   THE STATE OF EMPTINESS, MARKLESSNESS, AND WISHLESSNESS?

COMMENTARY:

These are the seven shares of Enlightenment, also called Seven Bodhi Shares, or Seven Limbs of Enlightenment. In the <u>Amitabha Sutra</u> they are referred to in the passage which says, "The seven Bodhi Shares, the Eight Sagely Way Shares" and so forth.

There are three kinds of emptiness mentioned here. "Emptiness" itself is emptied. "Markless-ness" and "wishlessness" mean that everything is

empty. This Sutra passage discusses the seven
enlightenment-shares and the three kinds of emptiness. Therefore, Foremost Wisdom Bodhisattva
again asks Manjushri Bodhisattva, "How does a
Bodhisattva cultivate the enlightenment-share of
mindfulness? How does he cultivate the enlightenment-share of selecting a dharma?" That is, how
do we know which kind of dharma is right and which
kind of dharma is wrong? How does one obtain the
Dharma selecting eye to cultivate the enlightenment-share of selecting a dharma? Right now, it
is not necessary to answer these questions. The
verse section of this Sutra text passage will
answer them quite clearly.

How does a Bodhisattva cultivate *THE ENLIGHTEN-
MENT-SHARE OF VIGOR?* That is, how does he cultivate the Dharma door of vigor and non-retreat? To
be vigorous means to not be lazy. But when faced
with the choice between laziness and vigor, most
people prefer to be lazy and do not wish to be
vigorous.

Furthermore, *THE ENLIGHTENMENT-SHARE OF JOY.*
How does a Bodhisattva cultivate to gain the Bodhi
mind of joy in studying Buddhism? How does he
maintain a joyful mind towards Buddhism without
letting it be cut off?

THE ENLIGHTENMENT-SHARE OF LIGHT EASE. How
does one cultivate and obtain the enlightenment-
share of ceaseless tranquility? Tranquility means
light ease. This is when one feels very comfortable when sitting in Dhyana. One has a feeling
of self-mastery and happiness. Once one sits there,
one doesn't want to get up. One feels sitting is
better than doing anything else. It's better than
eating good food! This means that one forgets
everything else. The state of tranquility is a
state which beginners experience while sitting in
Dhyana. They may experience this kind of feeling
of comfort and self-mastery.

THE ENLIGHTENMENT-SHARE OF SAMADHI. How does
a Bodhisattva attain the enlightenment-share of
Samadhi? How does he enter the state where *one
is always in Samadhi? There is no time where one is not
in Samadhi.*

THE ENLIGHTENMENT-SHARE OF RENUNCIATION. How
does a Bodhisattva discriminate between proper

Dharma and improper Dharmas? How does he renounce improper dharmas and renounce all greed and love?
THE STATE OF EMPTINESS. How does a Bodhisattva truly attain emptiness?
MARKLESSNESS. How does a Bodhisattva attain a state of being without marks?
WISHLESSNESS. How does a Bodhisattva attain a state of being without wishes?
Marks are empty and wishes are empty, too. How can he break through attachments and attain the three types of emptiness? Those are the questions that Foremost Wisdom Bodhisattva asked Manjushri Bodhisattva.

SUTRA:

HOW DOES A BODHISATTVA ATTAIN THE PERFECTION OF DANA PARAMITA? SHILA PARAMITA? KSHANTI PARAMITA? VIRYA PARAMITA? DHYANA PARAMITA? PRAJNA PARAMITA? AND ALSO THE PERFECTION OF KIND- NESS, COMPASSION, JOY, AND GIVING?

COMMENTARY:

Foremost Wisdom Bodhisattva asks Manjushri Bodhisattva, "How does a Bodhisattva cultivate to perfection the Dana Paramita?" "Dana" is San- skrit and translates as "giving." "Paramita" is also Sanskrit, and translates as "reaching the other shore," or "the other shore has been reached." That is, if you haven't finished a certain chore, then you don't have Paramita. After you have finished your chore, then that is Paramita. For example, after you finish eating, that is the paramita of eating food. After you have put on your clothes, that is the paramita of wearing clothes. After you wake up from your sleep, that is the paramita of sleeping. Somebody might say, "This Dharma Master always talks about eating, wearing clothes,or sleeping. We don't want to hear this any more." Although you don't want to listen, you cannot manage to go without eating, wearing clothes, or sleeping. Since you cannot do without any of these, why should it matter to you when we talk about them? Isn't it much better that I instruct you about the way to

reach the other shore, the way of paramita? It
is said,

  The Way is sought in shallow places.

You shouldn't expect something too lofty or too
far-reaching in your cultivation. Don't say, "I'm
going up to heaven to seek the Way. Right now
they've invented rockets, and I can take a rocket
to heaven and seek the Way." Probably you cannot
realize this false thought in this life. Although
scientists have invented the rockets, if you wish
them to take you to heaven to seek the Way, this
is just a big false thought which has no value at
all. But within the realm of what is possible,
whatever chore you perform perfectly and completely
is said to be "paramita."
  The paramita here refers to going "from the
shore of birth and death, across the current of
afflictions, and reaching the other shore of
Nirvana." Dana Paramita, then, is the "Perfection
of giving."
  The Paramita of Giving means reaching the
other shore through the act of giving. When we
give, we should have a mind wherein "the substance
of the three wheels is emptied (三輪體空)."
The "three wheels" refer to the gift, the giver,
and the receiver. To empty the three wheels is to
have no appearance of a giver, a gift, or a
receiver. If you maintain this kind of thought,
then your giving can extend to all of empty space
and pervade the Dharma Realm. Then this is really
the perfection of Dana Paramita.
  SHILA PARAMITA. "Shila" means "precepts,"
also Pratimoksha (liberation). When Shakyamuni
Buddha was about to enter Nirvana, the Venerable
Ananda asked the Buddha about four matters. One
of them involved the precepts. The Venerable
Ananda asked the Buddha, "When the Buddha dwells
in the world, we follow the Buddha as our teacher.
After the Buddha enters into Nirvana, who will
be our teacher?"
  Shakyamuni Buddha answered, "When I dwell in
the world, you take me as your teacher. After I
enter into Nirvana, you should take the precepts
as your teacher." Therefore, after the Buddha

entered Nirvana, all left-home people have to receive and uphold the precepts.

How did the precepts come about? When Shakyamuni Buddha dwelt in the world, there were six Bhikshus who always transgressed the rules. Everytime they transgressed, the Buddha would lay down a precept, and say, "From now on, you cannot transgress this precept any more. If you do, you will fall into the hells." It was by this process that the precepts were spoken. When the Buddha dwelt in the world and spoke the precepts, everybody followed them. After the Buddha entered Nirvana, all the left-home people should accord with precepts to cultivate. They should take the precepts as their teacher.

KSHANTI PARAMITA. "Kshanti" means "patience." The power of patience is very great. Whoever cultivates should practice this patience. Shakyamuni Buddha used to be a patient immortal. In the <u>Vajra Sutra</u> you will read about the king of Kalinga who dismembered the limbs of the patient immortal, but the latter did not produce a single thought of hatred. Now that we are the Buddha's disciples, if anyone comes to dismember our limbs, can we be patient? Somebody may say, "I can do it!" Others may say, "I'll wait to see what happens." And then others among you may say honestly, "I cannot do it!" Shakyamuni Buddha walked this path himself. Even though he had such great virtue, someone still came to dismember his body. So far nobody has come to dismember our bodies, but we still produce the mind of hatred. If we compare ourselves with Shakyamuni Buddha, shouldn't we feel ashamed? Since we are the Buddha's disciples, why shouldn't we emulate the Buddha's Dharma? Why can't we follow the door of conduct that the Buddha cultivated? At that time, nobody preached the Dharma door of the paramita of patience to Shakyamuni Buddha. Nobody instructed him in how to be patient. But he was able to be patient by himself. Now we listen to the Sutras and hear the Dharma everyday, but if someone criticizes us a bit we cannot endure it. We cannot be patient, but produce afflictions to the point that we die of anger! This is really pitiful!

Patience is a most wonderful Dharma door. You should not feel that patience is like tasting bitter medicine. On the contrary, you should feel it's as sweet as sweet dew. Then this is useful.

An example of patience is the story of "old man Chang tolerated a hundred things; the nine generations all lived together（張公百忍，九世同居）The elder Chang was a very sagacious and tolerant fellow. Nine generations of his household lived happily together under one roof. They co-existed in peace and didn't fight. This was considered very remarkable even by the most conservative of Chinese standards. How did they manage? It's because the Elder Chang tolerated a hundred things. He was always willing to concede. He never got angry.

Therefore, the Buddha extolled the virtues of the Paramita of patience. If we can personally practice it, then we will have great accomplishment. But how do you get into it when you begin to practice patience? Let me tell you--

you have to regard all things as very ordinary.

> *All conditioned dharmas are like dreams,*
> *illusions, bubbles,*
> *Like dew drops and a lightening flash.*

Thus one should observe and realize all the world's phenomena. You have to regard all dharmas as being like illusions and reflections. All dharmas refer to all phenomena, all the states that you experience or see in your daily life. At this time, you should face reality and recognize the state, have control over phenomena rather than being turned by states and ending up not knowing what to do. If you can see through it and put it down, then you can attain self-mastery. Let me tell you a wonderful motto that I use in America. What is it? It is *"everything is okay, no problem."* If you regard all things as being without any problem, then this is patience. You see all things as very ordinary and don't get uptight about them. All things are viewed as illusions and transformation. As it is said,

> *Basically there's not a thing in the world,*
> *But stupid people get worked up anyway.*

Why do you give rise to affliction? It's because you're very stupid. If you have wisdom, it's for sure you will not have any affliction. Affliction comes from ignorance. If you don't have affliction, then your wisdom will manifest. Why is your memory so bad? Somebody says, "When I was young, my memory was very good. But since I got older, my memory has disappeared." Today, I went to Upasaka Lee's residence. He inscribed a poem on a painting. I just glanced at it once and I memorized the poem. Now I will recite it to you. It goes like this:

> *The Black water gushes for a thousand years,*
> *The White Sand is valiant throughout ten*
> *   thousand generations.*
> *My home was located on the peak of an*
> *   obscure mountain.*

> *I plowed the fields and dug the well and enjoyed*
> *   life with my big family.*
> *When I was twenty years old, I threw away my*
> *   pen and joined the army.*
> *Now I'm old and the color of my face is faded,*
> *   and I lodge at the Island of P'eng.*
> *When can I return to my country,*
> *And walk around the oak tree in front of my*
> *   house again?*

The Black water gushes for a thousand years. He is a native of Manchuria and there's a mighty river called the Black Dragon River. The water gushes for thousands of years without stopping.

The White Sand is valiant throughout ten thousand generations. He lived near the Long White Mountain Range, which is the chief of Mountains among all mountains. It stands for ten thousand generations, just like a great hero. Because Upasaka Lee was a soldier, he likes to talk about heroes. He is into heroism.

My home was located on the peak of an obscure mountain. My residence was situated on the peak of an out-of-the-way mountain.

I plowed the fields and dug the well and enjoyed life with my big family. A verse that describes the reign of Emperor Yao says,

> *I go to work when the sun rises,*
> *And I go home to rest when sun sets.*
> *I drink water from the wells I dug; ;*
> *I eat food from the fields I plowed.*

To continue with General Lee's poem:

When I was twenty years old, I threw away my pen and joined the army. When he was twenty years, he threw away his pen and followed the style of Pan Ch'au (班超) who was a general in the Han Dynasty. Originally he wanted to study, but he decided to offer up his strength to serve his country, so he threw away his pen and joined the troops.

Now I am old and the color of my face is faded, and I lodge at the Island of P'eng. Now I lodge at the Island of P'eng (Taiwan) just like a traveller who lodges at a hotel.

When can I return to my country. When can I go back to my country to see Long White Mountain?

And walk around the oak tree in front of my house again? On the day when Upasaka Lee was born, his mother dreamt of an old oak tree in front of his house. After she woke up, she gave birth to Upasaka Lee. He wants to show his gratitude to his mother, and wishes to walk around the tree in front of his old house in every single thought. Maybe it means that he still wants to be his mother's son in his next live.

I recited this poem to him, he felt very surprised and said, "Your memory is so good!"

I said, "My memory's already bad. When I was young, my memory was better than right now."

If you can be patient, then your memory will get better. If somebody doesn't have any memory at all, it's because they cannot be patient. If you can be patient, then you can memorize everything. Memorizing everything is of no great use. However, if you can be patient, you can attain dhyana and you will be vigorous. The Bodhisattva who never slighted others always bowed to people when he saw them. He said, "I dare not look lightly upon you. You will all become Buddhas in the future." Although he acted in this way, people still scolded him and beat him. But he still bowed to them from afar and said, "I dare not look lightly upon you. You will all become Buddhas in the future." Those arrogant Bhikshus still wanted to beat him. But he just got up and fled!

So you see, our patience is far from the patience of the Bodhisattva who never slighted people. Our patience cannot compare with Shakyamuni Buddha's. Even when his body was dismembered by others he didn't give rise to hatred. If we can reach that level, then we have a little bit of skill, and we can say we've reached home. The Kshanti Paramita is the Perfection of Patience.

The fourth is the Virya Paramita. "Virya" is Sanskrit and translates as "vigor." There are two kinds of vigor:

      a.   The vigor of the body.

      b.   The vigor of the mind.

For example, if you read sutras and do not sleep too much, that's called vigor. I nicknamed Gold Mountain Monastery in San Fransisco the "Ice Box." Why? Because there's no heater inside that building. Sometimes people get so cold they can't take it, especially during the winters. People who cannot endure the cold, have to be that much more vigorous.

We follow the pattern of *"Investigating Dhyana in winter and studying Sutras in summer."* It's better to sit in Dhyana during winter when it's cold and not sleep too much. Summer is so hot that it's better to listen to the Sutras. This is the rule in most Way Places. However at Gold Mountain Monastery, one must be vigorous both winter and summer. Nobody can take a rest! Therefore, Virya Paramita is a method of being vigorous and arriving at the other shore.

The Paramita of Dhyana. "Dhyana" is a Sanskrit word and refers to meditation. It is said,

> *Sitting for a long time,*
> *One attains Dhyana.*

You should not sit for a while and feel it's meaningless and quit sitting. If you want to sit longer, you should use patience to help you out. Even if you sit there with your two legs aching like mad, you still have to endure it. Even if your waist feels painful, you should endure it anyway. You have to endure what cannot be endured. You should break through the gate of pain. After you pass the gate of pain, then you will not feel pain anymore. Sitting in Dhyana one will experience all kinds of states, but you should not be afraid of those states. Don't say, "When I was sitting in Dhyana, a tiger came and wanted to eat me up, and I was scared so that I got up and ran!" It turned out there wasn't tiger around after all. It was just a state. It will not eat you up, because it is only a state. If you see a tiger who wants to eat you, you should be even more concentrated and the tiger will not eat you. This is only a state to test you out, so you should not be afraid. No matter what kind of state appears, you should not be afraid, then all the demonic obstacles will disappear and you will subdue all demon armies. This is the Paramita of Dhyana.

THE PRAJNA PARAMITA. "Prajna" means wisdom. If you have wisdom, then you can reach the other shore. If you're stupid, can you reach the other shore? Well, I don't know the answer, but the Buddha didn't mention any "Paramita of Stupidity."

THE PERFECTION OF KINDNESS, COMPASSION, JOY, AND GIVING. Kindness, compassion, joy, and giving are the four unlimited minds. When unlimited kindness, unlimited compassion, unlimited joy, unlimited giving are all perfected, then that is just the Buddha.

A Bodhisattva will attain liberation after he completes the Six Perfections. After he attains liberation, eventually he will be certified to the fruition of Buddhahood.

The perfection of kindness, the perfection of compassion, the perfection of joy, the perfection of giving are the four unlimited minds of a Buddha. We who cultivate the Six Perfections also have to cultivate to perfection those four unlimited minds.

SUTRA:

HOW DOES HE ATTAIN THE WISDOM POWER OF EN-LIGHTENING TO WHAT IS AND WHAT IS NOT? THE WISDOM POWER OF KNOWING THE KARMIC RETRIBUTIONS OF LIVING BEINGS IN THE PAST, PRESENT, AND FUTURE? THE WISDOM POWER OF KNOWING THE SUPERIOR AND INFERIOR ROOTS OF LIVING BEINGS? THE WISDOM POWER OF KNOW-ING THE VARIOUS REALMS OF LIVING BEINGS? THE WISDOM POWER OF KNOWING THE VARIOUS UNDERSTANDINGS OF LIVING BEINGS? THE WISDOM POWER OF KNOWING THE DESTINATIONS OF ALL PATHS? THE WISDOM POWER OF KNOWING THE DEFILEMENT AND PURITY OF THE DHYANAS, LIBERATIONS, AND SAMADHIS? THE WISDOM POWER OF THE KNOWLEDGE OF PAST LIVES? THE WISDOM POWER OF THE HEAVENLY EYE? THE WISDOM POWER OF THE ENDING OF ALL HABITS?

COMMENTARY:

How does a Bodhisattva cultivate in order to attain the real powers of a Buddha? What are the ten powers of a Buddha? The first is *THE WISDOM*

POWER OF knowing WHAT IS AND WHAT IS NOT. There are a lot of ways of speaking about this one if we want to talk in detail.

THE WISDOM POWER OF KNOWING THE KARMIC RETRI-BUTIONS OF LIVING BEINGS IN THE PAST, PRESENT, AND FUTURE. How does one attain the wisdom power of knowing the karmic retribution of living beings in the past, knowing the karmic retribution of living beings of the present, and knowing the karmic retribution of living beings of the future? This is another of the Buddha's ten wisdom powers.

THE WISDOM POWER OF KNOWING THE SUPERIOR AND INFERIOR ROOTS OF LIVING BEINGS? How does one realize the basic foundation of all living beings? Which roots are superior? Which roots are inferior? Living beings who have inferior roots are very difficult to cross over. Even though they're very hard to cross over, are you not going to save them? No, you can't do that. Because they have inferior roots, you should cause them to increase and develop superior roots. For example, my principle in teaching and transforming is that I don't exclusively teach people who have goot roots. Those people with good roots will bring forth the Bodhi mind by themselves; they don't need me to teach and transform them. If people are already good, why do I need to teach and transform them? For instance, if people already believe in Bud-dhism, already have taken refuge with the Triple Jewel, and already have brought forth their Bodhi mind, but you still tell them, "You should believe in Buddhism, and you should take refuge with the Triple Jewel." What's the idea?

You should think of some method to cause people who haven't brought forth their Bodhi mind to do so. You should cause those who don't be-lieve in Buddhism to believe in Buddhism. You should cause those who haven't taken refuge with the Triple Jewel to take refuge with the Triple Jewel.

THE WISDOM POWER OF KNOWING THE VARIOUS REALMS OF LIVING BEINGS. How does one attain the wisdom power of knowing all kinds of realms of living beings?

THE WISDOM POWER OF KNOWING THE VARIOUS UNDERSTANDINGS OF LIVING BEINGS. How does one attain the wisdom power of knowing all kinds of understandings of living beings?

THE WISDOM POWER OF KNOWING THE DESTINATIONS OF ALL PATHS. How does one attain the wisdom power of knowing all the destinations of all paths?

THE WISDOM POWER OF KNOWING THE DEFILEMENT AND PURITY OF THE DHYANAS, LIBERATIONS, AND SAMA-. DHIS? How does one attain the wisdom power of knowing the respective defilement and purity of the four dhyanas, eight liberations, and eight samadhis?

<u>The Four Dhyanas:</u>

    a.   The first Dhyana: the ground of the joy of leaving Production.

    b.   The Second Dhyana: the ground of the joy of producing concentration.

    c.   The Third Dhyana: the ground of the wonderful bliss of leaving joy.

    d.   The Fourth Dhyana: the pure ground of renouncing thought.

To the Four Dhyanas one adds the Four Formless Samadhis to make up the Eight Samadhis:

    e.   The Samadhi of the Station of Boundless Emptiness.

    f.   The Samadhi of the Station of Boundless Consciousness.

    g.   The Samadhi of Nothing whatsoever.

    h.   The Samadhi of Neither perception nor Non-perception.

The gods dwelling in these samadhis stay in the heavens of the Formless Realm, for this reason these samadhis are called the formless samadhis. The gods have no material bodies, they only possess consciousness. These heavens are also called the four stations of emptiness.

The Eight Liberations:

    a.   The Liberation in which inwardly there is the mark of form, and outwardly form is contemplated.

    b.   The Liberation in which inwardly there is no mark of form, and outwardly form is contemplated.

    c.   The Liberation of the pure liberation body wherein pure liberation has been attained.

    d.   The Liberation of the Station of Boundless Space.

    e.   The Liberation of the Station of Boundless Consciousness.

    f.   The Liberation of the Station of Nothing Whatsoever.

    g.   The Liberation of the Station of Neither Perception nor Non-perception.

    h.   The Liberation of the Samadhi of the Extinction of Perception and Thought.

THE WISDOM POWER OF THE KNOWLEDGE OF PAST LIVES? How does one attain the wisdom power of knowing things in the past and present?

THE WISDOM POWER OF THE HEAVENLY EYE? How does one attain the wisdom power of the Heavenly Eye?

THE WISDOM POWER OF THE ENDING OF ALL HABITS? How does one attain the wisdom power of ending all outflows and habits?

Above are the Buddha's ten types of wisdom powers. Foremost Wisdom Bodhisattva asks Manjushri Bodhisattva, "How does a Bodhisattva attain these ten types of wisdom power?"

SUTRA:

HOW DOES A BODHISATTVA ATTAIN THE PROTECTION,

VENERATION, AND OFFERINGS OF HEAVENLY KINGS, DRAGON KINGS, YAKSHA KINGS, GANDHARVA KINGS, ASHURA KINGS, GARUDA KINGS, KINNARA KINGS, MAHO-RAGA KINGS, HUMAN KINGS, AND BRAHMA KINGS?

COMMENTARY:

HOW DOES A BODHISATTVA ATTAIN THE PROTECTION, RESPECT, AND OFFERINGS OF HEAVENLY KINGS? Heavenly Kings include all kings in the heavens. For example, Kings of the Four Heavens, Kings of the Trayastrimsha Heavens, King Shakra, Great Brahma Kings, and so forth. How does one attain the protection, respect, and offerings of these kings?
HOW DOES ONE ATTAIN THE PROTECTION, RESPECT, AND OFFERINGS OF DRAGON KINGS?
There are elephant dragon kings, snake dragon kings, horse dragon kings, fish dragon kings, shrimp dragon kings, and so forth. Although these belong to the animal kingdom, they have spiritual penetrations and guard the heavenly palaces. They also can stir up the cloud and send rain. They are Dharma protectors within Buddhism. In the past when they cultivated the Way, they preferred to practice Great Vehicle Dharmas and as a result obtained spiritual penetrations, but since they didn't keep the precepts, they fell into the animal realm.

HOW DOES ONE ATTAIN THE PROTECTION, RESPECT, AND OFFERINGS OF YAKSHA KINGS? Yaksha is a kind of swiftly-traveling ghost, or speedy ghost. There are Yakshas who fly in the sky, and Yakshas who travel on land. They also have kings. If the Yaksha King protects, respects, and makes offerings to you, then all the other Yakshas will also protect, respect, and make offerings to you.

HOW DOES ONE ATTAIN THE PROTECTION, RESPECT, AND OFFERINGS FROM GANDHARVA KINGS? The Gandharva is one of the eightfold division of ghosts and spirits. He is a music spirit, also called an incense-sniffing spirit, because he arrives when he smells the fragrant incense. The Jade Emperor has a kind of fragrant incense and whenever he lights it, the Gandharva King and his retinues will come to make music for him and dance as well.

HOW DOES ONE ATTAIN THE PROTECTION, RESPECT, AND OFFERINGS OF ASURA KINGS? Asuras only have heavenly blessings, but have no heavenly authority. They can live in the heavens, but they don't have heavenly authority or heavenly virtue. Asura translates as "not upright"; they are very ugly. Sometimes they are born with their noses on top of their heads or their eyes under their chins. They just look very grotesque, so they are called "not upright." But Asura women are very pretty.

HOW DOES ONE ATTAIN THE PROTECTION, RESPECT, AND OFFERINGS OF GARUDA KINGS? Garuda is Sanskrit, and translates as "golden-winged P'eng bird." The P'eng bird's wing span is three hundred Yojanas. When it flaps its wings, it can dry up the ocean. It used to do this and then feed on the exposed dragons. Later on, it became a Dharma Protector for the Buddha. It is one of the eightfold division of ghosts and spirits.

HOW DOES ONE ATTAIN THE PROTECTION, RESPECT, AND OFFERINGS OF KINNARA KINGS? Kinnaras are another type of music spirit.

HOW DOES ONE ATTAIN THE PROTECTION, RESPECT, AND OFFERINGS OF MAHORAGA KINGS? Mahoragas are the great python spirits.

HOW DOES ONE ATTAIN THE PROTECTION, RESPECT, AND OFFERINGS OF HUMAN KINGS? Human kings are emperors of the human world.

HOW DOES ONE ATTAIN THE PROTECTION, RESPECT, AND OFFERINGS OF GREAT BRAHMA KINGS? Brahma Kings are the kings in the Brahma Heaven.

How does one attain the protection, respect, and offerings of these ten types of kings? The answer to all those questions is that one has to keep precepts. When the virtue of precepts is perfected, you can go on to cultivate the power of samadhi. From this you will attain the power of wisdom. Once the virtue of your precepts, samadhi, and wisdom is perfected, then you will possess virtuous conduct. When you have virtuous conduct, those ten kings will naturally protect, respect, and make offerings to you.

SUTRA:

HOW DOES ONE BECOME THE RELIANCE, THE SAL-VATION, THE REFUGE, THE DESTINY, THE TORCH, THE LIGHT, THE ILLUMINATION, A GUIDE, A SUPREME GUIDE, A UNIVERSAL GUIDE FOR ALL LIVING BEINGS?

COMMENTARY:

THE RELIANCE. How does one become a place of reliance for living beings, one whom living beings depend and rely on?

THE SALVATION. How does one become a sal-vation for living beings who fall into the three evil destinies?

THE REFUGE. How does one enable living beings to take refuge with the Buddha's path, bring forth their Bodhi mind and take refuge with the Triple Jewel?

THE DESTINY. How does one cause all living beings to go on the Buddha's path and transcend the three realm?

THE TORCH. How does one become a bright torch for living beings, and illuminate the dark-ness?

THE LIGHT. How does one become the bright eyes for living beings to guide them out of their confusion?

THE ILLUMINATION. How does one become an illumination for living beings? This brightness always illuminates living beings and causes them to be without any darkness.

A GUIDE. How does one become a guide for living beings and gather them in?

A SUPREME GUIDE. How does one become a supreme guide and teacher for living beings?

A UNIVERSAL GUIDE. How does one become a universal guide for living beings?

Foremost Wisdom Bodhisattva asked Manjushri Bodhisattva these questions.

SUTRA:

HOW DOES ONE BECOME THE FOREMOST, THE GREAT, THE SUPREME, THE MOST SUPREME, THE WONDERFUL, THE ULTIMATELY WONDERFUL, THE SUPERIOR, THE UN-SURPASSED, UNEQUALLED, DOUBLY UNEQUALLED AMONG ALL LIVING BEINGS?

COMMENTARY:

Foremost Wisdom Bodhisattva again asks Manjushri Bodhisattva, "How does one cultivate to become foremost among living beings?" Who is the foremost among living beings? It's the Buddha, because the sea of the Buddha's merit and virtue is completely perfected, and there is nothing extraneous and nothing lacking. Therefore, the Buddha is foremost in the world.

How does one become the greatest among living beings? The Buddha's body is the greatest. His Dharma body contains everything. It contains the Dharmarealm. Therefore he is called the greatest.

SUPREME. What is meant by a supreme being among living beings? Supreme means outstanding. It is said,

> *One is far above the average,*
> *One is outstanding among one's peer.*

This means to be an uncommon person among living beings.

THE MOST SUPREME means an incomparable person among living beings. This is the Buddha's state. What is meant by supreme? To be supreme is to reach the perfection of benefitting oneself. One attains the final victory of the perfection of benefitting oneself. What is most supreme? To be most supreme means one has attained the perfection of benefitting others.

What is *WONDERFUL*? It means one has cut off all afflictions.

What is *ULTIMATELY WONDERFUL*? It means one cuts off the obstruction of what is known. Both the obstruction of affliction and the obstruction of what is known are cut off.

To have the obstruction of affliction means that no matter what happens, you give rise to affliction and it obstructs your Way karma. To have the obstruction of what is known means that you think you know more than other people. You may feel, "I know how to lecture the Sutras and I can speak Dharma. I also know how to recite sutras and I know how to bow to the Buddhas. See, other people just don't know how!" You have more knowledge, but it obstructs your Way karma. You have too much self-satisfaction, and it is bound to bring about a loss. So once you cut off the obstruction of what is known, then that is called "ultimately wonderful."

SUPERIOR. What is meant by superior? When you look down, there's no one higher than you. That's called being superior.

UNSURPASSED. What is meant by unsurpassed? When you look up, there's no one on top of you. That's called unsurpassed.

UNEQUALLED. When you look around, no one can compare with you.

DOUBLY UNEQUALLED. Not only does one person not compare with you, but all people cannot compare with you. If you reach this level, you have perfected the fruition of Buddhahood.

SUTRA:

AT THAT TIME, MANJUSHRI BODHISATTVA SAID TO FOREMOST WISDOM BODHISATTVA, "GOOD INDEED! DISCIPLE OF THE BUDDHA. NOW FOR THE SAKE OF WISHING TO BRING ABOUT MUCH BENEFIT FOR BEINGS, TO CAUSE THEM MUCH PEACE AND SECURITY, TO TAKE PITY ON THOSE OF THE WORLD, TO BENEFIT AND DELIGHT GODS AND HUMANS, YOU HAVE ASKED ABOUT SUCH MEANINGS."

COMMENTARY:

At this time, Manjushri Bodhisattva answers
Foremost Wisdom Bodhisattva, saying, "Good Indeed,
you are very wonderful, you're such a good disciple
of the Buddha!" You see, even Bodhisattvas
are very polite in their conversation. They also
like to praise each other first by saying, "You're
very wonderful, very good." No wonder we people
also learn their ways and say, "Thank you very
much," because Bodhisattvas are very polite in
their conversation.
     Manjushri Bodhisattva says, "Good Indeed,
disciple of the Buddha, you are very good! You're
the best one. Now you want to benefit all living
beings and cause them to attain advantages. You
also want living beings to attain peace and security. And you're very compassionate and sympa-
thetic toward living beings. You wish to cause
them to be happy, to cause the gods to attain
benefit, and to enable living beings to attain
peace and happiness. It is for those reasons
that you asked about such principles and meanings.
It's not for your own sake that you asked. You
are representing all living beings in asking
about such principle."

SUTRA:

DISCIPLE OF THE BUDDHA, IF ALL BODHISATTVAS
CAN SKILLFULLY USE THEIR MINDS, THEY WILL ATTAIN
ALL SUPREME AND WONDERFUL MERIT AND VIRTUE.
AMONG ALL BUDDHADHARMAS, THEIR MINDS WILL BE
WITHOUT ANY OBSTRUCTION. THEY CAN DWELL IN THE
WAY OF ALL BUDDHAS OF THE PAST, PRESENT, AND
FUTURE. THEY CAN DWELL IN ACCORD WITH LIVING BE-
INGS, AND ETERNALLY NOT RENOUNCE OR SEPARATE
FROM THEM. WITH REGARD TO THE SUCHNESS OF THE
TRUE APPEARANCE OF ALL DHARMAS, THEY CAN COMPLETE-
LY PENETRATE AND UNDERSTAND. THEY CAN CUT OFF
ALL EVIL AND BE ENDOWED WITH ALL GOOD. THEY WILL
BE LIKE UNIVERSAL WORTHY WHO IS FOREMOST IN HIS
PHYSICAL APPEARANCE. THEY WILL BE REPLETE WITH
CONDUCT AND VOWS. THERE IS NO DHARMA WITH WHICH
THEY DO NOT FEEL AT EASE. THEY ACT AS THE SECOND

GUIDING TEACHER FOR LIVING BEINGS. DISCIPLE OF THE BUDDHA, HOW DOES ONE USE HIS MIND TO ATTAIN ALL THE SUPREME AND WONDERFUL MERIT AND VIRTUE?

COMMENTARY:

Manjushri Bodhisattva also says, "You are such a good disciple of the Buddha! If all Bodhisattvas know how to use their minds skillfully, to make vast and great vows, then they will attain all supreme and inconceivable merit and virtue. Among all Buddhadharmas, their mind will be without any bit of obstruction. They can deeply enter into the store of sutras, and their wisdom will be as deep as the great sea. They can understand the real marks of all dharmas. They can dwell in the Way of all the Buddhas who cultivate in the past, present, and in the future. They eternally dwell according with all living beings, and do not renounce or depart from them. They can completely realize and understand all dharmas and principles of real mark. Once you understand all dharmas, you will follow the Dharma to cultivate. If you can accord with the Dharma and cultivate by it, then you can cut off all evil. Once you cut off all evil, then you attain pure good. So we say, "Affliction is Bodhi." If you turn the affliction around, then that's just Bodhi. Therefore, both left-home people and laypeople should recognize states in their cultivation. If you understand your state, then you will be patient. Once you penetrate and understand the real mark of all dharmas, then you will gain the power of endurance. Whether it is a good state or bad state, you can understand it and be patient. You won't give rise to happiness when a good state arrives. Also, you won't give rise to affliction when a bad state comes.

What is cultivation? It is said,

The ordinary mind is the Way.

It's to be very ordinary in your action, speech, and thought. What you do should be at peace and in harmony. Don't give rise to affliction. When you face a situation and give rise to affliction, then you will retreat from the Bodhi mind, which means you won't have a long and far-reaching Bodhi resolve. If you don't have a perservering mind, then it's not easy to accomplish your cultivation. Therefore, you have to bring forth a persevering mind. You should be patient. For example, there's a student who made an appointment with me yesterday to see me at 2:00 p.m. today. But today he went out and could not make it on time. So he came at 3 o'clock. When he came back, he didn't see me. He got so disappointed and gave rise to affliction. Once he gave rise to affliction, a demonic obstacle arose immediately, and he retreated. Fortunately, there was good spirit who came to protect him and gave him a state. He was happy with this state and recognized it. He understood he was wrong. He shouldn't have retreated from his resolve when he didn't see his teacher.

You can see this is a case of a swift response. Therefore, we who cultivate the Way should be patient. Be patient not only with your teacher, but also with all people. If we do not have endurance, we cannot attain real samadhi. Therefore, if you cut off all evil, then just that is perfect all good.

THEY WILL BE LIKE UNIVERSAL WORTHY WHO IS FOREMOST IN HIS PHYSICAL APPEARANCE. The physical appearance of this Bodhisattva who brings forth the initial resolve will be the same as Universal Worthy Bodhisattva who is foremost in his physical appearance. He also will be foremost in his physical appearance.

THEY WILL BE REPLETE WITH CONDUCT AND VOWS. All of the conducts and vows will be completed and perfected.

THERE IS NO DHARMA WITH WHICH THEY DO NOT FEEL AT EASE. They swim freely in the mark of the Dharma, penetrate and understand without obstruction. They can swim as freely as they wish in the sea of the Buddhadharma. You see, they really have a lot of fun!

THEY ACT AS THE SECOND GUIDING TEACHER FOR LIVING BEINGS. They become the second great guiding teacher for living beings. The first guiding teacher is the Buddha. Since this Bodhisattva resembles Universal Worthy Bodhisattva, he becomes the second guiding teacher.

DISCIPLE OF THE BUDDHA, HOW DOES ONE USE HIS MIND TO ATTAIN ALL THE SUPREME AND WONDERFUL MERIT AND VIRTUE? Manjushri Bodhisattva again calls out to Foremost Wisdom Bodhisattva, "Disciple of the Buddha, how does one use his mind to attain all supreme and wonderful merit and virtue?" Manjushri Bodhisattva is not afraid that Foremost Wisdom Bodhisattva isn't paying attention. He is afraid we living beings are not attentive, and--feeling the Sutra is ordinary--after listening for a while, fall asleep. So he calls out, "Disciple of the Buddha!" People who listen to the Sutra might feel he is calling them, and then wake up.

SUTRA:

> *A BODHISATTVA OF THE LAY LIFE,*
> *SHOULD VOW THAT LIVING BEINGS*
> *WILL REALIZE THE EMPTY NATURE OF THE*
> *   HOUSEHOLD,*
> *AND AVOID OPPRESSION FROM IT.*

菩薩在家　　當願眾生
知家性空　　免其逼迫

COMMENTARY:

A BODHISATTVA OF THE LAY LIFE. It says all the Bodhisattvas who are at home. But does this include left-home Bodhisattvas too? You will find out the answer in the text. Right here we are referring to lay Bodhisattvas, that is, those Upasikas and Upasakas who haven't left the home life. There are Bodhisattvas among laypeople. Once you receive the Bodhisattva precepts and practice the Bodhisattva conduct, you endure things that others cannot endure, renounce what others cannot renounce, eat what others cannot eat, suffer what others cannot suffer, practice what others cannot practice, and do what others cannot do. then you are practicing the Bodhisattva conduct. As it is said,

> *With kindness and compassion propagate and*
> *   teach for heaven,*
> *Use wisdom to save the citizens of the country.*

One who can adopt such conduct can be reckoned as a lay Bodhisattva.

SHOULD VOW THAT LIVING BEINGS WILL REALIZE THE EMPTY NATURE OF THE HOUSEHOLD. You should vow to help all living beings understand that the nature of the household is empty. Everything is empty! *AND AVOID OPPRESSION FROM IT.* Since you understand everything is empty, you will not be bound up by your home. Once you get tied up by your house, you cannot escape from it. You are just oppressed by it. If you understand it is empty, then you will not get attached to it or be burdened by it. You will feel that everything is just like a play. In the end it is all empty. If you understand this principle, you will not give rise to a lot of afflictions or be busy all day long. As it is said,

> *You're busy all day long to satisfy your hunger.*
> *Once you've had your fill of food, you start to*
> *   think of clothes.*
> *When clothes and food are felt to be sufficient,*
> *You feel your home requires a pretty wife.*
> *Once you have a pretty wife and then a stunning*
> *   concubine,*
> *You're out in search of horses and sedan-chairs to*
> *   ride on.*
> *When horses, mules, and palanquins are all prepared,*
> *You feel slighted that you are not holding office.*
> *You dismiss as trifling a position as a fourth or*
> *   fifty grade office,*
> *The third and second grades: even they are much*
> *   too low.*
> *The day you make the first grade and become the*
> *   chief,*
> *You dream of being emperor, who sits while facing*
> *   south.*
> *What at last you do become the emperor,*
> *You think of playing chess games with the immortal*
> *   spirits!*

So you see, there is no end   to these affairs!

SUTRA:

> WHEN I SERVE MY PARENTS IN FILIALITY,
> I VOW THAT LIVING BEINGS
> WILL SERVE THE BUDDHAS SKILLFULLY,
> AND PROTECT AND NOURISH EVERYTHING.

孝事父母　　當願衆生
善事於佛　　護養一切

COMMENTARY:

WHEN I SERVE MY PARENTS IN FILIALITY. If you are filial to your parents, you should also vow that all living beings serve the Buddhas skillfully, and be filial to the Buddhas. When the Buddha is not dwelling in the world, you should be filial to your parents. Your parents are living Buddhas at home. Because our parents gave us this physical body, we should be filial to them and repay their kindness. As it is said,

> *The heavens are vast, without limit;*
> *We should exhaust our bodies in toil.*

See how your mother carried you in her womb for nine months. Today, Cardinal Yu Pin said he is against abortion. Many people support the act of abortion right now. This is not a benevolent attitude. Therefore, no matter whether you are young or old, whether you have an old-fashioned brain, or new-fashioned brain, you should not support this dharma. This dharma does not accord with the nature of human beings. Cardinal Yu said, "Abortion is like killing the sprouts of the human species." He is right. Babies are just like sprouts of the human species. Abortion is killing those human sprouts. I really agree with him.

I VOW THAT LIVING BEINGS WILL SERVE THE BUDDHAS SKILLFULLY, AND PROTECT AND NOURISH EVERYTHING. Therefore, when you're filial to

your parents, you should also be filial to the
Buddha. By the way, if you protect and support
the Buddhadharma, that is the same as being filial
to your parents. When you're filial to your
parents,that is the same as being filial to the
Buddha. Therefore between the Buddha and your
parents there should not be any distinction. If
a person is filial to his parents, the Buddhas
will be very happy. The Buddhas surely will
praise you and say, "Good indeed! Good Indeed!"

SUTRA:

> WHEN I GET ALONG WITH MY WIFE,
> I VOW THAT LIVING BEINGS
> WILL TREAT ENEMY AND FRIEND EQUALLY,
> AND DEPART FOREVER FROM THE ATTACHMENTS
>   OF GREED.

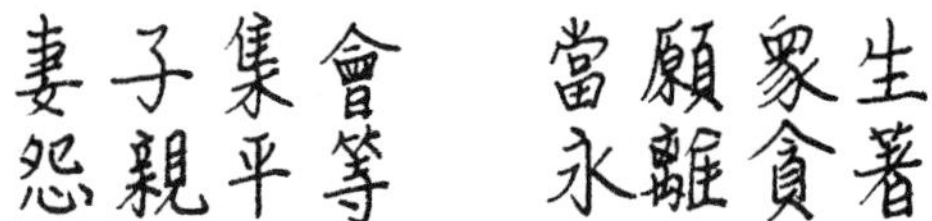

COMMENTARY:

WHEN I GET ALONG WITH MY WIFE, I VOW THAT
LIVING BEINGS WILL TREAT ENEMY AND FRIEND EQUALLY.
When you are harmonious with your wife, you should
vow that living beings treat foe and relative
alike. They should not get too close or too far
from people. Even if people harbor resentment
towards you, you should still treat them as your
relatives. This is true equality in Buddhadharma.
We treat even our enemies with equanimity. It's
not that we draw closer to our wives and get far
away from the rest of people. We treat everybody
equally.

AND DEPART FOREVER FROM THE ATTACHMENTS OF
GREED. We get away from greed and attachment to
our household, children, and wives. A Bodhisattva
can renounce his country, city, wife, and children.
If you can give away your country, city, wife,
and children, then you are a true Bodhisattva
with a Bodhi resolve.

SUTRA:

> WHEN I OBTAIN THE FIVE DESIRES,
> I VOW THAT LIVING BEINGS
> WILL PULL OUT THE ARROW OF DESIRE,
> AND ATTAIN ULTIMATE PEACE AND SECURITY.

若得五欲　　當願眾生
拔除欲箭　　究竟安隱

COMMENTARY:

WHEN I OBTAIN THE FIVE DESIRES. What are the five desires? They are wealth, form, fame, food, and sleep. Wealth is one of the five desires. Perhaps people are greedy for beautiful form, this is a great desire among human beings. Some people aren't greedy for wealth or form, but they're greedy for fame. They want to get a good reputation. They intend to be famous in the world, and this is also a desire. Some people have the a desire for leadership.

They're greedy for fame and benefit. Some people like to eat good food. Some people will compare the vegetarian food of this temple with another. They wonder which temple makes the best vegetarian food. We should not be like this, otherwise we'll become attached to the tastes of food. Some people are not greedy for wealth, fame, or food, but they're greedy for sleep. If you don't allow them to sleep, it's more bitter than if someone had cut off a piece of flesh from their bodies. So wealth, form, fame, food, and sleep are the five desires. They are also the five roots of hell. If you're greedy for wealth, it's very easy to fall into the hells. If you're greedy for form, you will fall into the hells easily. If you're greedy for fame, you will rub noses with King Yama pretty soon. And if you're greedy for food, then you will end up fighting for food with pigs or dogs. That's because they're afraid they will not get their share, so they have to grab and fight for it. They even fight to eat excrement. I'm not scolding people, but what I say is true. When they were human beings, they liked to eat food. When reborn as animals, if they cannot eat good food, they like to grab the foul-smelling food instead. Some people are greedy for sleep. When the Buddha dwelt in the world, he had a disciple who liked to sleep when the Buddha spoke the Dharma. Then the Buddha scolded him, and he changed his bad habits and didn't sleep for seven days straight.

So wealth, form, fame, food, and sleep are the five roots of hell. If you don't want to fall into the hells, you have to cut off those five desires.

I VOW THAT LIVING BEINGS WILL PULL OUT THE ARROW OF DESIRE. Desires are just like arrows which are shot into your body and cause pain. So you have to pull out the arrow of desire and get rid of it.

AND ATTAIN ULTIMATE PEACE AND SECURITY. Then you will obtain ultimate peace and wisdom.

SUTRA:

> *WHEN I AM IN A MUSICAL GATHERING OR*
> *   AMONG SONGSTRESSES,*
> *I VOW THAT LIVING BEINGS*
> *WILL USE DHARMA AS THEIR ENJOYMENT,*
> *AND UNDERSTAND THOSE TALENTS ARE NOT*
> *   REAL.*

伎樂聚會　　當願眾生
以法自娛　　了伎非實

COMMENTARY:

WHEN I AM IN A MUSICAL GATHERING OR AMONG SONG-STRESSES. When you go to a concert or some other form of entertainment *I VOW THAT LIVING BEINGS WILL USE DHARMA AS THEIR ENJOYMENT.* You

should resolve your mind on enlightenment and vow
that all living beings enjoy themselves with the
Buddhadharma. You see when you recite the Sutra
everyday, how happy you get! Reciting the name
of the Buddha or Sutras is the most enjoyable
pleasure.

AND UNDERSTAND THOSE TALENTS ARE NOT REAL.
You should know that the happiness from sensual
pleasures only lasts for a short time. It is not
permanent, not ultimate. Only the Buddhadharma is real.

SUTRA:

> *WHEN I AM IN A PALACE OR A HOUSE,*
> *I VOW THAT LIVING BEINGS*
> *WILL ENTER INTO A SAGE'S GROUND,*
> *AND ENTIRELY ERADICATE FILTHY DESIRES.*

若在宮室　　當願眾生
入於聖地　　永除穢欲

COMMENTARY:

WHEN I AM IN A PALACE OR A HOUSE. The palace
is the place where the emperor dwells. A house
is where ordinary people live.
*I VOW THAT LIVING BEINGS WILL ENTER INTO A
SAGE'S GROUND.* But no matter whether you're in
a palace or in a house, you should vow that living
beings will enter a sage's position, that is,
enter into a pure palace where Sages dwell.
AND ENTIRELY ERADICATE FILTHY DESIRES. And
entirely get rid of their filthy thoughts and
desires.

SUTRA:

> *WHEN I WEAR A NECKLACE OF PRECIOUS GEMS,*
> *I VOW THAT LIVING BEINGS*
> *WILL RENOUNCE ALL FALSE ORNAMENTS,*
> *AND REACH THE TRUE AND ACTUAL PLACE.*

著瓔珞時　　當願眾生
捨諸偽飾　　到真實處

COMMENTARY:

   WHEN I WEAR A NECKLACE OF PRECIOUS GEMS.
Sometimes you may wear precious beads on your
head or around your neck.
   *I VOW THAT LIVING BEINGS WILL RENOUNCE ALL
FALSE ORNAMENTS, AND REACH THE TRUE AND ACTUAL
PLACE.* At these times, you should vow that living
beings renounce all fake ornaments and arrive at
the true and real place, and that they should not
always do superfluous things or wear a false mask.

SUTRA:

WHEN I ASCEND A TOWER,
I VOW THAT LIVING BEINGS
WILL ASCEND THE TOWER OF PROPER DHARMA,
AND CLEARLY SEE THROUGH EVERYTHING.

上升樓閣　　當願眾生
升正法樓　　徹見一切

COMMENTARY:

WHEN I ASCEND A TOWER, I VOW THAT LIVING
BEINGS WILL ASCEND THE TOWER OF PROPER DHARMA.
When you ascend a tower, you should make such a
contemplation and vow that living beings ascend
the tower of the Proper Dharma.
AND CLEARLY SEE THROUGH EVERYTHING. They should
clearly understand all Buddhadharma.

SUTRA:

WHEN I HAVE SOMETHING TO GIVE,
I VOW THAT LIVING BEINGS
WILL BE ABLE TO RENOUNCE EVERYTHING,
AND BE WITHOUT ANY LOVE OR ATTACHMENT
    IN THEIR MINDS.

若有所施　　當願眾生
一切能捨　　心無愛著

COMMENTARY:

WHEN I HAVE SOMETHING TO GIVE. We should
renounce what cannot be renounced. If it is
impossible to renounce, but we give it away, then
this is true renunciation. For example, I have
500 million dollars, but I only give away one
dollar. That doesn't make any difference to me.
If I don't even possess a single penny, but when
people come to ask me, I try to find money to
give them, then I am practicing true giving.

If you have lots of money, and you only give away a small portion, you are not practicing true giving. However, you still have to measure your own capacity to do things. Don't force yourself when you cannot do it. For instance, suppose you accumulate debts that pile high like a mountain, on account of your giving. You carry heavy debts because you cultivate giving to the point that all day long you're involved with debtors, and you cannot pay it back. This is not giving of your own, so you shouldn't do that.

I VOW THAT LIVING BEINGS WILL BE ABLE TO RENOUNCE EVERYTHING. When you practice giving, you should vow that living beings can give away everything and give what they cannot give. What is the most important? Let me tell you, "Being without any love or attachment in their minds."

AND BE WITHOUT ANY LOVE OR ATTACHMENT IN THEIR MINDS. You shouldn't have greedy love. You should renounce those things you love. That is true giving. For example, suppose you love a precious antique so valuable that it has no price. You also think of it when you sleep at night. One day you dream this antique was stolen by a thief. You're so alarmed that you wake up and realize it was only a dream. The antique hasn't been lost, but you still worry about it in your dreams. Wouldn't you say this is really suffering? But if you can renounce this, then you are practicing true giving. This does not refer only to antiques, but also to the things that you love or are attached to. You should give them up.

SUTRA:

> *IN A GATHERING OF MULTITUDES AND*
> *   ASSEMBLIES,*
> *I VOW THAT LIVING BEINGS*
> *WILL RENOUNCE THE MULTIPLICITY*
> *   OF DHARMAS,*
> *AND ACCOMPLISH ALL-WISDOM.*

眾會聚集　　當願眾生
捨眾聚法　　成一切智

COMMENTARY:

IN A GATHERING OF MULTITUDES AND ASSEMBLIES.
Sometimes everybody gets together and there is a
meeting.
I VOW THAT LIVING BEINGS WILL RENOUNCE THE
MULYIPLICITY OF DHARMA. At these time,
you should vow that living beings renounce the
mulyiplicity of all dharmas. And not be
attached to them.
AND ACCOMPLISH ALL-WISDOM. Once you're not
attached to all dharmas and renounce them, then
you can accomplish All Wisdom. It's because you
have all kinds of attachments that you don't
possess All Wisdom. If you don't have these
attachments, then All Wisdom will naturally manifest.

SUTRA:

WHEN IN SUFFERING AND DIFFICULTY,
I VOW THAT LIVING BEINGS
WILL DO AS THEY WISH AND ATTAIN SELF-EASE,
SO THAT WHATEVER THEY DO WILL NOT BE
   OBSTRUCTED.

若在厄難　　當願眾生
隨意自在　　所行無礙

COMMENTARY:

WHEN IN SUFFERING AND DIFFICULTY, I VOW THAT
LIVING BEINGS WILL DO AS THEY WISH AND ATTAIN
SELF-EASE. When you're in suffering and difficulty, or undergoing disasters, or when you're
in danger --for example, you're laden with sickness, or you encounter fierce animals like wolves
snakes, tigers, or leopards while you're walking
--you should vow that living beings can do as
they wish and attain tranquility.
SO THAT WHATEVER THEY DO WILL NOT BE
OBSTRUCTED. Because you undergo such suffering
and difficulty, you should hope that living beings
won't be obstructed by them. This is the mind of
a Bodhisattva, the Bodhi mind.

SUTRA:

> WHEN I RENOUNCE THE HOUSEHOLD,
> I VOW THAT LIVING BEINGS
> WILL LEAVE THE HOME-LIFE WITHOUT ANY
>   OBSTRUCTION,
> AND ATTAIN LIBERATION IN THEIR MINDS.

捨居家時　　當願眾生
出家無礙　　心得解脫

COMMENTARY:

WHEN I RENOUNCE THE HOUSEHOLD. When you renounce your household means when you leave the home-life. After people leave home, they should truly cultivate. Don't break the precepts. Don't be a Bhikshu who frequently breaks the precepts. You should be a Bhikshu who holds the precepts all the time.

I VOW THAT LIVING BEINGS WILL LEAVE THE HOME-LIFE WITHOUT ANY OBSTRUCTION. So when you leave home and shave your head, dye your clothes black, and become a disciple of the Buddha, you should vow that living beings will not encounter obstructions when they leave home, that nobody will stop them from leaving home.

AND ATTAIN LIBERATION IN THEIR MINDS. You should make a vow that people will fullfill their wishes when they want to leave home; that their minds will attain liberation. Once your mind attains liberation, you will not have any impediments.

SUTRA:

> WHEN I ENTER INTO THE SANGHARAMA,
> I VOW THAT LIVING BEINGS
> WILL PROCLAIM ALL KINDS OF DHARMAS,
> AND BE WITHOUT THE DHARMAS OF ERROR OF
>   CONTENTION.

入僧伽藍　　當願眾生
演說種種　　無乖諍法

COMMENTARY:

WHEN I ENTER INTO THE SANGHARAMA. When you
enter into a place where left-home cultivators
live, such as a temple, a Way place, a monastery,
a "still and quiet" place, or any place where
left-home people cultivate their Way, you should
vow that living beings proclaim all kinds of
Buddhadharmas.

When you lecture the Sutras you should not
get stuck on a fixed way of speaking. Each person
has his own style. Each person has his own point
of view. As it is said,

> *The wise see wisdom.*
> *The benevolent see benevolence.*
> *The profound see the profound.*
> *The shallow see the shallow.*

In lecturing the Sutras one should contemplate
the dispositions of living beings and dispense
the teaching. Speak the Dharma according to the
people's needs. You have to investigate what
kinds of dispositions living beings possess, and
speak that kind of Dharma door to suit their
needs. Don't adhere to a fixed way, or lecture
according to any special kind of commentary. I
advocate speaking the Sutra with a lively style.
Don't be rigid or boring, or try to explain it
by reading the words from the book, or explain it
by reciting someone else's commentary. In the
beginning there were no commentaries. How did
the Buddha speak the Sutra when there were no
Sutras existing at that time?

> *The Buddha spoke all dharmas*
> *For the sake of all living beings' minds.*
> *If there are no minds,*
> *What's the use of all dharmas?*

Therefore, I emphasize speaking the Sutra with a lively style. What is meant by a lively style? You speak the Sutra in a relevant and animated way, so that it's not rigid or unchangeable. Therefore, young people like to listen to my lectures wherever I go, because my style suits their taste.

I VOW THAT LIVING BEINGS WILL PROCLAIM ALL KINDS OF DHARMAS. "All kinds of" means not only one dharma. It means to use various different ways to speak the Dharma. If you want to "deeply enter the Sutra treasury, and have wisdom like the sea," you should lecture Sutras like flowing water, and speak fluently and spontaneously.

AND BE WITHOUT THE DHARMAS OF ERROR OF CONTENTION. "Error" means what is not correct. One argues with people and contradicts the principles of the Sutras. What he lectures does not accord with the meaning of the Sutra. He departs from the theme. "Contention", as it is said,

> *Contention is the mind of winning or losing,*
> *It contradicts the Way.*
> *And gives rise to the mind of the four*
>   *marks,*
> *How can one attain Samadhi this way?*

This is the Samadhi-of-No-Contention mentioned in the Vajra Sutra. Once you fight, there's someone who wins and someone who loses. Once there is a winner and a loser, then one falls into the mark of self, and the mark of others. So it is said,

> *Contention is the mind of winning or losing,*
> *It contradicts the Way.*

It gives rise to the mind of the four marks. The four marks are:

1. The mark of self.

2. The mark of others.

3. The mark of living beings.

4. The mark of a life-span.

So how can you attain Samadhi__proper concentration and proper reception from arguing? You
cannot get it that way. So in proclaiming the
Dharma you can speak in any way, except speaking
erroneous or argumentative dharmas.

SUTRA:

> *WHEN I VISIT SENIOR OR JUNIOR TEACHERS,*
> *I VOW THAT LIVING BEINGS*
> *WILL SKILLFULLY SERVE THEIR TEACHERS*
>   *AND ELDERS,*
> *AND PRACTICE WHOLESOME DHARMAS.*

詣大小師　　當願眾生
巧事師長　　習行善法

COMMENTARY:

    WHEN I VISIT SENIOR OR JUNIOR TEACHERS. "To
visit" means you go to visit senior or junior
teachers, or a Dharma Master. A "Senior teacher"
refers to a great Acharya, a master of rules and
comportment. A "Junior teacher" refers to monks
in general, but not   great monks.
    *I VOW THAT LIVING BEINGS WILL SKILLFULLY
SERVE THEIR TEACHERS AND ELDERS, AND PRACTICE
WHOLESOME DHARMAS.* At this time, you should vow
that living beings serve their teachers and elders
skillfully, and learn to practice wholesome
dharmas. Don't learn to practice evil dharmas.
If you learn and practice wholesome dharmas, you
should hear the instructions and guidance of good
knowing ones, and not listen to the teachings of
evil knowing advisors. What is the teaching of
an evil knowing one? For example, in Buddhism
you have to hold precepts, but an evil knowing
one will tell you not to keep the precepts saying,
"The present time is the Dharma Ending Age. Since
we are just ordinary, common people, you can do
whatever you want to do. It's O.K. In this Dharma
Ending Age, nobody wants to cultivate!"
    So, what do you think about this? What is
meant by Dharma Ending Age? What is meant by
common ordinary people? Actually, the Dharma
Ending Age is created by people. If people prac-

tice proper Dharma, then that's the orthodox
Dharma Age. If people practice improper Dharma,
then that's the Dharma Ending Age. If you don't
cultivate in the Proper Dharma Age, even the
Proper Dharma will fail to exist. But if you
cultivate in the Dharma Ending Age, the Proper
Dharma will exist nonetheless. It's people who
make it so. It's not because of the Dharma. The
Dharma itself is neither proper nor ending. You
don't have any shame but just rationalize that you
are a common person; then who is a Sage? Anybody
in the world becomes a sage from the position of
a common person. But you want to descend from
sagehood to be a common person! Originally, you
left the home-life to become a Bhikshu, but all
the while you act as a defense attorney for yourself and say, "It's O.K. for me as a common person
to break the precepts." This is what the Buddha
called, "Really pathetic people!" It's pitiful
to the extreme! You protect yourself by making
this statement--"I am a common person!!!"

SUTRA:

> *WHEN I REQUEST PERMISSION TO LEAVE THE
>   HOME-LIFE,
> I VOW THAT LIVING BEINGS
> WILL ATTAIN NON-RETREATING DHARMAS,
> AND BE WITHOUT ANY OBSTRUCTION IN THEIR
>   MINDS.*

求請出家　　當願眾生
得不退法　　心無障礙

COMMENTARY:

   *WHEN I REQUEST PERMISSION TO LEAVE THE HOME-
LIFE.* If one wants to leave home, one has to
request and seek a good knowing advisor. The most
important thing for those of us who leave the home-
life is to find a good knowing one. A good knowing
advisor can point out the proper way for you in
your cultivation. If you cannot find a good
knowing one, but instead, you meet an evil knowing

When I request permission to leave the home-life,
I vow that living beings
Will attain non-treating dharmas,
And be without any obstruction in their minds.

advisor who is fond of saying, "It's the Dharma Ending Age, the Dharma doesn't exist. So you don't need to cultivate! Everybody just eats and waits to die." What do you think about that kind of talk?

It's for reasons such as the above that I vow that wherever I go, there must be the Proper Dharma. I don't like the Dharma Ending Age. The Proper Dharma and the Dharma Ending Age depend on people and are created by people. The Dharma itself is not divided. But people are divided into those who are vigorous and those who are lazy, and those who cultivate and those who don't cultivate.
Therefore, when you request permission to leave home, it is like "opening your eyes to get reborn." When we were born into this world, we didn't know which family was good or bad. We were like a fly buzzing around at random and we flew right into the net of ignorance, and then were born. We weren't in control but had to follow our karma and undergo our retribution. Now that we have already left the home-life, we should open our eyes, and truly look for a bright-eyed good know-ing advisor. If we follow the instructions of a good knowing advisor to study the Buddhadharma, we will not walk on a wrong path. This is very important! A good knowing one acts as a pair of bright eyes for us. Being unable to find a good knowing one is the same as not having any eyes. Therefore, when you ask permission to leave home, you have to look for a good knowing one. It's not for the sake of food stamps that you leave home. What do I mean by "food stamps"? That's the certificate of having received the precepts which allows you to stay at temples wherever you go. But it's a little different in this modern age. It's not as convenient as in China where you could find a dwelling at any temple. Even though it's not that convenient, you can still find a place to live after you leave the home-life. This is the meaning of "food stamps." But this is not the reason why you left the home life!

I VOW THAT LIVING BEINGS WILL ATTAIN NON-RETREATING DHARMAS, AND BE WITHOUT ANY OBSTRU-TION IN THEIR MINDS. When you request permission to leave the home life, you should vow that living

beings attain non-retreating dharmas, obtain
Anuttarasamyaksambodhi   , and be without any
obstruction in their minds. However, you should
not act as   your own defense attorney and say,
"Since this is the Dharma Ending Age, it's not :
necessary for one to cultivate." I've heard a
lot of people talk this way. They keep saying,
"It's the Dharma Ending Age, and there's no way
to cultivate. Let's forget it!" Forget it,
because of the Dharma Ending Age?! Since I've
heard many people talk this way, I am bringing it
up so you won't be turned by this kind of principle. If you say, "It's the Dharma Ending Age and
it's not necessary to cultivate," then you have
obstructions in your mind. If you didn't have
obstructions in your mind, you wouldn't say that.

SUTRA:

> *WHEN I CAST OFF MY WORLDLY CLOTHES,*
> *I VOW THAT LIVING BEINGS*
> *WILL DILIGENTLY CULTIVATE GOOD ROOTS,*
> *AND RENOUNCE ALL OFFENSES AND*
>   *OBSTRUCTIONS.*

脫去俗服　　當願眾生
勤修善根　　捨諸罪軛

COMMENTARY:

WHEN I CAST OFF MY WORLDLY CLOTHES. That is,
when you shave your head and dye your clothes.
To take off your worldly clothes means you leave
the home-life.
*I VOW THAT LIVING BEINGS WILL DILIGENTLY
CULTIVATE GOOD ROOTS.* At this time, you also
should vow that living beings cultivate good
roots diligently. You should diligently cultivate
precepts, samadhi, and wisdom, and nourish your
good roots.
AND RENOUNCE ALL OFFENSES AND OBSTRUCTIONS.
You should relinquish all the obstacles and
offense karma that block your cultivation.

SUTRA:

> WHEN SHAVING MY HEAD,
> I VOW THAT LIVING BEINGS
> WILL FOREVER DEPART FROM AFFLICTIONS,
> AND ACHIEVE ULTIMATELY STILL EXTINCTION.

剃除鬚髮　　當願眾生
永離煩惱　　究竟寂滅

COMMENTARY:

WHEN SHAVING MY HEAD, I VOW THAT LIVING BE-
INGS WILL FOREVER DEPART FROM AFFLICTIONS. When
you become a Bhikshu, you shave off your hair and
beard. At this time, you also should vow that
living beings be far removed from afflictions.
When shaving your head, you also should shave away
your afflictions, and vow to always attain the
bliss of ultimate still extinction.
AND ACHIEVE ULTIMATELY STILL EXTINCTION.
"Still extinction" means real quiescence, or pure
happiness. You attain the bliss of ultimate
still extinction.

SUTRA:

> WHEN I DON THE SASH,
> I VOW THAT LIVING BEINGS
> WILL NOT HAVE DEFILEMENT IN THEIR MINDS,
> BUT WILL COMPLETE THE WAY OF THE
>   GREAT IMMORTAL.

著袈裟衣　　當願眾生
心無所染　　具大仙道

COMMENTARY:

WHEN I DON THE SASH, I VOW THAT LIVING BEINGS WILL NOT HAVE DEFILEMENT IN THEIR MINDS. The sash is the robe worn by left-home people. There are three kinds of robes: the five piece robe, the seven piece robe, and the big robe. After a Bhikshu has left the home-life, he should never let his body be apart from his three robes, bowl, and sitting mat. This is the sign of a Bhikshu who holds the precepts. So when you wear the

sash, you should vow that living beings do not have defilements in their minds. A sash is also called the robe dyed with color. The robe is dyed a black color, but your mind should not be dyed by colors. Your mind should be pure.
BUT WILL COMPLETE THE WAY OF THE GREAT IMMORTAL. "The way of the great immortal" is the Buddha Way. The Buddha is also called the Golden Immortal. But most people think the Buddha is greatly different from an Immortal. Actually, Buddhist Sutras often mention the great immortal Way, which is just the Buddha Way. The Buddha is also called the Golden Immortal.

SUTRA:

> HAVING ACTUALLY LEFT THE HOME LIFE,
> I VOW THAT LIVING BEINGS
> WILL LEAVE THE HOME-LIFE WITH THE BUDDHA,
> AND SAVE AND PROTECT ALL.

正出家時　　當願眾生
同佛出家　　救護一切

COMMENTARY:

HAVING ACTUALLY LEFT THE HOME LIFE. The previous vow refers to the time when you wish to leave the home-life, but have not really left home yet. Meanwhile, you always wear the sash. *I VOW THAT LIVING BEINGS WILL LEAVE THE HOME-LIFE WITH THE BUDDHA, AND SAVE AND PROTECT ALL.* Now that you have actually left the home-life, you should vow that living beings leave the home-life at the same time as the Buddha, and save and protect all living beings. You should become a place of reliance for living beings.

SUTRA:

> IN TAKING REFUGE WITH THE BUDDHA,
> I VOW THAT LIVING BEINGS
> WILL CONTINUE AND PROPAGATE THE BUDDHAS'
>   LINEAGE,
> AND BRING FORTH THE UNSURPASSED INTENT.

自歸於佛　　當願眾生
紹隆佛種　　發無上意

COMMENTARY:

IN TAKING REFUGE WITH THE BUDDHA. Taking refuge with the Triple Jewel is very important. For example, the beginning lines of the Great Compassion Mantra, the Shurangama Mantra, or other mantras, all mean "to take refuge with the eternally dwelling inexhaustible Triple Jewel of the ten directions and three periods of time." The first line of the Great Compassion mantra "Na Mwo He La Da Nwo Dwo La Ye Ye" means to take refuge with the Triple Jewel of the ten directions. The line at the beginning of the Shurangama Mantra "Na Mwo Sa Dan Two, Su Chye Dwo Ye, E La He Di, San Myau San Pu Two Sye" also means to take refuge with the eternally dwelling inexhaustible Triple Jewel of the ten directions and three periods of time. Therefore, it's very important to take refuge with the Buddha, the Dharma, and the Sangha. When you recite and uphold the first line of the Shurangama Mantra, or the Great Compassion Mantra, and take refuge with the eternally dwelling inexhaustible Triple Jewel of the ten directions, the Buddhas of the ten directions will come to protect you. The 84,000 Vajra Treasury Bodhisattvas come last. After the Buddhas of the ten directions protect and are mindful of you, then the 84,000 Vajra Treasury Bodhisattvas will constantly follow and protect you. Therefore, it's very important to hold the ceremony of taking refuge with the Triple Jewel. We who are left-home people should always receive and uphold the refuge with the Triple Jewel, and also strictly and purely uphold the Vinaya.

I VOW THAT LIVING BEINGS WILL CONTINUE AND PROPAGATE THE BUDDHAS' LINEAGE, AND BRING FORTH THE UNSURPASSED INTENT. After you take refuge with the Buddha, you should vow that living beings support and propagate the Buddha's seed. Let the Buddha's seed continue to thrive without interruption. Let it be prosperous and flourishing. You should also produce the unsurpassed intent. As it is said,

> *Understand the Great Way,*
> *And produce the unsurpassed resolve.*

SUTRA:

> *IN TAKING REFUGE WITH THE DHARMA,*
> *I VOW THAT LIVING BEINGS*
> *WILL DEEPLY ENTER THE SUTRA TREASURY,*
> *AND HAVE WISDOM LIKE THE SEA.*

自歸於法　　當願眾生
深入經藏　　智慧如海

COMMENTARY:

IN TAKING REFUGE WITH THE DHARMA. The Dharma
is like a great sea. I VOW THAT LIVING BEINGS
WILL DEEPLY ENTER THE SUTRA TREASURY, the Sutra
Store. AND HAVE WISDOM LIKE THE SEA, have wisdom
like the great sea, which is without limit or
boundary.

SUTRA:

IN TAKING REFUGE WITH THE SANGHA,
I VOW THAT LIVING BEINGS
WILL UNITE AND LEAD THE GREAT ASSEMBLY,
ALL WITHOUT OBSTRUCTION.

自歸於僧　　當願眾生
統理大眾　　一切無礙

COMMENTARY:

IN TAKING REFUGE WITH THE SANGHA. That is,
in taking refuge with the worthies, sages and
saints of the ten directions.
I VOW THAT LIVING BEINGS WILL UNITE AND LEAD
THE GREAT ASSEMBLY, ALL WITHOUT OBSTRUCTION. At
this time, you should vow that living beings
unite and lead the great multitude, and be without
obstructions in all that they do.

SUTRA:

WHEN RECEIVING AND LEARNING PRECEPTS,
I VOW THAT LIVING BEINGS
WILL SKILLFULLY LEARN PRECEPTS,
AND NOT DO THE MULTITUDE OF EVILS.

受學戒時　當願衆生
善學於戒　不作衆惡

COMMENTARY:

WHEN RECEIVING AND LEARNING PRECEPTS. This means when you receive the precepts. The time of receiving the precepts is also called the time of learning the precepts. When we first receive the precepts, we should recite and memorize the ten precepts of a Sramanera, the 250 precepts of a Bhikshu, the 348 precepts of a Bhikshuni, and the 10 major and 48 minor Bodhisattva precepts. Only then are we allowed to receive the precepts. Besides we also should recite and memorize the 53 small mantras which are used daily by Sangha members. Therefore, this period is called the time of receiving and learning the precepts.
I VOW THAT LIVING BEINGS WILL SKILLFULLY LEARN PRECEPTS, AND NOT DO THE MULTITUDE OF EVILS. During such a time, you also should make a vow. As it is said,

From a vow give rise to practice.

You vow that living beings will learn precepts skillfully and know how to use the precepts, that they understand the Dharma of precepts, the mark of precepts, and the substance of precepts. Then they will deeply enter into the conduct door of precepts, and realize the principle of precepts. What is the meaning of learning precepts skillfully? It is, to "stop evil and prevent transgressions." You stop all evil and offer up your conduct to all good.

SUTRA:

WHEN RECEIVING THE ACHARYA'S TEACHING,
I VOW THAT LIVING BEINGS
WILL BE COMPLETE WITH AWESOME DEPORTMENTS,
AND BE TRUE IN WHAT THEY DO.

受闍梨教　當願眾生
具足威儀　所行真實

COMMENTARY:

WHEN RECEIVING THE ACHARYA'S TEACHING, I VOW THAT LIVING BEINGS WILL BE COMPLETE WITH AWESOME DEPORTMENTS. Acharya is Sanskrit, and translates as "master of regulations and rules (規範師)" or "master of pure teaching." When you receive the teaching from an Acharya, you should vow that living beings become replete with awesome deportments. The term "awesome deportment" is explained this way in Confucianism,

> *The three hundred rules of propriety,*
> *And the three thousand awesome deportments.*

In Buddhism we say,

> *Three thousand awesome deportments,*
> *And eighty thousand subtle conducts.*

Why does one need to be complete with awesome deportment? It is because deportment should be perfected so as to cause living beings to bring forth faith towards you when they see you. It is really unseemly if a left-home person does not have good deportment, for example, if he jumps around while he's walking, like a monkey or some other animal. I'm not scolding people, but this is really unsightly. Nobody will believe him. Therefore, we should emulate the Bhikshu Asvajit whose eyes didn't dart around when he was walking.

> *His eyes contemplated his nose.*
> *His nose contemplated his mouth.*
> *His mouth contemplated his mind.*

His posture was really dignified and proper. Therefore, when Mahamaudgalyayana and Shariputra saw his awesome deportment, they both brought forth the Bodhi mind and asked him, "What's your career?" They were confused because there were no left-home people at that time. Originally, Shariputra and Mahamaudgalyayana belonged to an outside path. But when they saw that Bhikshu Asvajit had such fine deportment, they asked him, "You must have a good teacher, who is he?"

Bhikshu Asvajit said, "My teacher is the Buddha."

When Shariputra and Mahamaudgalyayana heard the name of the Buddha, they got more confused. So they asked again, "What is the meaning of Buddha? We've never heard of such a word before."

Bhikshu Asvajit replied, "The principle that my teacher talks about is this:

> *All dharmas are produced from conditions.*
> *All dharmas are extinguished from conditions.*
> *The Buddha, the great Shramana,*
> *Always speaks in such a Way.*

This principle was propounded by the Buddha."

After Shariputra and Mahamaudgalyayana heard this principle, they were extremely delighted. They said, "This Dharma is really wonderful! It is unsurpassed, profound, and wonderful Dharma. We must meet your master!" So they followed Bhikshu Asvajit to see Shakyamuni Buddha and took refuge with the Triple Jewel.

This is because Bhikshu Asvajit's awesome deportment was really good. Therefore, he influenced Shariputra and Mahamaudgalyayana, who were two great adherents to an outside path, to take refuge with the Buddha. So no matter whether you are a left-home person or a lay-person, you should pay attention to your deportment. You shouldn't think, "I'm a lay-person and I don't need to have awesome deportment." That's a mistake. Lay-people are external protectors for Buddhism. If an external protector's deportment is good, as it is said,

> *He honors his words,*
> *And conducts himself with utmost sincerity*
> *and respect.*

AND BE TRUE IN WHAT THEY DO. When non-Buddhists see a person who is true to his words and reverent in his actions, one who doesn't lie or wear a false mask, one who isn't hypocritical like a tiger who puts on a necklace, then those unbelievers will be inspired to bring forth faith.

SUTRA:

> WHEN RECEIVING THE TEACHING FROM A
>   GREAT MONK,
> I VOW THAT LIVING BEINGS
> WILL ENTER THE WISDOM OF NON-PRODUCTION,
> AND REACH THE LOCATION OF NO-RELIANCE.

受和尚教　　當願衆生
入無生智　　到無依處

COMMENTARY:

WHEN RECEIVING THE TEACHING FROM A GREAT MONK. A great monk is "He Shang" in Chinese. "He (和)" refers to the six harmonies. "Shang (尚)" means elegant or lofty. The term stands for a pure, lofty, and elegant personality. It refers to the perfections of one's character. Therefore, we always refer to the abbot of a monastery as a great monk. One who is already retired is called an elder monk.

I VOW THAT LIVING BEINGS WILL ENTER THE WISDOM OF NON-PRODUCTION, AND REACH THE LOCATION OF NO-RELIANCE. When you receive the teaching from a great monk, you should vow that living beings enter into the wisdom of non-production and reach the place of no-reliance. A great monk is someone we rely upon. But you shouldn't bother him too much. If you create evils like killing, stealing, and sexual misconduct, the doors of the three evil paths will open for you and invite you to enter.

AND REACH THE LOCATION OF NO-RELIANCE. It means that you don't depend upon others. Instead, you should be self-confident, and not transgress precepts or create karmic offenses. Then you're

O.K. Don't produce a thought of reliance and think that after you've taken refuge with the Triple Jewel, it's for sure you will not become an animal. You never get off that cheaply.

SUTRA:

WHEN RECEIVING THE COMPLETE PRECEPTS,
I VOW THAT LIVING BEINGS
WILL BE ENDOWED WITH ALL EXPEDIENTS,
AND ATTAIN THE MOST SUPREME DHARMA.

受具足戒　　當願眾生
具諸方便　　得最勝法

COMMENTARY:

WHEN RECEIVING THE COMPLETE PRECEPTS, I VOW THAT LIVING BEINGS WILL BE ENDOWED WITH ALL EXPEDIENTS. When you receive the complete precepts, you should contemplate and vow that living beings become endowed with all the expedients. "Expedients": Originally, there are many expedient Dharma doors. But the most essential is to be kind and compassionate, and to protect and be mindful of living beings. It is an expedient to use these Dharma doors skillfully in your cultivation, to teach and transform living beings. Instead of renouncing birth and death, it is an expedient to always roam playfully in the wheel of birth and death, without being defiled by it, for the sake of teaching living beings. It is also an expedient to always be vigorous and diligent in cultivation, while teaching and transforming living beings at the same time. As it is said,

There are many doors of expedience,
But the path of return is non-dual.

"The path of return is non-dual"--this is the Buddha path. No matter which expedient method you cultivate, you will certainly become a Buddha.
AND ATTAIN THE MOST SUPREME DHARMA. Since

you are already endowed with all expedients, in the future you will attain the most supreme Dharma.

SUTRA:

> *WHEN ENTERING THE HALL,*
> *I VOW THAT LIVING BEINGS*
> *WILL ENTER THE UNSURPASSED HALL,*
> *AND DWELL PEACEFULLY IN UNMOVINGNESS.*

若入堂宇　　當願象生
升無上堂　　安住不動

COMMENTARY:

WHEN ENTERING THE HALL, I VOW THAT LIVING BEINGS WILL ENTER THE UNSURPASSED HALL. When you enter some kind of lecture hall or house, you should also contemplate and make a vow. Don't have too many false thoughts. Making a vow is a way to cure living beings' false thoughts. If you are making a vow, you will not have any false thoughts. If you don't make a vow, you will have another false thought and lose proper mindfulness. If you make a vow, you will protect and uphold proper mindfulness. Therefore, you make a vow at this time and bring forth the Bodhi mind. Your vow is to attain Bodhi. You vow that all living beings enter into the unsurpassed hall. The unsurpassed hall is Anuttarasamyaksambodhi the position of unsurpassed enlightenment.

AND DWELL PEACEFULLY IN UNMOVINGNESS. The position of the Buddha is thus, thus unmoving. If you are "thus thus unmoving", then you are "clearly, eternally bright." "Thus thus unmoving" refers to samadhi. "Clearly, eternally bright" refers to wisdom. This is the perfect brightness of samadhi and wisdom. Therefore, you dwell peacefully in the state of the perfect brightness of samadhi and wisdom.

SUTRA:

WHEN SPREADING OUT THE BED SHEET,
I VOW THAT LIVING BEINGS
WILL OPEN AND UNFOLD WHOLESOME DHARMAS,
AND SEE THE TRUE MARK.

若敷牀座　　當願眾生
開敷善法　　見真實相

COMMENTARY:

WHEN SPREADING OUT THE BED SHEET, I VOW THAT LIVING BEINGS WILL OPEN AND UNFOLD WHOLESOME DHARMAS, AND SEE THE TRUE MARK. When you spread out a bed sheet, you also should vow that living beings open and unfold wholesome dharmas, and understand how to foster good dharmas and see through the true mark. Originally, the true mark has no marks. Although it has no mark, there's nothing that's not marked by it. Therefore, you should vow that in every movement and each activity, you will cultivate awesome deportment.

SUTRA:

WHEN SITTING UPRIGHT AND PROPER,
I VOW THAT LIVING BEINGS
WILL SIT ON THE BODHI SEAT,
AND BE WITHOUT ANY ATTACHMENTS IN THEIR
MINDS.

正身端坐　　當願眾生
坐菩提座　　心無所著

COMMENTARY:

WHEN SITTING UPRIGHT AND PROPER. It means not leaning to your right side or left side, not bending forward or backward. You sit in a proper and upright posture while in meditation. You straighten your back-bone. Your head and shoulders should be level. Don't lower your head. You should sit like a bell.

I VOW THAT LIVING BEINGS WILL SIT ON THE BODHI SEAT. At this time, you also should vow that living beings will sit on the Bodhi seat, the seat of enlightenment. Sitting on the seat of enlightenment means not to sit in scatteredness. Don't fall asleep while you sit. Bodhi means enlightenment. You should cause yourself to bring forth the enlightened mind. Don't produce the mind of stupidity while sitting there. So you have to sit on the Bodhi seat.

AND BE WITHOUT ANY ATTACHMENTS IN THEIR MINDS. Bodhi is enlightenment. Even if you get enlightened, you still don't attach to any state. Often, when you sit in Ch'an, many kinds of states appear. Sometimes you will encounter a good state, sometimes you will happen on an evil state. Why? It is because if in your past life, you produced a good thought, this good state will appear while you sit in meditation. If you produced a bad thought, that demonic state will also appear while you sit in Ch'an. Therefore, no matter whether a favorable state or an adverse state, a good state, or an evil state appears, they are all produced from false thinking accumulated in your past lives. So we cultivators should not strike up false thoughts casually. As it is said,

> *When a single thought is not produced,*
> *The whole substance manifests.*

A single thought not produced is the great function of the whole substance. The original Buddha nature will manifest if you don't give rise to a single thought. "When a single thought is not produced" means you don't have any false thoughts and then you can become a Way cultivator of no mind. As the great Master Yung Chia (永嘉大師) says,

> *Gentlemen, don't you see the cultivator of*
> *leisure who has no learning and no activity,*
> *He does not eradicate false thoughts, he does*
> *not seek for truth.*

Why does he not eradicate false thoughts? Because there are no more false thoughts. Why doesn't he

seek for truth? Because he has already attained
the truth. Why is he a cultivator of leisure?
Because he's done what he should do, and does
not undergo further existence. Being a cultivator
of leisure, his mind does not have any attachment.
His mind unites with empty space in substance,
and fuses with the Dharma Realm as one. Therefore his mind doesn't have any attachments.

SUTRA:

*WHEN SITTING IN THE FULL-LOTUS POSTURE,
I VOW THAT LIVING BEINGS
WILL HAVE SOLID GOOD ROOTS,
AND ATTAIN THE GROUND OF UNMOVING.*

結跏趺坐　　當願眾生
善根堅固　　得不動地

COMMENTARY:

WHEN SITTING IN THE FULL-LOTUS POSTURE. All
the Buddhas and Bodhisattvas manifest the mark
of Samadhi when they sit in full-lotus position.
The full-lotus posture is also called the diamond
posture, or Bodhi posture. I just thought of a
public record which most of you already heard
before. Well, you can hear it one more time.
You should have a little bit of patience. Don't
complain, "I've already heard this public record
before. Don't talk about it again!" If you're
like that, it means you don't have patience.
Since you don't have patience, you cannot be
crossed over with the Paramita of Patience, one
of the Six Perfections. When you listen to the
Dharma it's not for sure that you never heard it
before. Since you heard it before, why not
listen one more time? Why don't you get tired
eating everyday? Why do you feel bored while
listening to the Dharma one more time? This is
a mistake. Those people who never heard it
before will increase in their Bodhi minds after
they have listened to it.

A long time ago in China, there was a monk

When sitting in the full-lotus posture,
I vow that living beings
Will have solid good roots,
And attain the ground of unmoving.

who recited Sutras for dead people. He always
recited the Sutras for others' sake, but not for
his own sake. He created merit and virtue for
other people, but not for himself. One day, he
came back from doing merit and virtue for others.
It was dark on his way back home. While he went
through a village, a dog barked at him. It woke
up some people from their sleep. He heard a
woman inside a house say, "Do you hear the dog
barking so loudly? Maybe there is a thief. We'd
better take a look." A man replied, "It cannot
be." Still he looked outside through the window.
The dog barked more fiercely.
     "Is that a thief?" His wife asked.
     "No, it's only a Sutra-reciting-ghost!"
That monk heard this man call him a Sutra-reciting-
ghost, but not a Sutra-reciting-god, and he felt
unhappy at heart.
     "Ha! What's the matter with reciting the
Sutras? How dare you call me a Sutra-reciting-
ghost? If I'm a real ghost, I'll let you have a
headache." So he passed through the village with
such thoughts. But it started to rain when he was
walking on a bridge, and he quickly ran down
under the bridge to get out of the rain. He heard
that if one sat in full-lotus, the result was not
bad. So he tried it out. Maybe he went crazy.
Suddenly, he saw two ghosts. They didn't bother
him, instead they bowed to him.
     They said, "This golden stupa must store
the Buddha's Sharira. We should respect it and
bow to it."
     Because he sat in full-lotus position, he
looked like a golden stupa in the eyes of those
two ghosts. The monk saw these two ghosts bow to
him. Probably he always saw ghosts when he crossed over dead people. Although he hadn't encounter ghosts before, he could feel the presence of
ghosts. So he was not afraid of them. After
sitting in full-lotus for awhile, he felt pain.
He could not endure the pain. Even if he clenched
his teeth, he still couldn't bear it. So he put
down the leg on top from the full-lotus position,
and sat in half-lotus position instead. When
these two ghosts raised their heads from bowing,
they were surprised, "Why has this golden stupa

become a Silver Stupa?" The full-lotus position
is a golden stupa, and the half-lotus position is
a silver stupa viewed from the eyes of the ghosts.

One ghost said, "Inside a golden stupa or a
silver stupa, there are still the Buddha's Sharira.
We should bow to the Buddha's Sharira so it will
eradicate our karmic offenses. We still have to
keep on bowing!"

Therefore, they kept on bowing to him. Probably he overheard the conversation between these
two ghosts. After one hour, he could not endure
the pain from sitting in half-lotus position.
Because he was used to reciting Sutras for dead
people to make his living, he couldn't endure
sitting in full-lotus for half an hour and half-
lotus for another full hour. So he put down
another leg and just sat casually. When those
two ghosts stood up from bowing, they saw him and
said, "Now this is neither a golden stupa, nor a
silver stupa. It's only a pile of mud!"

They wanted to hit him and kick him. This
monk was so scared that he quickly went back to
the full-lotus position. When these ghosts were
just about to hit him, they saw the mud pile had
become a golden stupa again!

They said, "This must be an inconceivable
state, we better bow quickly."

So these two ghosts continued to bow. After
this experience, the monk didn't dare to put down
his legs. No matter how painful his legs were,
he still endured it. And he recited the Buddha's
name while sitting in meditation.

Therefore he sat there in meditation and
recited the Buddha's name until the next morning.
And he felt his two legs didn't hurt any more.
Then he thought, "I was called a Sutra-reciting-
ghost before, because I recited Sutras for others.
But when I sat in full-lotus position, I was a
golden stupa. And when I sat in half-lotus position, I was a silver stupa. But when I sat casually, I was just a pile of mud. When one sits in
full-lotus position, even ghosts come to pay their
respects. This is really inconceivable."

So after this experience, he no longer dared
to recite sutras for others, but resolved to sit
in full-lotus position to help his own cultivation.

After cultivating for a period of time, he got enlightened and was certified to the fruition. After
he got enlightened, he found out that the source
of his enlightenment was these two ghosts who forced
him to resolve his mind to cultivate. So he gave
up his former name and called himself a very strange
name, "Forced by ghosts." Therefore, everybody
called him a Ch'an Master who was forced by ghosts,
because ghosts forced him to cultivate. Originally
this old cultivator only recited Sutras for others,
but he was also certified to the fruition through
cultivation. As it is said,

> *Don't concern yourself with the inferior background
> of a hero.*

No matter who you are, if you really can resolve
your mind to cultivate and endure a little bit of
pain, you certainly will have accomplishment. So
you can see the advantage from sitting in full-
lotus. You should *VOW THAT LIVING BEINGS WILL
HAVE SOLID GOOD ROOTS.* Sitting in full-lotus position, one should have a solid mind and plant good
roots that are solid, like vajra, and not retreat.
AND ATTAIN THE GROUND OF UNMOVING, that is, reach
to the ground where one will not be moved by any state.

SUTRA:

> *WHEN CULTIVATING SAMADHI,*
> *I VOW THAT LIVING BEINGS*
> *WILL SUBDUE THEIR MINDS WITH SAMADHI,*
> *AND BE ULTIMATELY WITHOUT RESIDUE.*

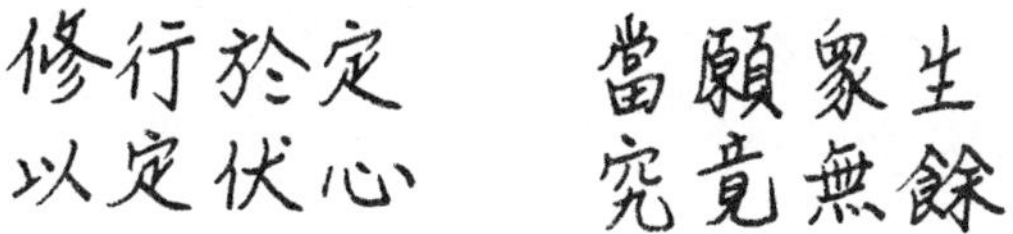

修行於定　　當願眾生
以定伏心　　究竟無餘

COMMENTARY:

  WHEN you *CULTIVATE SAMADHI*, you should *VOW
THAT LIVING BEINGS WILL SUBDUE THEIR MINDS WITH
SAMADHI*, use samadhi to subdue their scattered
minds. Therefore, I always say,

> *When the nature is in samadhi and demons are*
> *subdued,*
> *One is happy everyday.*

If your nature is in samadhi, then demons are subdued. Why are demons not subdued? It is because your nature is not in samadhi. Let me tell you, when I propagated the Buddhadharma in America, I encountered a lot of demonic obstacles. But I welcomed any kind of demons when they came to me. "I welcome them"--Have you ever heard such a way of speaking? I welcome demons to come to me. I make friends with any kind of demons. I say, "Welcome, welcome, sit down, please!" We sit down and have a nice chat. Why do I welcome them? Because of this principle, "Everything's O.K." Somebody might say, "You think everything is O.K? How about if someone steals a valuable thing from you, will that be O.K.?" But I say, "Since he steals it away from me and he uses it, that's the same as my using it. Why distinguish between his and mine? He steals it because he needs to use it. If it's useless, why would he bother to steal it? Since he utilizes it, why should I hold on to it? This is not a big problem!"

Another will say, "Probably you cannot put it down after people steal it from you." Well, you can try me out. But you don't have the guts to be a thief.

Therefore, it is said, "Once the nature is in samadhi and demons are subdued, one is happy every day." One is not only happy for one day; one is happy every day. "To understand the mind" is not hard at all. "To see through the nature," one does not have sorrow and difficulty. So it is said,

> *Once the nature is in samadhi and demons are*
> *subdued,*
> *One is happy every day*
> *If false thoughts do not arise,*
> *One is at peace everywhere.*

If you don't have false thoughts, you'll be happy and without any trouble wherever you go. So this verse says, "Will subdue their minds with samadhi."

AND BE ULTIMATELY WITHOUT RESIDUE. It means one doesn't have any habits left in the end. If you don't have Samadhi, you will have residual habits. For example, one of my disciples likes to drink milk and another one likes to eat ice cream that he steals. These are all residual habits. They think it's O.K. to steal ice cream in the afternoon. But mice also come to get their share. Because the mice think, "You're hungry, I'm also hungry. Since you don't keep the rules at Gold Mountain Monastery, I can also do as I wish. I will not create karmic offenses by stealing food from monks." Therefore they come to have a good meal. No matter how you try to keep them away, they won't go. Once you seize them, they flee. See, these mice have such great talent. That's because the mice come to teach and transform those two monks who steal food in the afternoon. You should be careful, otherwise you will become **mice.** Fortunately the two monks became enlightened to the fact that if they steal ice cream again, the mice will come to steal their bread. So it is said,

Such a cause will reap such an effect.

SUTRA:

WHEN CULTIVATING CONTEMPLATION,
I VOW THAT LIVING BEINGS
WILL SEE THROUGH PRINCIPLE AS IT TRULY IS,
AND ETERNALLY BE WITHOUT UNREASONABLE
CONTENTION.

若修於觀　當願眾生
見如實理　永無乖諍

COMMENTARY:

WHEN you *CULTIVATE CONTEMPLATION,* you practice "stopping and contemplation." From cultivating contemplation, one produces the Prajna of contemplation and illumination--the wisdom of investiga-

tion.   How does one give rise to the wisdom of
investigation? First of all, he has to cultivate
samadhi.   Samadhi means "stopping," and vice versa.
samadhi and stopping are just the same terms. Once
you can stop, you will have samadhi power. If you
are in samadhi, you will be in stillness. Therefore, you have to cultivate Ch'an samadhi. When
cultivating Ch'an samadhi, you should *VOW THAT
LIVING BEINGS SEE THROUGH PRINCIPLE AS IT TRULY IS.*
May they understand the principle of true suchness
and the real mark, and be eternally without obstruction, that they realize "everything's O.K." If you
can see everything as being empty, then this is to
be eternally without obstruction. You don't argue
and fight with anybody. You yield without fighting.
You are not fighting for fame, benefit, and power.
You are not fighting for anything. And this is to be
ETERNALLY WITHOUT UNREASONABLE CONTENTION. You
don't fight with people irrationally or force the
issue. You don't take the false as true principle.
But let me tell you, attorneys and lawyers have
these bad habits, so they'd better learn this
Dharma of being without unreasonable contention.

SUTRA:

> *WHEN COMING OUT OF THE LOTUS POSTURE,*
> *I VOW THAT LIVING BEINGS*
> *WILL CONTEMPLATE ALL DHARMAS OF*
> *   ACTIVITY,*
> *AS ENTIRELY RETURNING TO DISPERSAL AND*
> *   EXTINCTION.*

捨跏趺坐　　當願眾生
觀諸行法　　悉歸散滅

COMMENTARY:

WHEN COMING OUT OF THE LOTUS POSTURE. When
you put your legs down from the lotus position,
you are no longer sitting in full-lotus or in half-
lotus position. You become a pile of mud in the
eyes of ghosts. At this time, you should contemplate, and *VOW THAT LIVING BEINGS WILL CONTEMPLATE*

ALL kinds of *DHARMAS OF ACTIVITY*--all kinds of worldly dharmas, and all kinds of non-ultimate dharmas, *AS ENTIRELY RETURNING TO DISPERSAL AND EXTINCTION*, and emptiness. They are impermanent.

SUTRA:

> *WHEN PUTTING DOWN MY LEGS,*
> *I VOW THAT LIVING BEINGS*
> *WILL ATTAIN LIBERATION IN THEIR MINDS,*
> *AND PEACEFULLY DWELL IN UNMOVINGNESS.*

下足住時　　當願眾生
心得解脫　　安住不動

COMMENTARY:

WHEN you *PUT* your *LEGS DOWN* from lotus position and are about to walk, you also should *VOW THAT LIVING BEINGS WILL ATTAIN LIBERATION IN THEIR MINDS*, and be without any attachments. *LIBERATION* --if you don't have attachments, naturally you're liberated. Don't try to find liberation. In ancient times, there was an old cultivator who asked for instructions from a monk, "Great Monk, let me ask you, how can I attain liberation?" The Great monk said, "Who tied you up?" This old cultivator answered, "Nobody tied me up." The monk said, "Then why do you seek liberation?" This old cultivator immediately became enlightened when he heard this. Originally we are like this. Nobody tied us up. But you can't pretend to be enlightened, you have to actually become enlightened. The time when you get enlightened is the time you attain liberation. If you break through the "black energy barrel," then you get enlightened.

AND PEACEFULLY DWELL IN UNMOVINGNESS. That is, you always have the power of samadhi. You're in samadhi and not moved while walking, standing, sitting, or lying down. You're not moved. But what is meant by not being moved? You don't have false thoughts, nor do you give rise to deviant thoughts. What's not being moved? If at all times,

you are without sexual desire, then you're really
unmoving. Therefore Confucius said,

> *At age thirty I stood firm.*
> *At forty I was no longer deluded.*
> *At fifty I understood the decree of heaven.*
> *At sixty my ear was an organ of compliance.*
> *At seventy I could do whatever I wished but*
> *   still not transgress the proper limits.*

Mencius also said,

> *At age forty my mind did not move.*

That is the state of one "peacefully dwelling in
unmovingness." Somebody might say, "What's unmoving? Is it the body that is unmoving? If you die,
you can say your body is unmoving. Since you're
alive, how can you command your body to not move?
Is that right?" To be "unmoving" means you don't
move your mind. It is to be "thus thus unmoving,
understanding and constantly bright." If you're
really unmoving, you'll attain true wisdom. Once
you attain true wisdom, you will not be upside-down.
Not to move in your mind--this counts as being
truly unmoving. It's not seeking from outside.
But it's not like being a boulder which refuses to
budge. The wind cannot blow through it, and the
rain cannot seep in, but it is just a stone which
has no use. So it is said,

> *Dead water cannot bring a dragon to accomplishment.*

To be "unmoving" means not to make false thoughts,
not to give rise to deviant mindfulness, not to
produce any sexual desire. The most important
thing is that everybody return the light and illuminate within. Somebody says, "I've studied the
Buddhadharma for several decades." Do you still
give rise to sexual desire? If you don't give rise
to sexual desire, then I grant that you are a true
cultivator of the Buddhadharma. If you do, then
your skill is not yet ultimate. You still have
to cultivate, and to learn. You haven't cut off
your residual habits. So all of you good knowing
advisors, don't cheat yourselves! Don't proclaim

you are very wonderful and that your cultivation is ultimate. Well, what is wonderful? Your cheating yourself is wonderful!

SUTRA:

> AS I LIFT UP MY FOOT,
> I VOW THAT LIVING BEINGS
> WILL LEAVE THE SEA OF BIRTH AND DEATH,
> AND BE REPLETE WITH WHOLESOME DHARMAS.

若 舉 於 足　　當 願 眾 生
出 生 死 海　　具 眾 善 法

COMMENTARY:

AS you *LIFT UP* your *FOOT*. That's the time you start to walk. The previous vow is the time when you finish sitting and are about to walk. As you lift up your foot, you should recite a verse that says,

> From the break of dawn until the dusk,
> All you living beings best take care of
>   yourselves.
> If you should come to harm beneath my feet,
> I vow you will be reborn in the Pure Land.

It is explained very clearly in the *Shramanera Vinaya.* If you want to learn it, you can study it. As you lift up your foot is the time you are about to step forward. At this time, you should *VOW THAT LIVING BEINGS WILL LEAVE THE SEA OF BIRTH AND DEATH*, get out of the triple realm, *AND BE REPLETE WITH WHOLESOME DHARMAS*, be complete with good dharmas.

SUTRA:

> AS I PUT ON MY LOWER GARMENTS,
> I VOW THAT LIVING BEINGS
> WILL BE CLOTHED IN GOOD ROOTS,
> AND BE COMPLETE WITH SHAME AND REMORSE.

著下裙時　　當願眾生
服諸善根　　具足慚愧

COMMENTARY:

AS I PUT ON MY LOWER GARMENTS. "Lower garments" refers to the five-piece robe worn by left-home people in Cambodia, India, and Thailand, on account of the hot weather. But in China, lower garments refers to trousers. As you put on lower garments, you also should VOW THAT LIVING BEINGS WILL BE CLOTHED IN GOOD ROOTS, that is, be protected by their good roots. Good roots are like clothes that we wear.

AND BE COMPLETE WITH SHAME AND REMORSE. Why do we put on lower garments? Because we should have a sense of shame. If we don't put on lower garments, our appearance will be ugly, not elegant. If we're naked, we look awful. For example, last year in America there was a fad in which people ran around naked. They didn't wear clothes. They didn't have shame at all, therefore they ran around naked. They wanted people to see their original face. But why did they want to run? Wouldn't it have been much better to stand there and have people take a good look at them? But they still ran because their sense of shamelessness had not reached the ultimate point. Their skill was not perfected. They still had some sense of shame; therefore, they had to run. They just liked play-acting, they liked other people to look at them. But they wouldn't let you see them clearly. This is an example of one who hasn't the thought of shame, one who isn't complete with a sense of shame.

SUTRA:

> WHEN STRAIGHTENING MY CLOTHES AND
>   FASTENING MY BELT,
> I VOW THAT LIVING BEINGS
> WILL GATHER IN AND BIND UP THEIR GOOD ROOTS,
> AND NOT LET THEM BECOME SCATTERED OR LOST.

整衣束帶　當願眾生
檢束善根　不令散失

COMMENTARY:

WHEN you STRAIGHTEN your CLOTHES AND FASTEN your BELT, you accord with the mark of teaching and awesome deportment. You're well dressed and not sloppy about it. You are not naked, nor are you missing buttons on your shirt. You don't expose your chest or back. Sometimes laypeople wear Chinese style garments and boots to attend meetings or parties, and they conduct themselves with dignified awesome deportment.

Nowadays, left-home people do not wear belts around their waists. Before, left-home people had to fasten a vajra belt around their waists. They looked very awesome with those belts, just like the eighteen military generals who have all kinds of powers. The monks from Young Forest Temple (Shau Lin Temple 少林寺 , one of the most famous temples in China) were especially wonderful in their deportment.

When straightening your clothes and fastening your belts, at this time you should VOW THAT LIVING BEINGS WILL GATHER IN AND BIND UP THEIR GOOD ROOTS. They should check whether their good roots are perfect or imperfect; complete or imcomplete. Don't LET the skill in your cultivation and your good roots BECOME SCATTERED OR LOST.

"Scattered or lost" means you retreat from the Bodhi mind or produce a mind of laziness or an attitude that things are difficult--you think cultivation is a lot of hardship.

SUTRA:

> AS I PUT ON UPPER GARMENTS,
> I VOW THAT LIVING BEINGS
> WILL ATTAIN SUPERIOR GOOD ROOTS,
> AND REACH THE OTHER SHORE OF DHARMA.

若著上衣　　當願眾生
獲勝善根　　至法彼岸

COMMENTARY:

"Upper garments" refers to the seven-piece robe.
AS you *PUT ON* your *UPPER GARMENTS*, you *VOW THAT
LIVING BEINGS WILL ATTAIN SUPERIOR GOOD ROOTS, AND
REACH THE OTHER SHORE OF DHARMA.* You attain
Prajna Paramita and become perfected in the Six
Paramitas. Therefore it says, *REACH THE OTHER
SHORE OF DHARMA.* You reach the other shore of
Nirvana.

SUTRA:

> *WHEN PUTTING ON THE SANGHATTI,
> I VOW THAT LIVING BEINGS
> WILL ENTER INTO THE FOREMOST POSITION,
> AND ATTAIN THE UNMOVING DHARMA.*

著僧伽梨　　當願眾生
入第一位　　得不動法

COMMENTARY:

WHEN PUTTING ON THE SANGHATTI. THE SANGHATTI
is also called the Great Robe, the chief (host)
robe, or the patched robe. When you wear such a
robe, you should *VOW THAT LIVING BEINGS WILL ENTER
INTO THE FOREMOST POSITION,* the number one position.
The foremost position is just Buddhahood. You
vow that all living beings attain Buddhahood, the
fruition of the Buddha.
AND ATTAIN THE UNMOVING DHARMA. Since you
enter the foremost position, you will simultaneous-
ly attain the unmoving Sung Dharma. The unmoving
Dharma is without any attachments, meaning that
one attains true samadhi. The Buddhas dwell in
the Land of Constant and Still Light; they have
all attained the unmoving Dharma.

SUTRA:

AS MY HAND HOLDS MY TOOTHBRUSH,
I VOW THAT LIVING BEINGS
WILL COMPLETELY ATTAIN WONDERFUL DHARMA,
AND BE ULTIMATELY PURE.

手執楊枝　　當願眾生
皆得妙法　　究竟清淨

COMMENTARY:

AS MY HAND HOLDS MY TOOTHBRUSH. In ancient times, left-home people in China and India had a habit of chewing the willow branch. When they were about to chew the willow branch, they would pick up   and *VOW THAT LIVING BEINGS WILL COMPLETELY ATTAIN WONDERFUL,* inconceivable *DHARMA, AND BE ULTIMATELY PURE* in the future.

There are a lot of advantages from chewing the willow branch:

1. It can brighten the eyes. The willow branch has a certain kind of bitter taste which can counteract the fire in your head. Therefore, it can cause the eyes to become bright.

2. It can get rid of phlegm. When you chew the willow branch, you won't have phlegm in your throat. People have phlegm in their throats because of fire in their bodies. Not only can the bitter substance in the willow branch brighten the eyes, it can also cool the fire in your body.

3. It gets rid of bad breath. When you chew the willow branch, the bad odor in your mouth will disappear.

4. It can enhance flavor.

5. It can aid digestion.

So, chewing the willow branch has many advantages, but nowadays left-home people are using toothbrushes and toothpaste instead. When I lived in Liu Yin Mountain in Su Chou Province, the people there still maintained this old-fashioned habit of chewing the willow branch. Although it has so many advantages, people still give it up for newer things.

SUTRA:

WHEN I BRUSH MY TEETH,
I VOW THAT LIVING BEINGS
WILL BE HARMONIOUS AND PURE IN MIND,
AND BITE THROUGH ALL AFFLICTIONS.

嚼楊枝時　　當願眾生
其心調淨　　噬諸煩惱

COMMENTARY:

WHEN you BRUSH your TEETH, or chewing the
willow branch, you shouldn't be having false
thought; don't be sloppy about it. At this time,
you should VOW THAT LIVING BEINGS WILL BE HARMONI-
OUS AND PURE IN MIND, AND BITE THROUGH ALL AFFLIC-
TIONS, without any afflictions. People should
bite through all afflictions until they completely
disappear.

SUTRA:

> *AS I GO TO THE TOILET,*
> *I VOW THAT LIVING BEINGS*
> *WILL CAST OUT GREED, HATRED, AND STUPIDITY,*
> *AND CLEANSE THEMSELVES OF OFFENSE DHARMAS.*

大小便時　　當願象生
棄貪瞋癡　　蠲除罪法

COMMENTARY:

AS I GO TO THE TOILET. When left-home people
go to the toilet they should make a vow. Don't
hold meetings in the bathroom, because it is not
a place to have a chat. Therefore, you should
*VOW THAT LIVING BEINGS WILL CAST OUT GREED, HATRED,
AND STUPIDITY.* You don't want to hang on to your
greed, hatred, and stupidity anymore.
AND CLEANSE THEMSELVES OF OFFENSE DHARMA.
You should wipe away all offense dharmas. Offenses
are just like urine and excrement--they are very
filthy. You should not keep them with you, or be
unwilling to renounce them. You should wipe them
out!

SUTRA:

> *WHEN I USE WATER,*
> *I VOW THAT LIVING BEINGS*
> *WILL QUICKLY REACH*
> *TRANSCENDENTAL DHARMAS.*

事訖就水　　當願象生
出世法中　　速疾而往

COMMENTARY:

WHEN I USE WATER. After you finish going to
the toilet, you have to clean your hands. A
Bhikshu should clean his hands after he finishes
going to the toilet. At this time, you should

VOW THAT LIVING BEINGS WILL QUICKLY REACH TRANSCENDENTAL DHARMAS. They shouldn't keep on staying in the three realms.

SUTRA:

WHEN I WASH AWAY THE BODY'S FILTH,
I VOW THAT LIVING BEINGS
WILL BE PURE, REGULATED, AND COMPLIANT,
AND ULTIMATELY WITHOUT DEFILEMENT.

洗滌形穢　　當願眾生
清淨調柔　　畢竟無垢

COMMENTARY:

WHEN I WASH AWAY THE BODY'S FILTH. You should wash your hands after you finish urinating, and use water to clean your anus after you finish defacating. You should *VOW THAT LIVING BEINGS WILL BE PURE, REGULATED, AND COMPLIANT.* This means they should be patient. They won't have any temper, residual habits, or ignorance, *AND BE ULTIMATELY WITHOUT DEFILEMENT.* In the future they won't retain any filth.

SUTRA:

AS I USE THIS WATER TO WASH MY HANDS,
I VOW THAT LIVING BEINGS
WILL HAVE CLEAN HANDS
TO RECEIVE AND UPHOLD THE BUDDHADHARMA.

以水盥掌　　當願眾生
得清淨手　　受持佛法

COMMENTARY:

AS you USE WATER TO WASH your HANDS, you also should *VOW THAT LIVING BEINGS WILL HAVE CLEAN HANDS TO RECEIVE AND UPHOLD THE BUDDHADHARMA.* Why does one need to have hands that are clean? One

should have clean hands to open the Sutra and uphold all Dharmas. For example, people who are
cultivating the Forty-two Hands and Eyes from the
Great Compassion Mantra in the *Dharani Sutra* should
always clean their hands before they practice it.
Everybody can accomplish a thousand eyes and thousand hands. In ancient time, a person called Ma
Liu Tse (馬六子) was supposed to be Kuan Yin
Bodhisattva with a thousand eyes and a thousand
hands. But when we cultivate the Dharma door of a
thousand eyes and a thousand hands it's not for
the sake of becoming a thousand-eyed and a thousand-
handed Kuan Yin Bodhisattva. Nor is it for the
purpose of stealing things. Even though you're
equipped with so many hands, you can't steal
things while others are not watching. Also, to
have so many eyes is not for the purpose of stealing things. It's not for those kinds of reasons.
Rather, it's for this reason,

> *Prayers depart a thousand hearts,*
> *In a thousand hearts she answers.*
> *Sailing the sea of suffering,*
> *She crosses people over.*

As soon as someone obtains the Dharma door of the
thousand eyes and thousand hands, he certainly
will become Kuan Yin Bodhisattva with a thousand
eyes and a thousand hands. Not only will he have
just a thousand hands and eyes, but he'll have
limitless hands and eyes. There's a saying that
goes,

> *Hands and eyes penetrate to the heavens.*

That saying is used to describe someone with the
ability of a thousands hands and thousand eyes.
    Each one of us can have a thousand hands and
a thousand eyes like Kuan Yin Bodhisattva. But
we haven't cultivated the Dharma Door of Great
Compassion. The Forty-two Hands and Eyes is the
Dharma Door for obtaining a thousand hands and
a thousand eyes. Therefore, everyone of us should
clean our hands before we uphold the Buddhadharma.

SUTRA:

> AS I USE WATER TO WASH MY FACE,
> I VOW THAT LIVING BEINGS
> WILL ATTAIN PURE DHARMA DOORS,
> AND BE ETERNALLY WITHOUT DEFILEMENT.

以水洗面　　當願眾生
得淨法門　　永無垢染

COMMENTARY:

When you USE WATER TO WASH your FACE, you should also VOW THAT LIVING BEINGS WILL ATTAIN PURE DHARMA DOORS, AND BE ETERNALLY WITHOUT DEFILE-MENT.

SUTRA:

> AS I HOLD THE TIN STAFF,
> I VOW THAT LIVING BEINGS
> WILL ESTABLISH ASSEMBLIES OF GREAT GIVING,
> AND REVEAL THE WAY OF TRUE SUCHNESS.

手執錫杖　　當願眾生
設大施會　　示如實道

COMMENTARY:

When you HOLD THE TIN STAFF, you also should make a vow. Most people know the story of the Venerable Mahamaudgalyayana who opened the doors of hell with his tin staff.

At this time, you should VOW THAT LIVING BEINGS WILL ESTABLISH ASSEMBLIES OF GREAT GIVING, AND REVEAL THE WAY OF TRUE SUCHNESS, to display the true path for living beings.

An "assembly of great giving" refers to a big Dharma Assembly which can point out the path of cultivation for living beings.

SUTRA:

> AS I HOLD THE VESSEL,
> I VOW THAT LIVING BEINGS
> WILL BECOME DHARMA VESSELS,
> AND RECEIVE THE OFFERINGS OF GODS AND
>   PEOPLE.

執持應器　　當願眾生
成就法器　　受天人供

COMMENTARY:

AS I HOLD THE VESSEL, or bowl (the bowl is called the vessel of proper measurement). You also should VOW THAT LIVING BEINGS WILL BECOME DHARMA VESSELS, that is, become pure White Dharma vessels who can support and inherit the legacy of the Thus Come Ones, AND BE WORTHY OF RECEIVING OFFERINGS FROM GODS AND PEOPLE.

SUTRA:

> WHEN I TAKE THE FIRST STEP IN CULTIVATING
>   THE WAY,
> I VOW THAT LIVING BEINGS
> WILL TEND TOWARDS THE CONDUCT OF THE
>   BUDDHAS,
> AND ENTER THE PLACE OF NO-RELIANCE.

發趾向道　　當願眾生
趣佛所行　　入無依處

COMMENTARY:

WHEN I TAKE THE FIRST STEP IN CULTIVATING THE WAY. When you resolve to cultivate the Way, it's like taking the very first step of a journey. At this time, you also should make a vow. You VOW THAT LIVING BEINGS WILL TEND TOWARDS THE CON-DUCT OF THE BUDDHAS, that which all Buddhas practice, AND ENTER THE PLACE OF NO-RELIANCE. When we

cultivate the Way we should rely on the teaching
and offer up our conduct. We should practice the
methods that the Buddhas teach and enter a place
of no reliance. Don't bring forth a mind of laziness. If you are lazy, you will produce a mind
of dependence. For example, the Venerable Ananda
assumed that since he was the Buddha's cousin, he
didn't need to cultivate. He thought the Buddha
would naturally give him samadhi. But he didn't
understand this principle,

> *Each person gets full by eating his own share*
> *   of food;*
> *Everyone should end his own birth and death.*

Therefore, you shouldn't maintain a mind of dependence.

SUTRA:

> *WHEN TRAVELING ON A PATH,*
> *I VOW THAT LIVING BEINGS*
> *WILL WALK ON THE BUDDHA PATH,*
> *AND TEND TOWARD THE DHARMA OF NO-RESIDUE.*

若在於道　　當願眾生
能行佛道　　向無餘法

COMMENTARY:

WHEN you are *TRAVELING ON A PATH*, you should
also *VOW THAT LIVING BEINGS WILL WALK ON THE
BUDDHA PATH*, to cultivate the Buddha path and follow
the Dharma Door that the Buddhas cultivate.
AND TEND TOWARD THE DHARMA OF NO-RESIDUE. They
should head toward the Nirvana of no-impediment and
no-residue.

SUTRA:

> *WHILE WALKING ON A ROAD,*
> *I VOW THAT LIVING BEINGS*
> *WILL ENTER THE PURE DHARMA REALM,*
> *AND BE WITHOUT OBSTRUCTION IN THEIR MINDS.*

涉路而去　　當願眾生
履淨法界　　心無障礙

COMMENTARY:

WHILE WALKING ON A ROAD. When a left-home person walks on the road, he also should make a vow and not strike up any false thoughts. He should *VOW THAT LIVING BEINGS WILL ENTER THE PURE DHARMA REALM* wherever they go, *AND BE WITHOUT OBSTRUCTION* and attachments *IN THEIR MINDS.*

SUTRA:

> WHEN ASCENDING A STEEP PATH,
> I VOW THAT LIVING BEINGS
> WILL ETERNALLY TRANSCEND THE THREE REALMS,
> AND BE WITHOUT FEAR OR TIMIDITY IN THEIR
>   MINDS.

見升高路　　當願眾生
永出三界　　心無怯弱

COMMENTARY:

WHEN ASCENDING A STEEP PATH. When you ascend mountainous terrain and try to climb up step by step, you also should make a vow. You *VOW THAT LIVING BEINGS WILL ETERNALLY TRANSCEND THE THREE REALMS*--the desire realm, form realm, and formless realm.

AND BE WITHOUT FEAR OR TIMIDITY IN THEIR MINDS. For someone to get out of the three realms is not easy; he has to pass through a long time before getting out of it. Even though he has to go through such a long time, he still should not produce a mind of fear and think, "The Buddha path is so long and far--I cannot cultivate it." He produces a mind of retreat. If one produces a mind of retreat, his resolve and vows are no longer solid; they become soft and weak. This will undermine people's determination so they won't have any more strength to step forward.

SUTRA:

> WHEN GOING DOWNHILL ON A ROAD,
> I VOW THAT LIVING BEINGS
> WILL BE HUMBLE AND RESPECTFUL IN THEIR
>   MINDS,
> AND INCREASE IN THE BUDDHA'S GOOD ROOTS.

見趣下路　　當願衆生
其心謙下　　長佛善根

COMMENTARY:

WHEN GOING DOWNHILL ON A ROAD. When you're going downhill on a road, you should VOW THAT LIVING BEINGS WILL BE very HUMBLE AND RESPECTFUL IN THEIR MINDS, not to be proud or arrogant. You vow that they can get along with people with a humble and reverent attitude. As it is said,

> One is bright and eager to learn,
> And does not feel shame to consult those under
>   him.

He will go as far as consulting people who don't have as much knowledge as he does. Therefore, one should have the virtuous nature of humility and reverence so as to INCREASE IN THE BUDDHA'S GOOD ROOTS. If you don't bring forth arrogant thoughts toward all living beings, if you don't look down on people, you are "increasing in the Buddha's good roots."

The Buddha treats all living beings as Buddhas, and therefore he becomes a Buddha. If the Buddha treated all living beings as ghosts, then he wouldn't have become a Buddha. So, if we want to become Buddhas, we should use the mind of kindness, compassion, joy, and renunciation toward all living beings.

When going downhill on a road,
I vow that living beings
Will be humble and respectful in their minds,
And increase in the Buddha's good roots.

SUTRA:

> WHEN I WALK ON A SLANTING AND CROOKED
>   PATH,
> I VOW THAT LIVING BEINGS
> WILL RENOUNCE THE IMPROPER WAY,
> AND ETERNALLY ERADICATE EVIL VIEWS.

見斜曲路　　當願眾生
捨不正道　　永除惡見

COMMENTARY:

WHEN I WALK ON A SLANTING AND CROOKED PATH.
This means a path   which is not straight. It
is a winding, serpentine, tortuous path. There
are some kinds of roads that are shaped like silk-
worms. For example, the roads *in* S'ze Ch'uan
(四川) province of China are very precarious
and difficult to tread, so there's a verse that
describes this condition,

> *I heard someone talk about the worm-shaped road:*
> *It's rugged and difficult to walk on.*
> *Mountains appear right in front of people's faces,*
> *And clouds grow from the horse's head!*

It's very hard for one to travel on the paths of
S'ze Ch'uan. They are very treacherous and fraught
with danger. So, when you walk on a slanting and
crooked path, you should *VOW THAT LIVING BEINGS
WILL RENOUNCE* all *THE IMPROPER WAYS* and walk on
proper paths.
AND *ETERNALLY ERADICATE EVIL VIEWS*.   *EVIL
VIEWS* means deviant views and deviant knowledge,
not proper views and proper knowledge. Deviant
views and deviant knowledge are just like the
slanting and crooked path. Therefore, you should
vow to forever eradicate evil views.

SUTRA:

> WHEN I SEE A STRAIGHT ROAD,
> I VOW THAT LIVING BEINGS

WILL BECOME PROPER AND STRAIGHT IN THEIR
    MINDS,
AND BE WITHOUT FLATTERY OR DECEIT.

若見直路　　當願衆生
其心正直　　無諂無誑

COMMENTARY:

WHEN I SEE A STRAIGHT ROAD. A straight road
means that one's mind should be proper and straight.
As it is said,

A straight mind is the Way Place.

Why do I want to propagate the Buddhadharma in the
West? It's because I see that some Westerners are
very true, and not deviant at all. Their minds
are straight. They are not like Asian people who
are expert in lying. They are still in the stage
of learning how to lie. But they don't understand
the technique entirely. So, to propagate the
Buddhadharma in America during this period may
help them to maintain their straight-minds longer.
WHEN you SEE A STRAIGHT ROAD, at this time,
you should VOW THAT LIVING BEINGS WILL BECOME
PROPER AND STRAIGHT IN THEIR MINDS, AND BE WITHOUT
FLATTERY OR DECEIT. To "flatter" means to butter up
people. In general, people like to flatter those
who are rich, and be arrogant toward those who
are poor. They are in favor of something new,
but get tired of the things that are old. They
are disgusted with the old, but enjoy the new.
When they see a rich man, their faces light up.
They curry favors and display a fraudulent smile
when they encounter rich people, they toady up and
fawn on those who have power. Such an attitude is
shameful indeed!
"And be without flattery or deceit" means one
doesn't flatter rich people, nor look down on those
who are poor. If a rich person doesn't display
arrogance, then this is a virtuous conduct. If a
poor person doesn't butter up wealthy people, that
is also a virtuous conduct, a straight and proper

attitude.

What is meant by "being tired of the old, and enjoying the new"? When people see a new thing, they become very happy. But if a thing gets old, they don't like it any more. So the attitude of "forgetting the old, and enjoying the new", or flattering the rich, and scorning the poor" is the attitude which most people have. It's an old habit that most of them maintain. If you don't transgress with such false habits, then you will understand the principle of being a person. However, even if you don't flatter the rich, you also should not become arrogant towards the rich. It is a mistake if you butter up the rich; it's also false if you are arrogant towards the poor. In China during the Three Kingdoms period, there was a general called Kuan Ti Kung (關帝公). He was known for his sense of justice and righteousness. As it is said,

His sense of great justice reached the sky.

He stayed in Emperor Ts'ao's country for three years and received very respectful treatment from the Emperor. But that didn't change his determination; his mind was always faithful to his own country. One day, Emperor Ts'ao gave him a new green robe and expected him to put it on. But he didn't forget his elder brother Liu Pei's friendship. So he wore the new robe inside, and still wore the old one outside. When Emperor Ts'ao saw this he asked, "Why do you wear the green robe that I gave to you inside?"

Kuan Kung said, "Because this old robe was given to me by my elder brother Liu Pei. I'm not one who likes the new and forgets the old. Therefore, I wear the new robe which you gave me inside."

When Emperor Ts'ao' heard this, he was disappointed. He realized he couldn't move Kuan Kung's determination or utilize his ability. That's because Kuan Kung didn't flatter the wealthy, nor did he look down on the poor. He didn't get tired of old friends and toady up to new friends.

"Deceit"--Why does one want to lie? The reason one lies is selfishness. If one doesn't have the thought of selfishness, one will absolutely not lie.

SUTRA:

> *WHEN I SEE A DUSTY ROAD,*
> *I VOW THAT LIVING BEINGS*
> *WILL GET FAR APART FROM DUST,*
> *AND ATTAIN THE PURE DHARMA.*

見路多塵　　當願眾生
遠離塵坌　　獲清淨法

COMMENTARY:

WHEN you *SEE A DUSTY ROAD*, at this time, you
should make a *VOW THAT LIVING BEINGS WILL GET FAR
APART FROM DUST*, remove themselves from dust,
AND ATTAIN THE PURE DHARMA. When you encounter
such a situation, you should make a vow. You can
not eat too much dust! So you vow that living
beings will be far removed from dust,
that they will attain the pure and wonderful
Dharma and not be so dusty.

SUTRA:

> *WHEN I SEE A ROAD THAT IS FREE FROM DUST,*
> *I VOW THAT LIVING BEINGS*
> *WILL ALWAYS CULTIVATE GREAT COMPASSION,*
> *AND BE MOISTENED AND NOURISHED IN THEIR*
> *   MINDS.*

見路無塵　　當願眾生
常行大悲　　其心潤澤

COMMENTARY:

WHEN I SEE A ROAD THAT IS FREE FROM DUST,
which is very clean, like the roads in America.
American roads are coated with tar. At this time,
you should *VOW THAT LIVING BEINGS WILL ALWAYS
CULTIVATE* a *GREAT COMPASSION* mind. What is the

great compassion mind? It means you treat everybody the same. I have a verse which describes
this great compassion mind,

> *Truly recognize your own faults,*
> *Don't discuss others' mistakes.*
> *Their mistakes are just my mistakes,*
> *Sharing the same substance with everyone is*
>   *called Great Compassion.*

No matter what happens, you should not pick on
others' faults. You should admit your own mistakes. Don't try to cover up or protect your
faults, and let them go down the drain. As it
is said,

> *If one can change his mistakes,*
> *Then they will return to nothing.*
> *If one tries to cover them,*
> *Then they'll increase by the double.*

As Confucius said,

> *There's no greater good than in one who*
>   *changes his mistakes.*

If you can change your mistakes, then that is a
great good deed. He also said,

> *If you have mistakes, don't be afraid*
>   *to change them.*

If you're afraid to change your mistakes, then
you're trying to cover them and not admitting
that they exist. *But don't discuss others' mis-*
takes.   If people don't talk, there's no big
trouble. But if people get together, they always
gossip about others' faults. They only gossip
about other people's affairs, but they cannot
see through their own mistakes. As it is said,

> *The crow gets down on the pig's body.*

The crow sees that the body of a pig is black, but
it cannot see that its own body is black. This
is like people who all day long just talk about

others' faults, but they don't think they make any
mistakes themselves. This is very stupid behavior.
There's a saying,

> *People are not sages or worthies,*
> *Who can be without faults?*

From this line, we know that only sages do not
makes mistakes. A worthy person has very few mistakes. A superior person changes his mistakes,
while a petty person protects his mistakes.
     If you have mistakes, but you change them,
that's the best. But you shouldn't always look at
others' faults. Don't wash other people's clothes.
Why do I still feel happy when people scold me?
Because *their mistakes are just my mistakes!*
Others' mistakes are my mistakes I don't separate
myself from others. Somebody says, "Then you're
taking a loss!" Well, I'm not afraid of taking a
small loss. Why is this world going to ruin? It's
because people don't want to take losses. You
don't want to take a loss, neither does he. But
everybody wants to grab profit.
     When you see a road that is free from dust,
at this time, you should vow that living beings
will be without any discrimination between self
and others, and will always practice great compassion.
     AND BE MOISTENED AND NOURISHED IN THEIR MINDS.
You vow that they will become smart and wise, that
their minds will become brightened and enriched
by good Dharmas. As it is said,

> *Wealth enhances your household,*
> *Virtue enhances your body.*

If you have wealth, then wealth will ornament your
house so it looks elegant and fine. If you posses
virtue, then virtue will enrich you so that your
body radiates a healthy glow.

SUTRA:

> *WHEN I SEE A DANGEROUS ROAD,*
> *I VOW THAT LIVING BEINGS*
> *WILL DWELL IN THE PROPER-DHARMA REALM,*

AND SEPARATE FROM ALL OFFENSES AND
  DIFFICULTY.

若見險道　　當願眾生
住正法界　　離諸罪難

COMMENTARY:

WHEN I SEE A DANGEROUS ROAD. What is a dangerous path? This refers to the six destinies in which suddenly you ascend to the heavens, suddenly descend to hell, suddenly become a hungry ghost, and suddenly become an animal. The six paths contain a lot of danger. As it is said,

> Those who obtain a human body are like the dirt
>   in my palm,
> But those who lose their human bodies are like
>   the dirt on the great earth.

Therefore, a human body is very hard to obtain, and it is very dangerous to revolve back and forth in the six destinies.
At this time, you should VOW THAT LIVING BEINGS WILL DWELL IN THE PROPER-DHARMA REALM, AND SEPARATE FROM ALL OFFENSES AND DIFFICULTIES.

SUTRA:

AS I SEE A MULTITUDE ASSEMBLED,
I VOW THAT LIVING BEINGS
WILL PROCLAIM THE PROFOUND DHARMA,
AND BE HARMONIOUS WITH ALL.

若見眾會　　當願眾生
說甚深法　　一切和合

COMMENTARY:

AS you SEE A MULTITUDE ASSEMBLED, when you see everybody gathered together at a meeting, you also should *VOW THAT LIVING BEINGS WILL PROCLAIM THE PROFOUND DHARMA*, the subtle, wonderful Dharma, *AND BE HARMONIOUS WITH ALL.* There shouldn't be any fighting or strife among people when they get to-gether.

SUTRA:

> *WHEN I SEE A HUGE PILLAR,*
> *I VOW THAT LIVING BEINGS*
> *WILL DEPART FROM THE MIND OF A SELF AND*
>   *DISPUTE,*
> *AND BE WITHOUT RAGE OR HATRED.*

若見大柱　　當願眾生
離我諍心　　無有念恨

COMMENTARY:

WHEN I SEE A HUGE PILLAR. A "huge pillar" is translated as a "huge tree" in some Sutras. Well, a pillar and a tree are very similar to each other.

At this time, you should *VOW THAT LIVING BEINGS WILL DEPART FROM THE MIND OF A SELF AND DIS-PUTE*, get away from their egos and the mind of dispute, the mind of arrogance, and the mind of contention, *AND BE WITHOUT RAGE OR HATRED* in their thoughts.

SUTRA:

> *WHEN I SEE A FOREST,*
> *I VOW THAT LIVING BEINGS*
> *WILL BECOME WORTHY OF RESPECT AND*
>   *VENERATION*
> *BY ALL GODS AND PEOPLE.*

若見叢林　　當願眾生
諸天及人　　所應敬禮

COMMENTARY:

WHEN I SEE A FOREST. A forest is also called a "grove of trees." In China, the places where left-home people dwell are called "forests." Why are they called "forests"? It's because each left-home person is like a great tree, and since they live together, they are called a "forest," or a "grove." Another implication is that trees can benefit living beings. Therefore, *WHEN* you *SEE A FOREST* or a grove, you should *VOW THAT LIVING BEINGS WILL BECOME WORTHY OF RESPECT AND VENERATION BY ALL GODS AND PEOPLE.*

SUTRA:

> *WHEN I SEE A HIGH MOUNTAIN,*
> *I VOW THAT LIVING BEINGS*
> *WILL HAVE SUCH TRANSCENDENT GOOD ROOTS*
> *THAT NONE CAN REACH THEIR SUMMIT.*

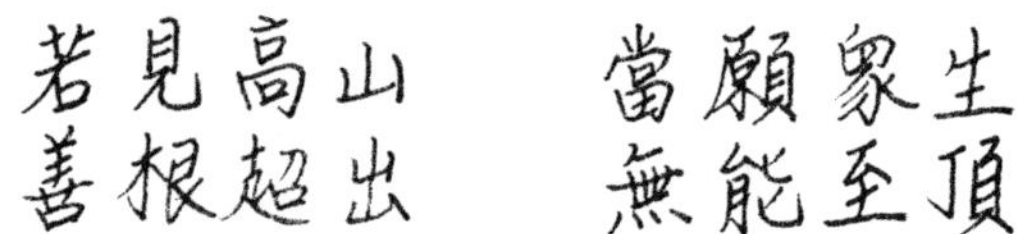

若見高山　　當願眾生
善根超出　　無能至頂

COMMENTARY:

WHEN you *SEE A HIGH MOUNTAIN.* At this time, you *VOW THAT LIVING BEINGS WILL HAVE SUCH TRANS-CENDENT GOOD ROOTS* that they are outstanding and excel all. As it is said,

> *One is outstanding from the average,*
> *And superior among one's peers.*

THAT NONE CAN REACH THEIR SUMMIT. Their good roots reach a peak which nobody can surpass. This means they become very lofty, very transcendental.

When I see a high mountain,
I vow that living beings
will have such transcendent good roots
that none can reach their summit.

SUTRA:

> WHEN I SEE A THORNY BUSH,
> I VOW THAT LIVING BEINGS
> WILL QUICKLY CUT OFF AND ERADICATE
> THE THORN OF THE THREE POISONS.

見棘刺樹　　當願眾生
疾得翦除　　三毒之刺

COMMENTARY:

WHEN you SEE THORNY BUSHES such as brambles or briers, you should VOW THAT LIVING BEINGS WILL QUICKLY CUT OFF AND ERADICATE THE THORN OF THE THREE POISONS, that is, greed, anger, and stupidity. They are like poisonous arrows. You should quickly cut them off, and not wait until it's too late. If you're too slow, it is to be feared that you won't have the strength to cut them off. Therefore, you should cut off the three poisons as soon as possible.

SUTRA:

> WHEN I SEE THE LUXURIANT FOLIAGE ON TREES,
> I VOW THAT LIVING BEINGS
> WILL BECOME LIBERATED THROUGH CONCENTRATION,
> AND ACT AS A SHELTER.

見樹葉茂　　當願眾生
以定解脫　　而為蔭映

COMMENTARY:

WHEN you SEE THE LUXURIANT, verdant and lush FOLIAGE ON TREES, you should make a vow. You VOW THAT LIVING BEINGS WILL BECOME LIBERATED THROUGH CONCENTRATION--use samadhi to become liberated.

The analogy of luxuriant foliage on a tree symbolizes that one cultivates concentration to attain liberation, so as to become A SHELTER for

When I see the luxuriant foliage on trees,
I vow that living beings
Will become liberated through concentration,
And act as a shelter.

living beings.

SUTRA:

> WHEN I SEE BLOSSOMING FLOWERS,
> I VOW THAT LIVING BEINGS
> WILL ATTAIN SPIRITUAL PENETRATIONS AND
>   SIMILAR DHARMAS,
> JUST AS A FLOWER BLOOMS.

若見華開　　當願眾生
神通等法　　如華開敷

COMMENTARY:

WHEN you SEE BLOSSOMING FLOWERS, you also should make a vow. You shouldn't engage in false thinking when you see such a situation. You VOW THAT LIVING BEINGS WILL ATTAIN SPIRITUAL PENETRATIONS AND SIMILAR DHARMAS, dharmas such as spiritual penetrations that are wonderful and inconceivable functions, JUST AS A FLOWER BLOOMS. The Dharmas should be very profuse and beautiful, just like flowers in full bloom.

SUTRA:

> WHEN I SEE A BLOSSOMING TREE,
> I VOW THAT LIVING BEINGS
> WILL ATTAIN ALL THE CHARACTERISTICS OF
>   A FLOWER,
> AND BE REPLETE WITH THE THIRTY-TWO MARKS.

若見樹華　　當願眾生
眾相如華　　具三十二

COMMENTARY:

WHEN you SEE A BLOSSOMING TREE, a tree which carries all kinds of flowers in bloom, you also should VOW THAT LIVING BEINGS WILL ATTAIN ALL THE CHARACTERISTICS OF A FLOWER, AND BE REPLETE WITH

THE THIRTY-TWO MARKS--complete with the thirty-two marks of the Buddhas and be splendid and magnificent like the blossoms on those trees.

SUTRA:

> *WHEN I SEE A FRUIT,*
> *I VOW THAT LIVING BEINGS*
> *WILL ATTAIN THE MOST SUPREME DHARMA,*
> *AND CERTIFY TO THE WAY OF BODHI.*

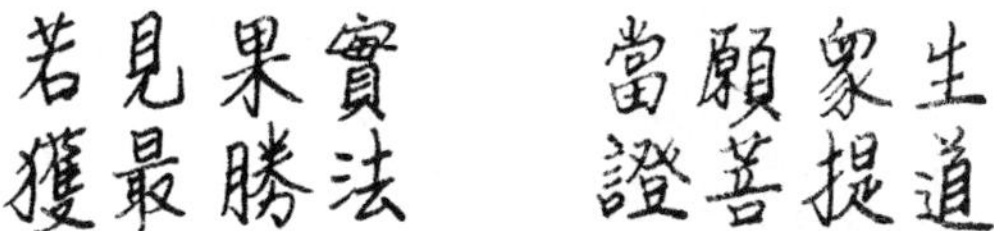

COMMENTARY:

WHEN you *SEE A FRUIT* tree , such as an apple tree, an orange tree, or a papaya tree, you also *VOW THAT LIVING BEINGS WILL ATTAIN THE MOST SUPREME,* inconceivable *DHARMA, AND CERTIFY TO THE WAY OF BODHI.* You wish living beings to certify to the enlightened Way of Nirvana.

SUTRA:

> *WHEN I SEE A GREAT RIVER,*
> *I VOW THAT LIVING BEINGS*
> *WILL ENTER THE FLOW OF DHARMA,*
> *AND STEP INTO THE SEA OF THE BUDDHA'S*
>   *WISDOM.*

COMMENTARY:

WHEN you *SEE A GREAT RIVER,* like the Ganges River or any other large river, you *VOW THAT LIVING BEINGS WILL* desire to *ENTER THE FLOW OF DHARMA,* the flow of the Dharma-nature of sages, *AND STEP INTO THE SEA OF THE BUDDHA'S WISDOM.* If you desire to enter the current of Dharma, you first have to enter the sea of Buddha's wisdom.

When I see a great river,
I vow that living beings.
Will enter the flow of Dharma,
And step into the sea of the Buddha's wisdom.

SUTRA:

WHEN I SEE A SWAMP,
I VOW THAT LIVING BEINGS
WILL QUICKLY ENLIGHTEN TO ALL BUDDHA'S
SINGLE FLAVOR OF DHARMA.

若見波澤　　當願衆生
疾悟諸佛　　一味之法

COMMENTARY:

WHEN I SEE A SWAMP, if you see a swamp. This
means a marsh where still water gathers, that water
does not move. At this time, you also should VOW
THAT LIVING BEINGS WILL QUICKLY ENLIGHTEN TO ALL
BUDDHA'S SINGLE FLAVOR OF DHARMA, that is, the
principle of real mark.

SUTRA:

WHEN I SEE A POND OR A LAKE,
I VOW THAT LIVING BEINGS
WILL PERFECT THEIR SPEECH KARMA,
AND BECOME SKILLFUL AT SPEAKING.

若見池沼　　當願衆生
語業滿足　　巧能演說

COMMENTARY:

WHEN I SEE A POND OR A LAKE. A pond is just
a lake. In the <u>Book of Poetry</u>, it is said,

When he started to build the magical tower,
He devoted painstaking toil to it,
And the people all worked on it,
So that in less than a day it was completed.
When he began to build the tower he said to them,
    "Do not go out of your way,"
But the people came as if they were his children.

The king was in his menagerie.
The deer lay about in ease,
The doe were sleek and fat,
The white birds were bright and shining.
The king was in his pond,
How the fish jumped about!

King Wen used the strength of the people to build
  his tower and his pond.
The people delighted in doing it,
Calling it "the magical tower," and "the magical
  pond," and were happy that there were deer, fishes
  and turtles it.
The ancients shared their pleasures with the people;
Therefore they themselves could enjoy them too.

When Emperor Wen of the Chou dynasty built his
imperial tombs, he made a platform which was called
the imperial glade, and he made a marsh which was
called the imperial pond. The imperial glade is
also a pond. Therefore, when you see a pond, you
should also make a vow. You *VOW THAT LIVING BEINGS
WILL PERFECT THEIR SPEECH* and fulfill their speech
karma, that they do not create evil karma, but
instead perfect their good karma, *AND BECOME SKILL-
FUL AT SPEAKING.* You wish living beings to use
clever expedient Dharma doors to proclaim the real
mark of all Dharmas.

SUTRA:

> *WHEN I SEE A WELL,*
> *I VOW THAT LIVING BEINGS*
> *WILL BE COMPLETE WITH ELOQUENCE*
> *TO PROCLAIM ALL DHARMAS.*

若見汲井　　當願眾生
具足辯才　　演一切法

COMMENTARY:

WHEN I SEE A WELL. This is a place from
which you can draw water. Nowadays we use chain
pumps. When we turn on the generator, the water
will come up by itself. But in ancient times they

had to use a rope and pulley to draw out water from wells.

When you see such a well, you also should make a vow. You *VOW THAT LIVING BEINGS WILL BE COMPLETE WITH great ELOQUENCE.* If you recite Kuan Yin Bodhisattva's name, you will attain great wisdom, great eloquence, great fearlessness, and great peace. There are four kinds of eloquences:

1. Unobstructed eloquence in meaning.
2. Unobstructed eloquence in Dharma.
3. Unobstructed eloquence in phrasing.
4. Unobstructed eloquence of delight in speech.

You will be replete with these four unobstructed eloquences to skillfully proclaim all wonderful Dharma, just like the Venerable Purnamaitreyaniputra who was foremost in speaking Dharma among the Buddha's disciples.

SUTRA:

WHEN I SEE A BUBBLING SPRING,
I VOW THAT LIVING BEINGS
WILL INCREASE AND GROW IN EXPEDIENT
*   DEVICES,*
AND THAT THEIR GOOD ROOTS BECOME
*   INEXHAUSTIBLE.*

COMMENTARY:

WHEN I SEE A BUBBLING SPRING. A bubbling spring refers to water which wells up from the ground. When you see such a state, you also should make a vow.

The purpose of the *Pure Conduct Chapter* is to aid a cultivator to remain unmoved when coming face to face with different states. Instead, he should turn the state. He can change a bad state into a good state. But how can he turn it over? He has to make vows. If you see a bubbling spring, you should *VOW THAT* all *LIVING BEINGS*, not just one person, but all beings, *WILL INCREASE AND GROW IN EXPEDIENT DEVICES*. You vow that their wisdom will increase *AND THAT THEIR GOOD ROOTS BECOME IN-EXHAUSTIBLE*. Their good roots will never be exhausted and their wisdom will emerge flowingly without cease.

If living beings haven't planted good roots, you should cause them to plant good roots. If they've already planted good roots, you should cause them to increase. If their good roots have already increased, you should cause them to become liberated. In this way, their good roots will become inexhaustible and limitless.

SUTRA:

> *WHEN I SEE A BRIDGE-CROSSING,*
> *I VOW THAT LIVING BEINGS*
> *WILL EXPANSIVELY CROSS OVER ALL,*
> *AND ACT AS A BRIDGE.*

若見橋道　　當願眾生
廣度一切　　猶如橋梁

COMMENTARY:

WHEN I SEE A BRIDGE-CROSSING, I also should make a vow. A bridge is a conduit that can cross you over from this shore of birth and death to the other shore of Nirvana. If you want to cross over the river of birth and death, you have to rely on Prajna bridge. The Prajna bridge can help you end birth and death.

Therefore, when you see a bridge-crossing, you *VOW THAT LIVING BEINGS WILL EXPANSIVELY CROSS OVER ALL* other living beings *AND ACT AS A BRIDGE*. They should enable people to go from this shore to the other shore, and also to come from the other shore to this shore.

SUTRA:

WHEN I SEE FLOWING WATER,
I VOW THAT LIVING BEINGS
WILL ATTAIN THE ASPIRATION TOWARDS
   WHOLESOME INTENT,
AND WASH OFF THE FILTH OF DELUSION.

若見流水　　當願眾生
得善意欲　　洗除惑垢

COMMENTARY:

WHEN I SEE FLOWING WATER, I VOW THAT LIVING
BEINGS WILL ATTAIN THE ASPIRATION TOWARDS WHOLESOME
INTENT. This "Aspiration" refers to wholesome vows
that one makes.
AND WASH OFF THE FILTH OF DELUSION. From
limitless kalpas until now, we have all given rise
to delusion, created karma, and undergone retribution. This is what is meant by the delusion of
filth; it is just unclean and defiled dharma.

SUTRA:

WHEN I SEE A PERSON CULTIVATE A GARDEN,
I VOW THAT LIVING BEINGS
WILL HOE OUT THE WEEDS OF LOVE
FROM THE GARDEN OF THE FIVE DESIRES.

見修園圃　　當願眾生
五欲圃中　　耘除愛草

COMMENTARY:

WHEN I SEE A PERSON CULTIVATE A GARDEN. This
may be a flower garden or a vegetable garden. Cultivating the Way is like planting flowers or vegetables. Therefore, when you see people working in
the garden and planting vegetables, or trimming
flowers, you also should make a VOW THAT LIVING
BEINGS WILL HOE OUT THE WEEDS OF LOVE FROM THE

When I see flowing water,
I vow that living beings
Will attain the aspiration towards wholesome
    intent,
And wash off the filth of delusion.

GARDEN OF THE FIVE DESIRES. The five desires are wealth, sex, name, food, and sleep. This weed of love is an obstruction in our garden of Bodhi. It can cause us to fall, so we have to get rid of it.

SUTRA:

> *WHEN I SEE AN UNTROUBLED FOREST,*
> *I VOW THAT LIVING BEINGS*
> *WILL FOREVER SEPARATE FROM GREED AND LOVE,*
> *AND NOT PRODUCE GRIEF AND TERROR.*

見無憂林　　當願眾生
永離貪愛　　不生憂怖

COMMENTARY:

WHEN I SEE AN UNTROUBLED FOREST. That is, when you see a place that is full of happiness, without any melancholy or sadness. This also means a person of clean, bright resolve who has no yearning for profit. He is patient, knows content- ment and is without worries. At this time, you also should *VOW THAT LIVING BEINGS WILL FOREVER SEPARATE FROM GREED AND LOVE.* Once you have greedy thoughts, love and desire, your Bodhi mind will not flourish.

The Buddha is a person whose "karma is exhausted and whose emotions are empty." But living beings are those who have heavy karma and confused emotions. If we can exhaust our karma and empty our emotions, then we will become Buddhas, too. Why are we still not empty? It's because we have greed and love.

SUTRA:

> WHEN I SEE A GARDEN,
> I VOW THAT LIVING BEINGS
> WILL DILIGENTLY CULTIVATE ALL CONDUCTS,
> AND TEND TOWARD THE BUDDHA'S BODHI.

若見園苑　　當願眾生
勤修諸行　　趣佛菩提

COMMENTARY:

WHEN I SEE A GARDEN or an orchard. In the T'ang Dynasty, the empress Wu Tse T'ien once wrote a poem commanding the flower spirits to make all the flowers bloom the next morning. The poem went like this,

> Tomorrow morning I will go to the garden to play.
> The fruit trees should spring buds on their branches,
> And flowers should all bloom right this very
>   night.
> Don't wait until the morning breezes come along!

At that time, it was in the heart of winter. All the flowers hadn't started to blossom yet. But she wanted to see if the flowers and trees would listen to her order. She wanted to see if her order was effective or not. Therefore she told them, "Although it is winter, you should behave as if in spring."

After she wrote this poem, the next morning she went to the garden to take a look. And all the flowers did blossom! Then she knew she truly possessed the imperial mandate. Even the trees had to listen to her decree.

Empress Wu Tse T'ien was a great Dharma protector of Buddhism. A long time ago the Buddha gave her a prediction that she would become a woman emperor in China, and that she would be a great Dharma protector, although her personality and behavior were not so good. She was a provisional manifestion, an expedient manifestion to help people to understand some inconceivable states.

Since even the flowers, grass, and trees had to
obey her orders, all the people also gladly came
under her reign.
    WHEN you *SEE A GARDEN*, you should *VOW THAT
LIVING BEINGS WILL DILIGENTLY CULTIVATE ALL CONDUCTS*.
They shouldn't be lazy. They should cultivate all
the doors of conduct, and go *TOWARD BUDDHA'S BODHI*--
quickly arrive at the enlightened fruition of
Buddhahood.

SUTRA:

*WHEN I SEE A PERSON ADORNED WITH ORNAMENTS,
I VOW THAT LIVING BEINGS
WILL TAKE THE THIRTY-TWO MARKS
AS THEIR WONDERFUL ADORNMENTS.*

見嚴飾人　　當願眾生
三十二相　　以為嚴好

COMMENTARY:

    WHEN I SEE A PERSON ADORNED WITH ORNAMENTS,
who likes to decorate his appearance so as to look
very upright, adorned, and elegant. But this
doesn't mean he looks seductive. Rather, this
means that the appearance of his virtuous conduct
is very refined and calm. The first poem in the
Book of Poetry says,

> *Kuan Kuan* coo the ospreys,
> On the island by the river.
> The modern and charming young lady,
> A fine mate she'll be for our prince.

It is also said,

> The mind of a cultivator
> is exemplified by the things in which he vests
>   his interest--
> That is, in the odes that he recites.
> The Lord of Chou had profound virtue.
> He also attained the speech of the sages.
> His people searched for a worthy spouse for him.

> *When those at court saw the arrival of Lady Sze,*
> *And upon watching her virtue of elegance, refinement,*
> *   and quietness.*
> *They composed this ode in praise of her.*

Ancient people also adorned themselves. Their attitude was very elegant and graceful. They did not put on weird styles. Therefore, when you see a person ornamented with such adornments, you *VOW THAT LIVING BEINGS WILL* attain *THE THIRTY-TWO MARKS* and eighty subtle characteristics *AS THEIR WONDERFUL ADORNMENTS.*

SUTRA:

> *WHEN I SEE A PERSON WHO IS DEVOID OF ANY*
> *   ADORNING ORNAMENTS,*
> *I VOW THAT LIVING BEINGS*
> *WILL RENOUNCE ALL FINE ORNAMENTS,*
> *AND BE COMPLETE WITH DHUTA PRACTICES.*

見無嚴飾　　當願眾生
捨諸飾好　　具頭陀行

COMMENTARY:

WHEN you *SEE A PERSON WHO IS DEVOID OF ANY ADORNING ORNAMENTS.* This refers to those who appear in their original face, to the point they don't brush their hair, nor seek to improve their appearances. They are careless and sloppy. But they don't look like American hippies. American hippies are really a mess! They're out of the range of "adorned ornaments" spoken of here.

When you see such a person who is devoid of any adorning ornaments, you also should *VOW THAT LIVING BEINGS WILL RENOUNCE ALL FINE,* wonderful *ORNAMENTS--* give up all adorned objects, *AND BE COMPLETE WITH DHUTA PRACTICES.* Dhuta is Sanskrit, and translates as "to strike up one's energy." One always strikes up one's spirit. Originally one wants to fall asleep, but one strikes up one's spirit and energy and doesn't allow oneself to fall sleep. Originally one wants to eat, but one strikes up one's spirit not to eat. Originally one wishes to wear more clothes to keep warm, but one frequently exercises, such as running or walking, and in this way maintains one's vitality and energy, so one is not afraid of the heat, cold, or hunger. There's no   time when one is exhausted. This is called "striking up one's spirits." It also means "always being vigorous." There isn't a time when one is not cultivating. There are twelve kinds of Dhuta Practice:

1. Wearing rag-robes. One wears robes taken out of   the dust heap.
2. Wearing only three robes: The five piece robe, seven piece robe, and the great robe.
3. Always begging for food. One doesn't prepare one's own food; one goes out to beg.
4. Begging in succession. One begs at each house in succession, regardless of whether the inhabitants are rich or poor.
5. Eating only once in the middle of the day. One doesn't eat after lunch.
6. Reducing the measure of what one eats. One only eats the amount that one needs.
7. Not drinking juices after noon. After lunch, one doesn't drink milk, honey or juice.
8. Dwelling in an aranya. One gets away from noisy places and lives in a quiet place.
9. Dwelling at the foot of a tree. One stays under a tree, but not over three nights.
10. Dwelling under the open sky. One lives in a place in the open, without any shelter over one's head.
11. Dwelling in a graveyard. Living here, one is always on the alert. Dwelling in a graveyard is a good cure for laziness.
12. Ribs not touching the mat. This means always sitting and never lying down, cultivating vigorously and not fearing suffering.

SUTRA:

> *WHEN I SEE A PERSON ATTACHED TO HAPPINESS,*
> *I VOW THAT LIVING BEINGS*
> *WILL USE THE DHARMA AS SELF-ENJOYMENT,*
> *DELIGHT IN IT AND NEVER RENOUNCE IT.*

見樂著人　　當願眾生
以法自娛　　歡愛不捨

COMMENTARY:

WHEN I SEE A PERSON ATTACHED TO HAPPINESS.
This refers to those who are attached to pleasures
which are not ultimate. This type of happiness is
ephemeral and doesn't last forever. At the present,
giant rock concerts are the fad all over America.
Men and women don't wear clothes, and they congre-
gate to dance and make music. Whenever they hold
such concerts, it's not known how many people
attend--maybe thirty or fifty thousand people get
together. People crowd against people, to the
point they crush each other to death, or many
children get crushed to death. They have this
crazy style! The cars also bump against one another.
All those people are squeezing and spinning around
without stop. They shake and rock until they can't
move--it's that fierce and dangerous!
    But not many people attend places where there
are Sutra and Dharma lectures. There are only
thirty, fifty, one hundred, or two hundred people
at most. The most would be three hundred to one
thousand in attendance. But as to rock concerts--
they can easily draw thirty, fifty, three hundred,
up to five hundred thousand ....to the point that
you can't even figure out how many people are
there. One of my disciples said, "The most popular
fad among young American men and women is to co-
habitate. They do their own thing. They don't
have any constraints or restrictions. They really
have no impediments. They act as if they don't
have the mark of people and mark of self. This
type of upside-down and inconceivable situation
is very prevelant in America."

People who are "attached to happiness" refers to upside-down people such as those who think rock and roll concerts are the happiest events in the world. They're not afraid of being crushed to death. They still want to go and see it, and to be upside-down; they don't even care about their life. When faced with such situations, you also should *VOW THAT LIVING BEINGS WILL USE THE DHARMA AS SELF-ENJOYMENT.* But they shouldn't produce passion for the Dharma. Once you want to grasp on to Dharma, you bring forth an attachment to it. Even if you have emptied the attachment to self, you still haven't emptied the attachment to Dharma. You still wouldn't be able to conduct yourself with ease.

DELIGHT IN IT AND NEVER RENOUNCE IT. So you should take the Dharma as your happiness, and not ever give it up. But at the same time don't become attached to the Dharma. If you take the Dharma as the greatest bliss, this will help you break through the attachment to worldly and impermanent happiness.

SUTRA:

> *WHEN I SEE A PERSON WHO IS WITHOUT THE*
> *   ATTACHMENT TO HAPPINESS,*
> *I VOW THAT LIVING BEINGS' MINDS*
> *WILL NOT TAKE PLEASURE*
> *IN CONDITIONED EVENTS.*

見無樂著　　當願眾生
有爲事中　　心無所樂

COMMENTARY:

WHEN I SEE A PERSON WHO IS WITHOUT THE ATTACH-MENT TO HAPPINESS, one who is not upside-down. At this time, you also should *VOW THAT LIVING BEINGS' MIND WILL NOT TAKE PLEASURE IN CONDITIONED EVENTS.* They will have no greedy attachments in their minds when they encounter conditioned affairs. Conditioned affairs refer to things that have shape and marks. Living beings should not be trapped by form and marks. They should be without the attachments of form and mark.

SUTRA:

> WHEN I SEE A HAPPY PERSON,
> I VOW THAT LIVING BEINGS
> WILL ALWAYS ATTAIN PEACE AND BLISS,
> AND DELIGHT IN MAKING OFFERINGS TO THE
>   BUDDHAS.

見歡樂人　　當願眾生
常得安樂　　樂供養佛

COMMENTARY:

WHEN I SEE A HAPPY PERSON, a person who is very joyous and happy. When you encounter such a state, you also should make a *VOW THAT LIVING BEINGS WILL ALWAYS ATTAIN PEACE AND BLISS.* This means in whatever they do, they will attain tranquility and joy. How do they attain this state? First of all, they have to be content and patient. As it is said,

> One who is content will be peaceful and blissful,
> One who can be patient will be naturally at ease.

AND DELIGHT IN MAKING OFFERINGS TO THE BUDDHAS. They delightedly make offerings to the Buddhas and Bodhisattvas.

SUTRA:

> WHEN I SEE A PERSON UNDERGOING SUFFERING
>   AND AFFLICTIONS,
> I VOW THAT LIVING BEINGS
> WILL ATTAIN BASIC WISDOM
> TO EXTINGUISH AND ERADICATE ALL SUFFERINGS.

見苦惱人　　當願眾生
獲根本智　　滅除眾苦

COMMENTARY:

WHEN I SEE A PERSON UNDERGOING SUFFERING AND AFFLICTIONS--when you see a person undergo suffering and afflictions, when you encounter such a state, you should *VOW THAT LIVING BEINGS WILL ATTAIN BASIC WISDOM TO EXTINGUISH AND ERADICATE ALL SUFFERINGS.*
There are three kinds of sufferings, known as the Three Sufferings, The Eight Sufferings, and The Limitless Sufferings.

A. Three Sufferings:

1. the suffering within suffering.
2. the suffering of decay.
3. the suffering of activities.

B. Eight Sufferings:

1. the suffering of birth.
2. the suffering of age.
3. the suffering of sickness.
4. the suffering of death.
5. the suffering of being apart from the one you love.
6. the suffering of being together with the one you hate.
7. the suffering of not being able to attain what one wishes.
8. the suffering of the blazing fire of the five Skandhas.

C. Limitless Sufferings:

This world is full of a myriad of sufferings and evils.

Everyone has his own suffering and afflictions. When you encounter such a state, you should vow that living beings will attain basic wisdom, in order to extinguish and eradicate all sufferings.
What is basic wisdom? This is the fundamental wisdom that is originally enlightened. If you attain such wisdom, you will extinguish and eradicate all sufferings and afflictions. Why do

people have suffering and afflictions? Why do they
have ignorance? It's because they don't have
wisdom. Being stupid, they are unclear about affairs, and don't recognize what's before them.
Therefore they produce afflictions. A person who
has wisdom can see through it and put it down. He
attains self-mastery. Being sovereign is being
happy. How does one get rid of suffering and afflictions? One can do so by diligently cultivating
precepts, samadhi, and wisdom, and by eradicating
greed, hatred, and stupidity. There's no better
method than this.

SUTRA:

> WHEN I SEE A HEALTHY PERSON,
> I VOW THAT LIVING BEINGS
> WILL ENTER TRUE AND ACTUAL WISDOM,
> AND FOREVER BE WITHOUT SICKNESS
>   AND AFFLICTION.

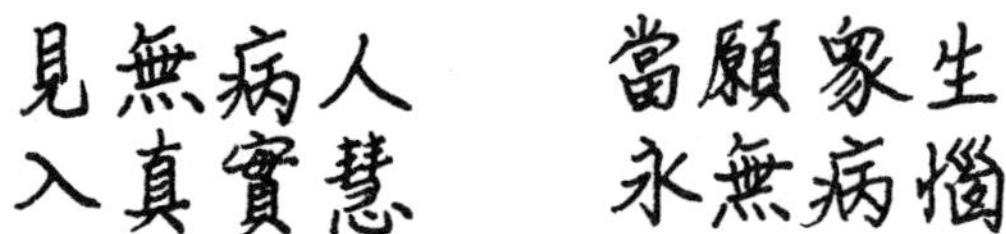

見無病人　　當願眾生
入真實慧　　永無病惱

COMMENTARY:

When you see a person who doesn't have any
sickness, you also should make a vow. You *VOW
THAT LIVING BEINGS WILL ENTER TRUE AND ACTUAL
WISDOM*, attain true wisdom, *AND FOREVER BE WITHOUT
SICKNESS AND AFFLICTION*. Why does one get sick?
Because one is not happy. As it is said,

> *From ancient times until now, immortals and spirits
>   had no other method,*
> *But to expansively rejoice in their minds and not
>   bring forth sorrow.*

This is the secret method for health in one's body
and mind.

SUTRA:

> WHEN I SEE A SICK PERSON,
> I VOW THAT LIVING BEINGS

*WILL REALIZE THEIR BODIES ARE EMPTY
    AND EXTINCT,
AND DEPART FROM THE DHARMA OF CONTENTION.*

見疾病人　　　當願眾生
知身空寂　　　離乖諍法

COMMENTARY:

A person who cultivates the Bodhisattva conduct will go to visit sick persons. *WHEN you SEE
A SICK PERSON*, you should make a vow. You *VOW
THAT LIVING BEINGS WILL REALIZE THEIR BODIES ARE
EMPTY AND EXTINCT*, recognize that the body is a
false combination of the four elements--earth,
water, fire, and wind. Basically it is empty and
extinct, therefore one should not attach to one's
physical body.

When the four elements disperse, they will
transform into nothing and return to the source.
Right now you are relying on this false body to
cultivate true suchness; you are cultivating the
Dharma body of true-suchness. Since you know the
body is empty and extinct, you should separate
FROM THE DHARMA OF CONTENTION, that is, you don't
argue with people and you don't fight with the
world. You reach the state of samadhi of no contention and arguing.

SUTRA:

*WHEN I SEE AN UPRIGHT AND PROPER PERSON,
I VOW THAT LIVING BEINGS
WILL ALWAYS PRODUCE PURE FAITH
TOWARD THE BUDDHAS AND BODHISATTVAS.*

見端正人　　　當願眾生
於佛菩薩　　　常生淨信

COMMENTARY:

WHEN I SEE AN UPRIGHT AND PROPER PERSON, this means a person who has full and perfect features. What is meant by an upright and proper person? And what is meant by perfect features? This means the five facial features are upright and proper. The nose is not found where the mouth is located. The eyes will not be grown in a place where the nose is supposed to be. The eyes will not be found on top of the head. That way one only sees people on top, but they cannot see people at the bottom. Having upright and proper features means that one's eyes, nose, ears, and head are all located in their own positions.

At this time, you should *VOW THAT LIVING BEINGS WILL ALWAYS PRODUCE PURE FAITH* before *THE BUDDHAS AND BODHISATTVAS.* Don't produce the thought of doubt and slander. The Buddhas all have thirty-two marks and eighty subtle characteristics. An upright and proper person may have in the past bowed to the Buddhas, or recited the Buddha's name, or made offerings of flowers to the Buddhas. In the <u>Sutra of Cause and Effect of the Three Periods of Time</u>, it is said,

> *If in this life, one's appearance is proper and*
> > *fine,*
> *This is because one made offerings of flowers*
> > *and lamps before the Buddhas in previous lives.*

In the <u>Avatamsaka Sutra</u> it is said,

> *The Faith is the source of the Way, the mother*
> > *of merit and virtue,*
> *It constantly nourishes all wholesome dharmas.*

It is also said,

> *The Buddhadharma is like a great sea,*
> *Only with faith can one enter.*

If you don't have faith, then you can't deeply enter the Sutra Treasury and have wisdom like a great sea. Therefore you have to always bring forth pure faith. Don't produce faith for one day, and then retreat the next day. It's not that you only believe some time, and retreat other time.

You have to produce deep faith constantly, and not retreat at all.

SUTRA:

> *WHEN I SEE AN UGLY PERSON,*
> *I VOW THAT LIVING BEINGS*
> *WILL NOT PRODUCE DELIGHT AND ATTACHMENT*
> *TOWARDS UNWHOLESOME AFFAIRS.*

見醜陋人　　當願眾生
於不善事　　不生樂著

COMMENTARY:

Because of the heavy karma, some people have very ugly appearances. If one's karma is heavy, one's appearance will not be upright. One will be like asuras whose name means "not upright." Why are they not upright? It's because they like to fight. Sometimes they harm people by chopping off their noses. Therefore when they become asuras they themselves are without noses. This is the retribution they receive.

Those who are born ugly all had the karma of killing. People who kill a lot of living beings will receive the retribution of being ugly. *WHEN* you *SEE* such *AN UGLY PERSON,* you should make a vow. You *VOW THAT LIVING BEINGS WILL NOT PRODUCE DELIGHT AND ATTACHMENTS,* or pleasures *TOWARDS UNWHOLESOME AFFAIRS.* Don't get attached to bad things. Don't be greedily attached to deviant knowledge and deviant view.

SUTRA:

> *WHEN I SEE A PERSON WHO REPAYS KINDNESS,*
> *I VOW THAT LIVING BEINGS*
> *WILL BE ABLE TO UNDERSTAND THE VIRTUE OF*
> *   THE KINDNESS*
> *OF THE BUDDHAS AND BODHISATTVAS.*

見報恩人　　當願眾生
於佛菩薩　　能知恩德

COMMENTARY:

WHEN I SEE A PERSON WHO REPAYS KINDNESS.
When you see a person who understands gratitude
and knows how to return the virtue of his parents'
kindness by being filial to his parents, or by
respecting his teachers and elders; at this time,
you should make a vow. In China, there's a saying,

> *Upon receiving kindness of a drop of water,*
> *One seeks to repay it with a bubbling spring.*

Therefore, you should understand the virtue of
paying back kindness. Don't be like the person who
realizes the debt of kindness, but doesn't return
it. At this time, you should *VOW THAT LIVING
BEINGS WILL BE ABLE TO UNDERSTAND THE VIRTUE OF
THE KINDNESS OF THE BUDDHAS AND BODHISATTVAS.* They
should return the kindness of the Buddhas and Bodhisattvas, and also repay the kindness of their parents, teachers, elders, and rulers. What is the
parents, teachers, elders, and rulers. What is the
virtue of the kindness of the Buddhas and Bodhisattvas toward us? You should know that the
Buddhas, in their past lives, renounced their heads,
eyes, brains, and marrow in order to teach and
transform living beings, so as to cause them to
bring forth the Bodhi mind and quickly accomplish
the Buddha path. Therefore we living beings should
return the kindness of the Buddhas and Budhisattvas.
SUTRA:

> *WHEN I SEE A PERSON WHO TURNS HIS BACK ON*
> *   KINDNESS,*
> *I VOW THAT LIVING BEINGS*
> *WILL NOT REDOUBLE THEIR REVENGE*
> *ON EVIL PEOPLE.*

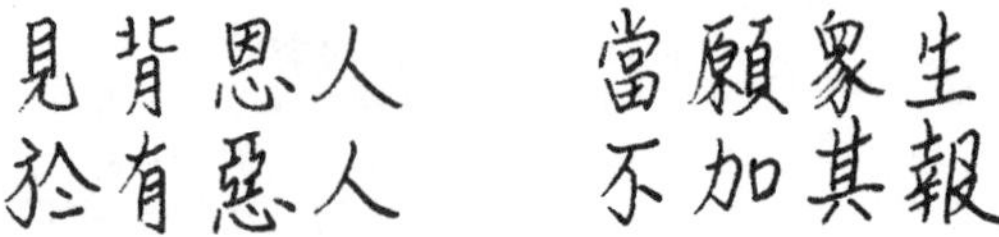

見背恩人　　當願眾生
於有惡人　　不加其報

COMMENTARY:

WHEN I SEE A PERSON WHO TURNS HIS BACK ON

KINDNESS. This is someone who realizes kindness but doesn't return it. He doesn't return the kindness of his parents, teachers, and elders, neither does he return the kindness of the Buddhas and Bodhisattvas. This person isn't filial to his parents, nor does he respect his teachers and elders. People who slander the Buddha, the Dharma, and the Sangha are called those who turn their backs on kindness.

At this time, you also should *VOW THAT LIVING BEINGS WILL NOT REDOUBLE THEIR REVENGE ON EVIL PEOPLE.* They shouldn't hate vile people, and they shouldn't produce a mind of revenge. In general, you should always use the nature of virtue to influence such people. Don't bring forth a mind of vengeance!

SUTRA:

> *WHEN I SEE A SHRAMANA,*
> *I VOW THAT LIVING BEINGS*
> *WILL BECOME SUBDUED, GENTLE, STILL AND*
> *   QUIET,*
> *AND ULTIMATELY FOREMOST.*

COMMENTARY:

WHEN I SEE A SHRAMANA. Shramanas refer to left-home people. It's Sanskrit, and translates as "diligently putting to rest."   It also means to "diligently cultivate precepts, samadhi, and wisdom, and put to rest greed, hatred, and stupidity."

If you see a left-home person, you should *VOW THAT LIVING BEINGS WILL BECOME SUBDUED, GENTLE, STILL AND QUIET,* that is, without afflictions. Your mind is still and quiet. What do you subdue? You should subdue your own stubborn and brittle mind, that which is hard to subdue, and cause your rough thoughts to become gentle and soft.

What is stillness? This means being without

affliction or temper. If you have affliction and the fire of ignorance inside, then you will not be still and quiet.
   AND ULTIMATELY FOREMOST. If you can subdue your mind to become gentle, still and quiet, then you will be number one in the future. You will become a Buddha. Accomplishing Buddhahood is the foremost thing to do.

SUTRA:

> *WHEN I SEE A BRAHMAN,*
> *I VOW THAT LIVING BEINGS*
> *WILL FOREVER UPHOLD BRAHMA CONDUCT,*
> *AND DEPART FROM ALL EVIL.*

見婆羅門　　當願眾生
永持梵行　　離一切惡

COMMENTARY:

   WHEN I SEE A BRAHMAN. In India, there is a kind of Brahman religion in which the cultivators practice pure conduct. They also cultivate very hard. They eat vegetarian food, and practice various kinds of ascetic practices. But some people of the Brahman religion still have a mind of hatred. When they encounter unpleasant states, they get angry.
   When you see a Brahman, you also should *VOW THAT LIVING BEINGS WILL FOREVER UPHOLD BRAHMA CONDUCT,* that is, always cultivate the door of pure conduct. *AND DEPART FROM ALL EVIL,* and get away from the mind of hatred.

SUTRA:

> *WHEN I SEE A PERSON WHO ENGAGES IN ASCETIC*
>   *PRACTICES,*
> *I VOW THAT LIVING BEINGS*
> *WILL RELY ON ASCETIC PRACTICES,*
> *AND ARRIVE AT THE ULTIMATE PLACE.*

見苦行人　　當願眾生
依於苦行　　至究竟處

COMMENTARY:

WHEN I SEE A PERSON WHO ENGAGES IN ASCETIC PRACTICES. The ascetic practices referred to are not the unbeneficial ascetic practices. In India, there are people who cultivate the precepts of cows and the precepts of dogs. They emulate cows and dogs and undergo suffering to the extreme. Such practices are called "unbeneficial ascetic conduct."

Once they saw a cow ascend to heaven, so they

started to follow the style of cows; they started
to eat grass. At another time they saw a dog
ascend to heaven, and so they started to emulate
the behavior of dogs. Those people had no true
wisdom. Although they may have gained some spiritual powers through their cultivation, those powers
were not ultimate. They didn't realize that the
cows or dogs ascended to heaven because in former
lives, they planted the causes of being reborn in
the heavens. After they had undergone retribution
for other offenses, their former good causes
ripened, and so they were reborn in the heavens.
But it wasn't because they were cows or dogs that
they got reborn in the heavens.
     On the other hand, "beneficial ascetic conduct"
refers to Dhuta practices, the conduct of "striking
up one's spirits." This means to endure what
others cannot endure, yield what others cannot
yield, eat what others cannot eat, and undergo
what others cannot undergo. You take suffering
as your own happiness. As it is said,

> *To undergo suffering is to end your suffering,*
> *To enjoy blessing is to exhaust your blessings.*

I always bring up these two verses, and one of my
disciples got enlightened. He said,

> *To eat rice is to finish the rice.*
> *To sleep is to put an end to sleep.*

Because he likes to eat, he says, "to eat rice is
to finish the rice." This means that for everyday he finishes with his eating, he has completed
that job.
     When you practice ascetic conduct, you should
not force it. You should do it naturally. You
*VOW THAT LIVING BEINGS WILL RELY ON ASCETIC PRA-
CTICES, AND ARRIVE AT THE ULTIMATE PLACE*, that is,
Buddhahood.

SUTRA:

> *WHEN I SEE A PERSON WITH INTEGRITY,*
> *I VOW THAT LIVING BEINGS*
> *WILL MAINTAIN THEIR RESOLVE WITH*
> *   DETERMINATION,*
> *AND NOT RENOUNCE THE BUDDHA WAY.*

見操行人　　當願眾生
堅持志行　　不捨佛道

COMMENTARY:

WHEN I SEE A PERSON WITH INTEGRITY. This means a person who has personality, who is not casual in doing things. He has integrity and can uphold his pure and lofty attitude. It means he will not do what he's not supposed to do. He will not be sloppy or transgress the rules. His conduct is pure and elegant; he will not conform to what's defiled or flow with what's mundane. He will not act as a thief among virtuous people.

In general, even an ordinary person who does not cultivate should have integrity. He should have a pure and lofty personality. How much more a cultivator! He should not drift along in a defiled and lowly current. He should not enter a defiled room, and become a thief among the virtuous. At this time, you *VOW THAT LIVING BEINGS WILL MAINTAIN THEIR RESOLVE WITH DETERMINATION.* You should have a resolve that soars to the heavens, the kind of resolve that can turn over heaven and move the earth. You should behave in a manner whereby you can influence people's customs and change their habits, so that upon hearing about you, they'll be moved to change for the better. You should also vow that living beings will *NOT RENOUNCE THE BUDDHA WAY.* You wish that living beings cultivate in accord with the Buddha's teaching method and guidance.

SUTRA:

WHEN I SEE A PERSON DRESSED IN ARMOR,
I VOW THAT LIVING BEINGS
WILL ALWAYS BE EQUIPPED WITH THE ARMOR
*   OF GOODNESS,*
AND WILL TEND TOWARD THE DHARMA THAT
*   REQUIRES NO TEACHER.*

見著甲冑　　當願眾生
常服善鎧　　趣無師法

COMMENTARY:

WHEN I SEE A PERSON DRESSED IN ARMOR. Armor
is a kind of military gear worn by soldiers in
ancient times. As it is said,

> They wore helmets on the heads,
> And armor on their bodies.

Armor can protect one against weapons. Once you
wear armor, you will not get harmed even if people
try to stab you with sharp knives. Cultivators of
the Way also should wear a kind of armor. What is
that? The armor of good deeds. Therefore when
you see a person equipped with armor, you should
make a vow. You VOW THAT LIVING BEINGS WILL ALWAYS
BE EQUIPPED WITH THE ARMOR OF GOODNESS, the armor
of wholesomeness. We should don the armor of
vigor, and bravely advance.
AND WILL TEND TOWARD THE DHARMA THAT REQUIRES
NO TEACHER. You tend toward dharmas that do not
require the instructions of a teacher; you can
understand by yourself. That means you are not
afraid of suffering, difficulty, and demonic
obstacles. You don't need to rely on a certain
kind of dharma. You should not produce a mind of
dependence.

SUTRA:

> WHEN I SEE A PERSON WHO IS NOT EQUIPPED
>   WITH ARMOR OR WEAPONRY,
> I VOW THAT LIVING BEINGS
> WILL FOREVER DEPART FROM ALL
> UNWHOLESOME KARMA.

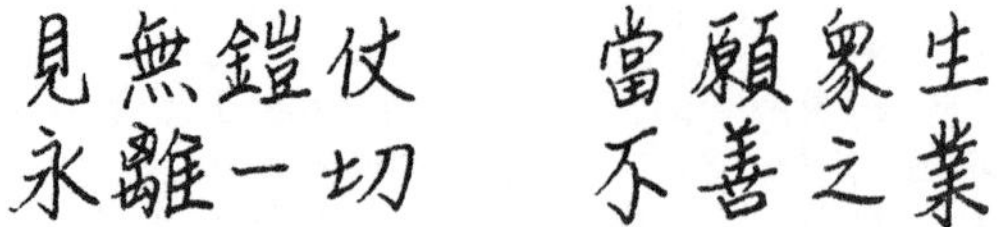

見無鎧仗　　當願眾生
永離一切　　不善之業

COMMENTARY:

WHEN I SEE A PERSON WHO IS NOT EQUIPPED WITH
ARMOR OR WEAPONRY. This is someone who doesn't
carry any weapons. When you encounter such a

state, you also should *VOW THAT LIVING BEINGS WILL FOREVER DEPART FROM ALL UNWHOLESOME KARMA;* they will leave all the bad karma behind. Once they separate from unwholesome karma, their good karma will increase and they will attain liberation.

SUTRA:

> *WHEN I SEE A PERSON WHO ENGAGES IN DISPUTE*
> * AND ARGUMENT,*
> *I VOW THAT LIVING BEINGS*
> *WILL COMPLETELY SUBDUE*
> *ALL KINDS OF HETERODOX DEBATES.*

見論議人　　當願眾生
於諸異論　　悉能摧伏

COMMENTARY:

WHEN I SEE A PERSON WHO ENGAGES IN DISPUTE AND ARGUMENT. In India there were masters of debate who had unobstructed eloquence. Even if a thing had absolutely no principle, they could still come up with some reasoning for it. They concentrated on studying the books of external paths in order to argue and discuss with people. They had "worldly knowledge and argumentative intelligence." They had perfected worldly wisdom and the art of debate. Their aim was to defeat other people through the skill of rhetoric and argument. Therefore, if you say something is right, they will come up against you by saying it is wrong. They always stick to a kind of principle and reasoning which is different from yours. Because they use rhetorical skills and florid language, they can easily clarify principle. But instead they engage in all manner of heterodox and bizarre discourses.

At this time, you should *VOW THAT LIVING BE-INGS WILL COMPLETELY SUBDUE ALL KINDS OF HETERODOX DEBATES.* You wish that living beings will be victorious over the deviant theories that take black for white, and right for wrong. Living beings should be victorious over them.

SUTRA:

> *WHEN I SEE A PERSON WHO HAS PROPER*
> *LIVELIHOOD,*
> *I VOW THAT LIVING BEINGS*
> *WILL ATTAIN PURE LIVELIHOODS,*
> *AND NOT   FEIGN AWESOME DEPORTMENT.*

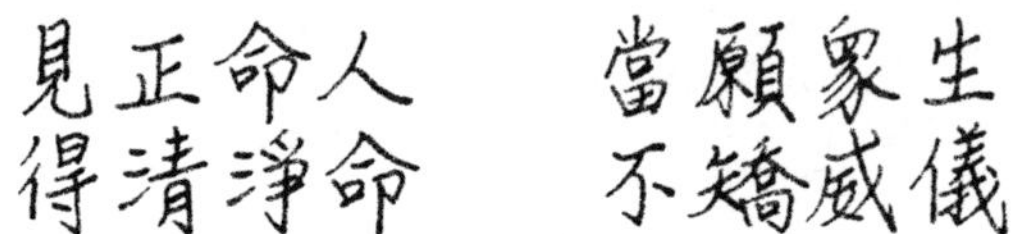

COMMENTARY:

WHEN I SEE A PERSON WHO HAS PROPER LIVELIHOOD.
This means a proper career. There are proper
careers and deviant careers. A person with a proper career can cultivate in accord with the Dharma.
He is not greedy for offerings. A person with a
deviant career will manifest a very strange and
weird appearance. He will deliberately show off
a style which differs from other people. Why does
he want to assume such a strange appearance? It's
because he wants to cause people to pay attention
to him. But he does not cultivate according to
the Buddhadharma. There are five kinds of deviant
livelihoods:

1. One manifests a strange style, which is
not in accord with the Buddhadharma.
2. One advertises one's own merit and virtue,
such as saying, "I already have done such and such
a good deed," or "I have made such and such a contri-
bution to living beings." He always praises himself. This situation is described in Confuciusiam
as,

> *One exaggerate one's own good.*

This means one exaggerates one's capabilities.
One boasts of one's own abilities. One day, Yen
Yuan (顏淵) and Tse Lu (子路) were standing by
Confucius' side, and Confucius asked them, "Come,
let each of you tell me your wishes."
Tse Lu was a rather gruff and coarse person.

He said, "I should like to have a plump horse, and chariot, and light fur coats, to share them with my friends. And even if they should spoil them, I would not be displeased or complain about it."

Yen Yuan said, "I should like not to boast of my excellence nor to make a display of my meritorious deeds." That is, he didn't want to exaggerate his own merit and virtue. One should benefit other people, but not advertise one's own efforts. This is Yen Yuan's resolve and vow, which is far superior to Tse Lu's. Tse Lu's resolve had shape and form, but Yen Yuan's resolve could not be pinned down by shape and form.

3.   One practices divination, such as foretelling auspicious or ill omens. One practices prognostication. Such a person casts fortunes for people. He might say to someone, "You better be careful, otherwise..." He tries to scare that person. So that person will say, "Is there a way to save me from this impending disaster?"

4.   One makes a display of one's awesomeness by shouting and bragging. He purposely shouts at the top of his lungs so that his face becomes as red as Kuan Kung, who is foremost in having a red face. This way he awes and intimidates people. They say, "He's really something!" This is also a deviant livelihood.

5.   One talks about the offerings of others. Whenever he goes to a new place, he says to people, "Do you know? In the place I came from, people made a lot of offerings to me. Those laypeople really bring forth the resolve!" When these laypeople hear this, they'll be influenced to pile offerings upon this monk so they won't be out-done. Or, he may say, "When I went to India, although that place was poverty-stricken, the temples made offerings of lunch meals to me." The laypeople in Taiwan, upon hearing this, will fight to make offerings to him.

Cultivation sounds easy, but it isn't easy to actually do it. Real cultivators are very, very rare. Think it over--how many left-home people in the world can be innocent of the five deviant livelihoods?

Therefore, when you see a person who has proper

livelihood, you vow that living beings attain pure
livelihoods, and not only   pretend they have
awesome deportment.
     In cultivation, one should follow the precepts
set up by the Buddha. One should accord with the
Buddha's system to cultivate. You cannot select
an unusual style for yourself. Somebody says,
"Dharma Master, since Chinese Dharma Masters don't
wear their sashes at all times, why do you wear
your sash and show off a special style?" Well,
the style we manifest is the way it was originally;
it's not unusual. All the disciples of the Buddha,
--all Bhikshus--have to wear the sash at all times.
Because of the environment, weather and customs
in China, people didn't wear the sash anymore.
Although they don't wear the sash, you still cannot
say this is the right thing to do. Because people
got so used to it, they overlooked its significance,
so it turned out that nobody wears the sash. But
we have to wear the sash all the time. Since
Chinese people didn't have the habit of wearing
the sash, after a period of time, they started
assuming that wearing the sash is wrong. This is
a mistake!
     Last spring when I came to Taiwan to lecture
the Sutras, a person questioned me on the telephone.
He said, "You monks who come from America wear
your sashes everyday and eat one meal a day, and
also claim that you sit up to sleep without lying
down. You're just pretending to be a model and
showing off a new style. If you are right, then
Chinese Buddhism is wrong. But if you are wrong,
then Chinese Buddhism is right. Can you make a
statement and tell me who is right, and who is
wrong?" What a hot question! I answered him,
"Chinese Buddhists think that not wearing the sash
is right. Ultimately is it right or wrong? Nobody knows. Nobody understands. Since you don't
wear the sash, he doesn't wear the sash, nobody
wears the sash--eventually everybody assumes the
same appearance. Everybody looks the same way.
Sometimes they will wear their robes when attend-
ing the ceremonies, but still they won't wear the
sash."
     The long robe is a style of clothing handed
down from ancient times in China, but it's not the

proper attire or trademark of a left-home person.
Take a look at the Theravadan   monks in Tailand
and Cambodia--the robes they wear accord with the
Buddha's system. But because of the cold weather
in China, left-home people had to wear more clothes
to keep the body warm. They wore their sashes on
top of their clothes, and it was easy for the sash
to get lost without people even knowing it. Later,
some smart Dharma Masters and stupid monks devised
a method. They sewed a hook and clasp onto the
end of the sash, so that the sash could be kept in
place and wouldn't slide down off people's bodies.
Originally Chinese left-home people wore the sash.
But later on, people saw that one after another didn't
wear the sash, and so gradually they didn't wear
it any more. This is the situation described by
the saying,

> *It evolves into a habit and so people don't
> even recognize it.*

Therefore they think that not wearing a sash is
correct. This question is something that merits
further investigation. However, there is a great
difference between one who wears a sash and one
who doesn't wear a sash. Wearing a sash, you
manifest the mark of a Bhikshu, and are worthy of
receiving offerings and reverence from gods and
humans. But if you don't wear a sash, you aren't
considered to be manifesting the mark of a Bhikshu.
Therefore, when I saw Theravadan   Buddhists, I
said to them, "The Great Vehicle is too great; the
Small Vehicle is too small, and so the great and
small cannot connect with each other. They don't
cooperate. If we want Buddhism to be prosperous
in the world, the Theravadan   should go forward
one step, and the Great Vehicle should go backward
one step. Then they can meet each other. Once
they connect with each other, they will cooperate."
By this I meant that the Small Vehicle should
break through their attachments, and the Great
Vehicle should withdraw their expedients. The
Small Vehicle Buddhists are too attached. They
bind their own feet and fail to make any progress.
They constrain themselves within certain boundaries.
They are too conservative in following traditional

regulations. They only know about themselves but don't know about other people. But Great Vehicle Buddhists are so expedient that they become sloppy in everythng. They think everything is no problem --even not wearing a sash is O.K. There are no problems at all!! Therefore, this causes people to ignore the importance of wearing the sash. They think that not wearing the sash is not a big error. How about if they don't eat rice--is that a big deal? If monks don't eat rice, then people will make a lot of offerings. Why? If you don't eat, then the offerings will be there all the time, for they will not be digested. But if you think, "I won't eat, so as to obtain more offerings," that is also a mistake! You just get yourself into the five deviant livelihoods.

AND NOT TO FEIGN AWESOME DEPORTMENT. This means not showing off a strange and different appearance and pretending that one has proper conportment.

SUTRA:

WHEN I SEE A KING,
I VOW THAT LIVING BEINGS
WILL BECOME DHARMA KINGS,
AND FOREVER PROPAGATE THE PROPER DHARMA.

若見於王　　當願衆生
得為法王　　恒轉正法

COMMENTARY:

WHEN I SEE A KING. Sometimes a Bhikshu gets an opportunity to meet an emperor or a king. At this time, he also should make a vow. *I VOW THAT LIVING BEINGS WILL BECOME DHARMA KINGS,* that is, will become Buddhas, *AND FOREVER PROPAGATE THE PROPER DHARMA.* One constantly turns the Dharma wheel to save living beings.

SUTRA:

WHEN I SEE A PRINCE
I VOW THAT LIVING BEINGS

WILL GET BORN BY TRANSFORMATION FROM THE
    DHARMA,
AND BECOME DISCIPLES OF THE BUDDHA.

若見王子　　當願眾生
從法化生　　而爲佛子

COMMENTARY:

WHEN I SEE A PRINCE. When you see a member
of the imperial clan, such as the emperor or a
prince, you also should VOW THAT LIVING BEINGS
WILL GET BORN BY TRANSFORMATION FROM THE DHARMA,
AND BECOME DISCIPLES OF THE BUDDHA.

SUTRA:

WHEN I SEE AN ELDER,
I VOW THAT LIVING BEINGS
WILL SKILLFULLY BE ABLE TO MAKE CLEAR
    DISTINCTIONS,
AND NOT PRACTICE EVIL DHARMAS.

若見長者　　當願眾生
善能明斷　　不行惡法

COMMENTARY:

WHEN I SEE AN ELDER. In the preceding gatha
kings and princes were discussed. Now an elder is
mentioned. "Elders" includes prime ministers and
court ministers.
I VOW THAT LIVING BEINGS WILL SKILLFULLY BE
ABLE TO MAKE CLEAR DISTINCTIONS. At this time
you should vow that living beings will acquire
proficiency in determining everything with bright,
clear understanding, and will not engage in vile
dharmas.
An elder is one who litigates legal affairs
with a proper sense of justice. You should make
a vow that all living beings will be able to clearly distinguish between what is right bund what is

wrong, *AND NOT PRACTICE EVIL DHARMA.* They will judge all court cases with impartiality and fairness.

SUTRA:

> WHEN I SEE A GREAT OFFICIAL,
> I VOW THAT LIVING BEINGS
> WILL ETERNALLY GUARD THEIR PROPER
>   MINDFULNESS,
> AND LEARN TO PRACTICE THE MULTITUDE OF
>   WHOLESOME DEEDS.

若見大臣　　當願眾生
恒守正念　　習行眾善

COMMENTARY:

WHEN I SEE A GREAT OFFICIAL-- A great official is one who works for the government. *I VOW THAT LIVING BEINGS WILL ETERNALLY GUARD THEIR PROPER MINDFULNESS.* At this time, you should vow that living beings will always guard and uphold their proper mindfulness, *AND LEARN TO PRACTICE THE MULTITUDE OF WHOLESOME DEEDS.* And always cultivate all kinds of good deeds.

SUTRA:

> WHEN I SEE A CITY AND CITY RAMPARTS,
> I VOW THAT LIVING BEINGS
> WILL ATTAIN THE SOLID BODY,
> AND BE WITHOUT DEVIOUSNESS IN THEIR MINDS.

若見城郭　　當願眾生
得堅固身　　心無所屈

COMMENTARY:

WHEN I SEE A CITY AND CITY RAMPARTS. In
ancient times, a city was three *li* in width. A
rampart was seven *li* in length (one Chinese *li* is
1/3 English mile). Every city contained an inner
city and an outer city. When you see such a city
or city wall, you should make a vow. I VOW THAT
LIVING BEINGS WILL ATTAIN THE SOLID BODY. You vow
that living beings will attain a solid body which
is very sturdy and durable, like the city and city
ramparts, AND BE WITHOUT DEVIOUSNESS IN THEIR
MINDS. Their minds should always be proper and
straight.

SUTRA:

> WHEN I SEE A CAPITAL CITY,
> I VOW THAT LIVING BEINGS
> WILL ACCUMULATE A MULTITUDE OF MERIT AND
>   VIRTUE,
> AND ETERNALLY BE JOYOUS AND HAPPY IN THEIR
>   MINDS.

COMMENTARY:

WHEN I SEE A CAPITAL CITY, where the emperor
lives. At this time, you also should make a vow.
I VOW THAT LIVING BEINGS WILL ACCUMULATE A MULTI-
TUDE OF MERIT AND VIRTUE. You vow that living
beings' merit and virtue will amass.
AND ETERNALLY BE JOYOUS AND HAPPY IN THEIR
MINDS. They should be joyous and exultant in their
minds.

SUTRA:

> WHEN I SEE A COPPICE OF TREES,
> I VOW THAT LIVING BEINGS
> WILL BE WORTHY OF PRAISE AND RESPECT
> FROM GODS AND PEOPLE.

見處林藪　　當願眾生
應為天人　　之所歎仰

COMMENTARY:

WHEN I SEE A COPPICE OF TREE. A coppice
refers to a grove filled with bushes. At this
time, you also should make a vow. *I VOW THAT LIV-
ING BEINGS WILL BE WORTHY OF PRAISE AND RESPECT
FROM GODS AND PEOPLE.* You vow that living beings
will be   praised, venerated and admired by
people and gods.

SUTRA:

*WHEN I ENTER A VILLAGE TO BEG FOR FOOD,
I VOW THAT LIVING BEINGS
WILL DEEPLY ENTER THE PROFOUND DHARMA
   REALM,
WITHOUT ANY OBSTRUCTIONS IN THEIR MINDS.*

入里乞食　　當願眾生
入深法界　　心無障礙

COMMENTARY:

WHEN I ENTER A VILLAGE or a city, or a very
small alley *TO BEG FOR FOOD.* At this time, you
should make a vow. You *VOW THAT LIVING BEINGS
WILL DEEPLY ENTER* into *THE PROFOUND DHARMA REALM,
WITHOUT ANY OBSTRUCTIONS IN THEIR MINDS,* that is,
that they will be without any affliction. If you
have affliction, then you have obstructions. There
are two kinds of obstruction: the obstruction of
affliction and the obstruction of that which is
known.

SUTRA:

WHEN I REACH THE DOOR OF A RESIDENCE,
I VOW THAT LIVING BEINGS
WILL ENTER THE DOOR OF
ALL BUDDHADHARMAS.

到人門戶　　當願眾生
入於一切　　佛法之門

COMMENTARY:

WHEN I REACH THE DOOR OF A RESIDENCE. When
you're at the threshold of a layperson's house,
you should make a vow.
*I VOW THAT LIVING BEINGS WILL ENTER THE DOOR
OF ALL BUDDHADHARMAS.* You vow that living beings
enter the doors of all the Buddhadharmas. You
enter all of the 84,000 doors of the Buddhadharma,
so you will clearly understand them all.

SUTRA:

WHEN I ENTER A RESIDENCE,
I VOW THAT LIVING BEINGS
WILL GET TO ENTER THE BUDDHA-VEHICLE,
AND BE EQUAL IN THE THREE PERIODS OF TIME.

入其家已　　當願眾生
得入佛乘　　三世平等

COMMENTARY:

WHEN I ENTER A RESIDENCE. When you go into
a village and go to a house to beg for food, first
you reach the door of that house. Each household
has its own door; after you enter the house, you
find that every household is about the same. When
you enter a residence, at this time, you also
should make a vow.
*I VOW THAT LIVING BEINGS WILL GET TO ENTER
THE BUDDHA-VEHICLE.* You vow that living beings
can all get to enter the Buddha-Vehicle, which is
the only vehicle. There are no other vehicles.

AND BE EQUAL IN THE THREE PERIODS OF TIME.
All living beings should attain the equality with
all the Buddhas of the past, all the Buddhas of
the present, and all the Buddhas of the future.
All Buddhas are equal, they are without duality.
You vow that living beings will all attain the
Buddha-Vehicle.

SUTRA:

WHEN I SEE A PERSON WHO DOESN'T GIVE,
I VOW THAT LIVING BEINGS
WILL NEVER RENOUNCE OR DEPART FROM
THE DHARMA OF SUPERIOR MERIT AND VIRTUE.

COMMENTARY:

WHEN I SEE A PERSON WHO DOESN'T GIVE. When
you go out begging for food, some people might
give, while others might not give to you. For
example, The Living Buddha of Gold-Mountain (金山
活佛), went out one day to beg for food. Someone
gave him two buckets of paint and said, "I give
this paint to you, you can drink it." He did drink
it. Now the householder was a person who refused
to give. But the Living Buddha of Gold-Mountain
wanted to teach and transform him, and therefore
he drank those two buckets of paint. After he
drank it, that person recognized his faults, and
immediately made a repentance before the Living
Buddha.
       When you see such people, you also should
make a vow. *I VOW THAT LIVING BEINGS WILL NEVER*
RENOUNCE OR DEPART FROM THE DHARMA OF SUPERIOR
MERIT AND VIRTUE. You vow that living beings will
always be able to bring forth a mind of giving,
and never renounce or depart from the Dharma of
superior merit and virtue. This means you cultivate and study all the Buddhadharmas, and establish
all merit and virtue. When you cultivate, if you
don't have offenses, then you have merit. Superior

merit and virtue means you keep on doing more meritorious acts. The Dharma of merit and virtue
refers to all kinds of good deeds that you have to
do. As it is said,

> *Do not do any evil even if it's very small;*
> *Do not bypass any good because it is insignificant.*

Even if it's a small good, you should go ahead and
do it. Although the evil is minimal, still you
shouldn't do it. By doing more good deeds, then as
time goes by, you will accomplish the Dharma of
superior merit and virtue.

SUTRA:

> WHEN I SEE A PERSON CAPABLE OF RENOUNCING,
> I VOW THAT LIVING BEINGS
> WILL FOREVER ATTAIN THE RENUNCIATION
> OF THE SUFFERINGS OF THE THREE EVIL PATHS.

見能捨人　　當願眾生
永得捨離　　三惡道苦

COMMENTARY:

   WHEN I SEE A PERSON CAPABLE OF RENOUNCING.
This means a person who can give away what he
possesses. When you see such a state, you also
should make a vow.
   *I VOW THAT LIVING BEINGS WILL FOREVER ATTAIN
THE RENUNCIATION OF THE SUFFERINGS OF THE THREE
EVIL PATHS.* You vow that living beings eternally
attain the renunciation of sufferings in the three
evil paths. What are the three evil paths? They
are the hells, hungry ghosts, and the animal realms.
How does one fall into the three evil paths?
Because one has greed, hatred, and stupidity. If
you have greedy thoughts, you will become a hungry
ghost. If you have a mind of hatred, you will
become an animal. If you're stupid, then you will
go to the hells. The three evil paths have sufferings so extreme that you cannot describe them with
words. Therefore you have to eternally depart

from the sufferings of the three evil paths.

SUTRA:

> *WHEN I SEE AN EMPTY BOWL,*
> *I VOW THAT LIVING BEINGS*
> *WILL BE CLEAN AND PURE IN MIND;*
> *EMPTY, AND WITHOUT AFFLICTION.*

若見空鉢　　當願眾生
其心清淨　　空無煩惱

COMMENTARY:

Left-home people eat from a special bowl. As it is said,

> *One holds the bowl to beg for food.*

Before a left-home person obtains some food from begging, his bowl is empty. Therefore the Sutra says *WHEN I SEE AN EMPTY BOWL.* You should make a vow when you encounter such a state. You should produce the power of vows from this kind of contemplation. *I VOW THAT LIVING BEINGS WILL BE CLEAN AND PURE IN MIND.* You vow that living beings will be ultimately pure in their minds, without greed, hatred, and stupidity. Once you don't have greed, hatred, and stupidity, you won't have afflictions. Therefore, it says *EMPTY, AND WITHOUT AFFLICTION.*

The most important thing for a cultivator is to not give rise to afflictions. Therefore, it is said,

> *Afflictions are inexhaustible;*
> *I vow to cut them off.*

But affliction is Bodhi, and birth and death is Nirvana. You don't seek outside of affliction for Bodhi. Also it's not outside of birth and death that you find Nirvana. Right within affliction, there is Bodhi. If you understand and get enlightened, Nirvana is right within birth and

When I see an empty bowl,
I vow that living beings
Will be clean and pure in mind;
Empty, and without affliction.

death.   It's as easy as turning over your palm.
    Ice is an analogy for affliction, while water
is an analogy for Bodhi.   If you use a piece of
ice and hit a person over the head with it, that
person might die.   But if you use a bowl of water
and splash it over a person's head, that person
might not even feel pain.   Once we have afflictions,
we produce all kinds of obstructions.   If we don't
have afflictions, but only the Bodhi mind, then we
discover affinities with everybody.

SUTRA:

> WHEN I SEE A FULL BOWL,
> I VOW THAT LIVING BEINGS
> WILL COMPLETELY PERFECT AND FULFILL
> ALL WHOLESOME DHARMAS.

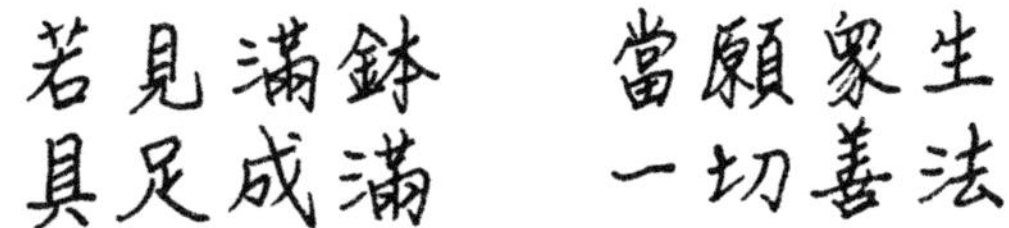

若見滿鉢　　當願眾生
具足成滿　　一切善法

COMMENTARY:

    WHEN I SEE A FULL BOWL.   When you go out to
beg for food, and somebody makes offerings to fill
up your bowl, you should make a vow.   I VOW THAT
LIVING BEINGS WILL COMPLETELY PERFECT AND FULFILL
ALL WHOLESOME DHARMAS.   "Complete" means everything is without obstruction and perfectly fused.
"Fulfill" means all good dharmas are perfectly
blended without obstruction.   All wholesome dharmas
are completely realized and brought to accomplishment.   When you see a full bowl, you wish that
all living beings will attain perfection and
success in their conduct, that all their wishes
will be fulfilled.

SUTRA:

> WHEN I RECEIVE VENERATION AND RESPECT,
> I VOW THAT LIVING BEINGS
> WILL REVERENTLY AND RESPECTFULLY CULTIVATE
> ALL BUDDHADHARMAS.

若得恭敬　　當願眾生
恭敬修行　　一切佛法

COMMENTARY:

When a Bhikshu holds his bowl to beg for food, people will come to pay their respects, make offerings, and bow to him. If the Bhikshu doesn't have samadhi power, he will give rise to a mind of delight. But if nobody makes offerings, then he will give rise to afflictions. *WHEN I RECEIVE VENERATION AND RESPECT.* When a Bhikshu happens upon a person who comes to pay respects and make offerings, he also should make a vow. The reason for making a vow is to counteract one's faults.

I VOW THAT LIVING BEINGS WILL COMPLETELY PERFECT AND FULFILL ALL WHOLESOME DHARMAS. Therefore you vow that living beings will reverently and respectfully cultivate all Buddhadharmas. You have to revere the Buddhas, revere the Dharma, and revere the Sangha. As it is said,

You should revere and respect the Triple Jewel.

You cultivate the three karmas of body, mouth, and mind so they are purified. You have to follow the regulations to cultivate all Buddhadharmas. You should get rid of the conduct of self-pride and smash down your mount Sumeru!

SUTRA:

*WHEN I DON'T RECEIVE REVERENCE AND
    RESPECT,
I VOW THAT LIVING BEINGS
WILL NOT PRACTICE
THE MANY UNWHOLESOME DHARMAS.*

不得恭敬　　當願眾生
不行一切　　不善之法

COMMENTARY:

WHEN I DON'T RECEIVE REVERENCE AND RESPECT from people, I also should make a vow. *I VOW THAT LIVING BEINGS WILL NOT PRACTICE THE MANY UNWHOLE-SOME DHARMAS,* that instead they will practice all good dharmas. First one has to attain the perfection and fullness of merit and virtue, then people will come to pay their reverence and respect.

When you receive reverence and respect, you also shouldn't be pleased. And when people don't render you respect, you shouldn't feel shameful and remorese. You should reflect and examine your own Way-virtue to see where it is incomplete and imperfect. You should consider with discernment the places which are lacking and not full. As it is said,

> *Returning the light and illuminate within,*
> *One seek the fullness of self.*

You certainly shouldn't complain to heaven of gripe to people!

SUTRA:

> *WHEN I SEE A PERSON WITH A SENSE OF SHAME*
>   *AND REMORSE,*
> *I VOW THAT LIVING BEINGS*
> *WILL BECOME ENDOWED WITH THE CONDUCT*
>   *OF SHAME AND REMORSE,*
> *AND STORE AND PROTECT ALL THEIR FACULTIES.*

見慚恥人　　當願眾生
具慚恥行　　藏護諸根

COMMENTARY:

WHEN I SEE A PERSON WITH A SENSE OF SHAME AND REMORSE. A cultivator should always bring forth a mind of shame and remorse. One shouldn't be shameless. I am really unfortunate: I took an American disciple who doesn't understand the meaning of being ashamed. He's shameless. He asked me, "What is the meaning of shame?" This is a Westerner who is hard to teach and transform. Therefore I say,

> *Although going to the heavens is hard, still it's*
>   *not hard,*
> *But to teach and transform westerners is most*
>   *difficult.*
> *Although penetrating into the ground is hard, still*
>   *it's not hard,*
> *But to teach and transform westerners is most*
>   *difficult.*

Basically, he doesn't want to have a sense of shame. He just goes ahead and does what he wants to do. He says, "This is just the way to handle things. You just go ahead to do it. What's the use of having a sense of shame?" Well, it sounds reasonable. He's very self-righteous about it. But this attitude of shamelessness is not right.

To have "shame" means to be modest and humble. If you have done something wrong, sometimes your face will turn red. When you can feel bashful, then you know the sense of shame. The ancients said,

> One who is clever and fond of study,
> Is not ashamed to inquire from those who are
> beneath him.

However, this can only be brought up by other people, not something you use to describe yourself. For example, you cannot say, "Why do I inquire from you? It's because I'm clever and fond of study that I don't feel ashamed to consult those who are beneath me." When you say this, you are just looking down on other people, thinking that they are below you. This is equal to scolding people--"I'm so clever and fond of study that I am not ashamed to inquire from you who are beneath me." For instance, I'm a teacher, and you're a student. Therefore,if I inquire, then I'm one who is not ashamed to inquire from people who are beneath me. Now if other people say , "Ah! That person is so knowledgeable, but he still inquires from those who have no knowledge. Well, he is clever and fond of study but he is not ashamed to inquire from those who are beneath him." That is O.K. But you cannot put a high hat on yourself and proclaim, "Do you know? I consult you because I am so clever and fond of study that I am not ashamed to inquire from those who are beneath me." If a person without any common sense hears, that won't be a big matter. But if a person with some knowledge hears this he will put a question mark on your statement.

Therefore, to have shame and remorse means that "one is afraid to do incorrect things; one is scared to do evil deeds." This is a person who has a sense of shame.

This is like a person, who on hearing that he has done something wrong, will turn red in the face whenever you mention it. The face of Kuan Kung will appear. This is because he has a sense of shame.

To be "modest" means to be pure, sparing, and frugal. Shame means that one recognizes the things he has done wrong. A person with a sense of shame and remorse is one who knows how to be ashamed. When you encounter such a person you *VOW THAT LIVING BEINGS WILL BECOME ENDOWED WITH THE CONDUCT OF SHAME AND REMORSE.*

AND STORE AND PROTECT ALL THEIR FACULTIES.   To "store" here doesn't mean to hide something away. It means to eradicate faults before they have time to appear. "Store and protect" also means to guard.   Although the Sutra translates it as "store", actually it also contains the meaning of "being careful." You carefully protect and handle all of your faculties. "All faculties" refer to the eyes, ears, nose, tongue, body, and mind. None of those faculties will be turned by states. You are very careful and cautious to protect and guard all of your faculties. Your eyes don't look at things which are not proper; you don't look at things that are unreasonable. Your ears don't listen to things that are not in accord with propriety. You don't listen to unreasonable music. Some music is really terrible. It confuses people and makes them upside-down, as if drunk, always muddled and not awake. Therefore, your ears don't listen to evil sounds. Your eyes don't watch evil form. As it is said,

> *Things that are not proper, I don't watch,*
> *Things that are not proper, I don't listen to,*
> *Things that are not proper, I don't speak,*
> *Things that are not proper, I don't do.*

This is a good method to store and protect all of your faculties.

SUTRA:

> *WHEN I SEE ONE WHO IS SHAMELESS AND*
> *   WITHOUT REMORSE,*
> *I VOW THAT LIVING BEINGS*
> *WILL RENOUNCE AND DEPART FROM SHAMELESSNESS,*
> *AND DWELL IN THE WAY OF GREAT KINDNESS.*

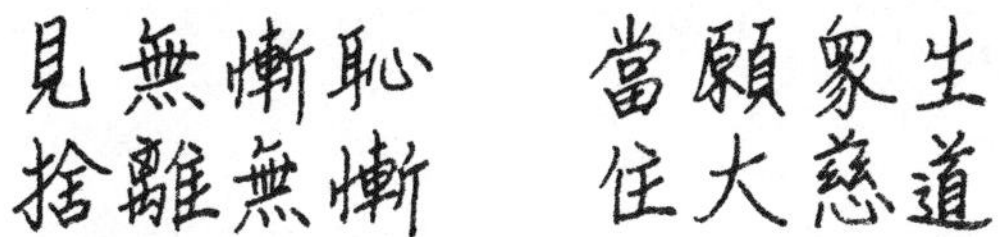

見無慚恥　　當願眾生
捨離無慚　　住大慈道

COMMENTARY:

WHEN I SEE ONE WHO IS SHAMELESS AND WITHOUT REMORSE. Before, the Sutra says that one has to

make a vow while encountering a person who has a
sense of shame and remorse. Here it refers to one
who doesn't recognize a sense of shame. One who
doesn't have a sense of shame is like a person
who doesn't have blood or breath. He's spineless!
He is shameless and remorseless. While encountering such a state, you also should make a vow. You
*VOW THAT LIVING BEINGS WILL RENOUNCE AND DEPART
FROM* the conduct of *SHAMELESSNESS.*
     AND DWELL IN THE WAY OF GREAT KINDNESS. One
abides on the road of great kindness and compassion.

SUTRA:

> *WHEN I OBTAIN DELICIOUS FOOD,*
> *I VOW THAT LIVING BEINGS*
> *WILL FULFILL THEIR VOWS*
> *AND BE WITHOUT ENVY IN THEIR MINDS.*

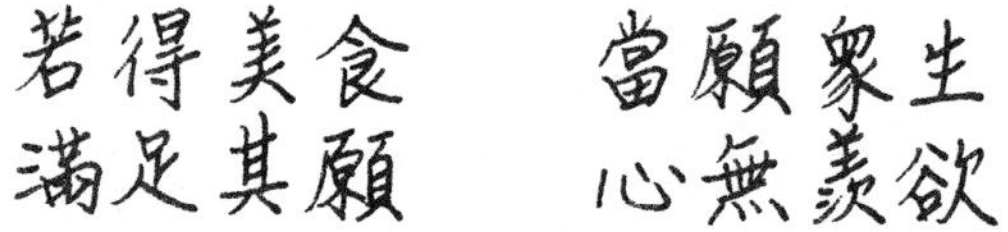

若得美食　　當願眾生
滿足其願　　心無羨欲

COMMENTARY:

     WHEN I OBTAIN DELICIOUS FOOD. Delicious food
refers to flavorable, fine food, replete with
wonderful taste and colorful appearance. As it is
said,

> *Form, fragrance, and flavor are all complete.*

Whether food is delicious or not also depends on
what type of people are eating it. For example,
Northern people like to eat dumplings. If they
obtain some dumplings, they think that is the most
delicious food. Southern people like to eat rice.
If they obtain some rice, they think that's the
most delicious food. Westerners like to eat butter,
bread, and cheese. If you give them a little bit
of butter and bread, then they won't get angry.
If they cannot eat butter and bread because you
hide them away, their mind of hatred will arise,
and they'll be impolite to their teacher. "Why

don't you give me some bread? Why do you hide such
good butter and not let me eat it?" Their anger
arises and they blow up. Therefore, whether food
is delicious or not depends on what kind of people
get it. Each has his own liking. For instance,
if a pig gets some fermented grains left over from
the wine vat, then it thinks that's the most delicious food to eat. If you give it some leftover
soy bean husks, it also thinks that's the most
flavorful food. But if you give it to people,
people won't eat it. Dogs like to eat human beings'
excrement. They eat it as if there's a lot of
flavor in it. They think that's the most flavorable food.

WHEN I OBTAIN DELICIOUS FOOD. Food which
suits your taste is called "delicious food." At
this time, you should *VOW THAT LIVING BEINGS WILL
FULFILL THEIR VOWS*. They will attain whatever
they're seeking for. For example, Kuan Yin Bodhisattva always fulfills people's wishes. As it is
said,

> *Seeking for wealth and honor,*
> *One will attain wealth and honor.*
> *Seeking for long life,*
> *One will attain long life.*
> *Seeking for a son,*
> *One will attain a son.*
> *Seeking for a daughter,*
> *One will attain a daughter.*

Therefore, whoever wishes to get a son or a daughter
should bow to Kuan Yin Bodhisattva, recite Kuan
Yin Bodhisattva's name, and he certainly will
have his wishes fulfilled.

AND BE WITHOUT ENVY IN THEIR MINDS. To envy
means to convet, to long for. For instance, you
see other people attain delicious food, and your
mouth waters--that is envy. You envy other people
getting delicious food. "He gets to eat such good
cheese, and also bread and butter, but I don't get
to eat them--Oh! this is really suffering!"

To be without envy in their minds means that
they don't have such convetous thoughts, or gult-
tonous thoughts. Their mouths will not water.

SUTRA:

WHEN I OBTAIN FOOD WHICH IS NOT DELICIOUS,
I VOW THAT AMONG LIVING BEINGS
THERE ARE NONE WHO WILL NOT ATTAIN
THE FLAVORS OF ALL SAMADHIS.

得不美食　　當願眾生
莫不獲得　　諸三昧味

COMMENTARY:

WHEN I OBTAIN FOOD WHICH IS NOT DELICIOUS.
For example, the bread is stale, the butter is
spoiled, the cheese has long mold on it.However,
the longer the mold gets on cheese, the better they
like it. Westerners like to eat cheese. They
say if cheese grows long mold then it's even more
delicious.

"Food which is not delicious" refers to food
which you don't wish to eat. At this time, you
also should make a vow. You vow that among living
beings, there are none who will not attain the
flavors of all samadhis.   Samadhi is "proper
concentration and proper reception." All living
beings will attain the flavor of samadhi, or the
flavor of proper concentration and proper reception, all without exception.

SUTRA:

WHEN I OBTAIN SOFT FOOD,
I VOW THAT LIVING BEINGS
WILL BE PERMEATED BY GREAT COMPASSION,
SO THEIR MINDS AND INTENTIONS ARE SUPPLE
AND SOFT.

得柔軟食　　當願眾生
大悲所熏　　心意柔軟

COMMENTARY:

WHEN I OBTAIN SOFT FOOD. Some foods are hard, and some are soft. For example, there's soft bread that makes people get very fat when they eat it, and there are hard breads that make people get thin when they eat it. Nowadays almost all Westerners are afraid of getting fat. Everybody wishes to get thinner. Therefore the breads in the markets have signs that read "this kind of bread is guaranteed non-fattening." Those non-fattening breads must not be very **soft**, because soft bread tastes very sweet and delicious, and is pleasant to eat. When you eat soft food, you also should make a vow. *I VOW THAT LIVING BEINGS WILL BE PERMEATED BY GREAT COMPASSION, SO THEIR MINDS AND INTENTIONS ARE SUPPLE AND SOFT.* What is supple and soft? Supple and soft means to be patient. Patience is just a soft food. As it is said,

> *Kindness can bestow happiness on living beings.*
> *Compassion can pull out living beings' sufferings.*

The greatly compassionate heart can bestow happiness on all living beings. That is, one does not fight with living beings. If you don't fight with living beings, you are patient. Patience is the greatly compassionate heart. Therefore the Sutra says, "Permeated by great compassion, so their minds and intentions are supple and soft." One doesn't have hatred in one's mind. One's mind is always happy.

SUTRA:

WHEN I OBTAIN COARSE AND ROUGH FOOD,
I VOW THAT LIVING BEINGS
WILL HAVE NO DEFILED ATTACHMENTS IN THEIR
*   MINDS,*
AND CUT OFF WORLDLY GREED AND LOVE.

得粗澀食　　當願眾生
心無染著　　絕世貪愛

COMMENTARY:

WHEN I OBTAIN COARSE AND ROUGH FOOD. This
food is harsh-textured and hard to digest. Although
it is not easy to eat, you still are able to eat
it. This is being patient, and also cultivating
the practice of "eating what others cannot eat."

One day a bhikshu offered me a big basket of
steamed dumplings. They were made from corn meal
or some other cheap cereal, and of the kind eaten
by poor people in North China. Those dumplings
have a colloquial name, which is "inside two and
outside eight." There's a public record concerning this type of dumpling, entered in the history
of the travels of Dhyana Master Chao Chou (趙州).
At that time Chao Chou was over eighty years old.
One day someone asked him, "Do you know what an
inside two and outside eight is?" The old monk
was unable to answer the question. He knew it was
food, but didn't know the reason behind that name.
So he said, "Bring them to me, and I will eat them."
That person had assumed that Chao Chou knew he
was talking about steamed dumplings, but actually
Chao Chou didn't know. As a result Chao Chou
brought forth a mind of remorse. He thought,
Here I have been cultivating for such a long time,
and I don't even know the meaning behind the name
of this kind of food. What have I been cultivating? A muddle path? I should go out and investigate and see what is behind that name. But my eyes
are dim, my teeth are falling out, and my legs have
gone into retirement. What can I do?"

He decided to have a chat with his servant.
He called him in and asked him, "May I borrow
something from you?" The servant thought, "If my
master wants something, how can I not lend it to
him?" Therefore he said, "Anything that the Venerable Master would like, I am willing to lend him."
Chao Chou said, "As long as you agree to it, that's
fine. You don't have to ask me what thing I want
to borrow. Now run along and go back to sleep."

The servant felt this was a rather strange
request, but he went back to sleep. The next morning on waking up he took a look at the mirror and
just about had a fit! He saw that he now had a long
beard and teeth that were falling out; in fact,
he looked exactly like the old monk Chao Chou.
He was panic stricken, "Oh no, this is terrible!

How did I come into this body of the old master?"
He ran to find Chao Chou. When he entered the
master's room, he found himself standing there.
This terrified him even more, so that he was
screaming and yelling, "What's happening?"

Chao Chou comforted him in a gentle voice,
"Don't stir up a scene. I will return your body
to you eventually. You needn't be afraid. Now
you better stand in for me as the Abbot, while I
go out to investigate a little." So Chao Chou
went from the south to the north in his investigation. In the northern region, he saw people
making steamed dumplings. As they kneaded the
dough, they used two fingers to knead the inside
of the dumpling, while eight fingers remained
outside to shape the exterior of the dumpling.
He asked the people, "What is the name of this
food?" They answered, "You don't know what this
is called?! This is 'inside two and outside eight'
--steamed dumplings!"

Suddenly Chao Chou understood. There was
nothing else to do, so he came home and returned
the young body to his servant, and crept back into
his old, weak, and worn body--his own. That's
the story of "inside two and outside eight."

At that time, a bhikshu sent me a basket of
those dumplings, also called "Wo Wo T'ou," about
fifty or sixty of them. This was a bhikshu who
ate one meal a day. He was afraid I would starve
to death when I was mourning beside my mother's
grave. So he offered me these dumplings. I ate
them slowly and took three weeks to finish them.
On the last day, the steamed dumplings had
developed long mold, about 1 1/2 inches thick. I
didn't expose them under the sun or let them blow
in the wind. I was very lazy at that time. After
eating, I usually sat there and didn't pay attention to anything. As a result, the food developed
long mold when the weather got hot. At that time
I wiped away the mold and ate all the Wo Wo T'ous.
This kind of food was really hard to eat--it was
really "coarse and rough food." It was too coarse
to eat. It stank even worse than excrement. It
was very hard to eat when it got into my mouth,
but I swallowed them up anyway, not wishing to
waste them. So, *WHEN I OBTAIN COARSE AND ROUGH*

FOOD, I VOW THAT LIVING BEINGS WILL HAVE NO DEFILED ATTACHMENTS IN THEIR MINDS. In their minds, there's no defiled attachment, no thoughts of good or bad flavors. *AND CUT OFF WORLDLY GREED AND LOVE.* They should eradicate the thought of being greedy for delicious food.

SUTRA:

> *WHEN THERE IS FOOD TO EAT,*
> *I VOW THAT LIVING BEINGS*
> *WILL TAKE DHYANA BLISS AS FOOD,*
> *AND BE FILLED WITH THE JOY OF DHARMA.*

若飯食時　　當願眾生
禪悅爲食　　法喜充滿

COMMENTARY:

All left-home people should perform the three kinds of mindfulness and five contemplations before eating. The three kinds of mindfulness are:

1. I vow to cut off all evil.
2. I vow to cultivate all good.
3. I vow to cross over all living beings.

Before you start to eat, you have to take three spoonfuls of soup. When you swallow the first spoonful, you contemplate,"I vow to cut off all evil." Bhikshus, Bhikshunis, Upasakas, and Upasikas, should all perform this contemplation before they eat. As you swallow the second spoonful of soup you contemplate,"I vow to cultivate all good." Since we vow to cut off all evil, we should not always be gossiping about others' faults. If you gossip about others' faults, that's just an evil. "I vow to cultivate all good," means to praise other people. One should cover up others' evil and expose others' good. To "cover up evil" does not mean to cover over your own faults, but to cover others' faults. To "expose good" does not mean to expose your own good points, but others' good points. Remember, you should not praise yourself and slander others. You don't praise yourself and say how wonderful you are and complain how bad other people's behavior is. The reason this world has so much strife is that people only recognize themselves, but do not care about other people. Because we don't recognize that there are other people, we always bring forth the mind of fighting and greed. When you are about to drink the third spoonful of soup, you "vow to cross over all living beings." You should vow, "I shall cross over all my relatives and friends, and lead them first to take refuge with the Triple Jewel, and then to take the Five Precepts. Futhermore, I'll cross them over to bring forth the Bodhi mind, to leave the home life, and to cultivate the Way." With regard to leaving home to cultivate the Way, all of you who have this idea should consider very carefully before you make such a decision. Don't leave home recklessly and then regret it later on. After leaving home, you must act like a left-home person. If you're a lay-person, then act like a lay-person. Don't become a person who doesn't fit into any category. A left-home person should not do the things that lay-people do. As it is said,

> Although the body leaves the home life,
> The mind is still not in the Way.

It means that a person looks like a left-home person on the outside, but his mind doesn't want to cultivate. He doesn't do any work that left-home people should do to the point that he doesn't even do morning and evening recitation. He's lazy to the extreme! One certainly cannot obtain any benefit from this. Therefore, these three kinds of mindfulness are very important. Also, you have to perform the five contemplations before you eat.

    1. Consider the amount of work involved to bring the food to where it is eaten. You think it over. How much human labor was necessary to bring even a single grain of rice to the table? There's a verse which says,

> *The farmer hoes in the midday sun,*
> *His sweat falls on the soil,*
> *Who can guess how much toil it took*
> *   to bring the food to the bowl?*

It says that when the farmer hoes the grain under the midday sun, his sweat falls on the ground, and wets the soil. It means he sweats a lot. "Who can guess how much toil it took to bring the food to the bowl?" Who really knows the amount of work it took to get even a single grain of rice in the bowl. There's also a saying,

> *The donor's one grain of rice*
> *Is as heavy as Mount Sumeru.*
> *If you don't cultivate the Way after you eat it,*
> *You'll return the debt by wearing fur and horns.*

This verse sounds very serious. Therefore, since left-home people and lay-people have food to eat, clothes to wear, and a house to dwell in, they should make use of this good opportunity to culti-vate the Way quickly! Don't let the time pass in vain. So it says, WHEN THERE IS FOOD TO EAT, I VOW THAT LIVING BEINGS WILL TAKE DHYANA BLISS AS FOOD, AND BE FILLED WITH THE JOY OF DHARMA. You vow that everyone will attain the joy of dhyana as his food. When one sits in meditation, one produces the happiness of tranquility.
One takes this kind of happiness as his own meal. It means as one sits in meditation, one doesn't feel hungry even if one doesn't eat. One takes the bliss of dhyana as food, and is "filled with the joy of dharma." One attains the happiness of the Buddhadharma.
    2.   Consider whether or not one's virtuous conduct is sufficient to enable one to accept the offering. You should think about it. "Is my virtuous conduct sufficient to receive this offer-ing?" In the Vinaya it is said,

> *If one doesn't sit in Dhyana or recite the Sutras,*
> *Nor handle the affairs of the Buddha, Dharma,*
> *   and Sangha,*
> *But still goes ahead to receive offerings from*
> *   donors,*
> *Then one certainly will fall.*

3. Guard the mind from transgression, of which greed is the principle cause. As it is said,

If one gives rise to greed towards good food,
One will fall into the path of the hungry ghosts.
If one gives rise to hatred towards inferior food,
One will fall into the path of animals.
If one gives rise to stupidity towards mediocre food,
One will fall into the hells.

All the karmic obstacles of living beings come from greed, hatred, and stupidity.

4. Properly taken, the food is like medicine, to keep the body from wasting away. When you eat the food, you should not seek for either good or bad flavor. You should rely on the false to cultivate the true. This is the purpose of eating food.

5. This food is accepted only in order to accomplish the Way. In order to seek the Buddha-dharma, and to accomplish our Way-karma, we have to accept the offering of food. But one cannot be greedy for it. One eats it only as an aid to realize the Way.

SUTRA:

WHEN I TASTE FLAVOR,
I VOW THAT LIVING BEINGS
WILL OBTAIN THE BUDDHA'S FLAVOR
AND BE SATISFIED WITH SWEET DEW.

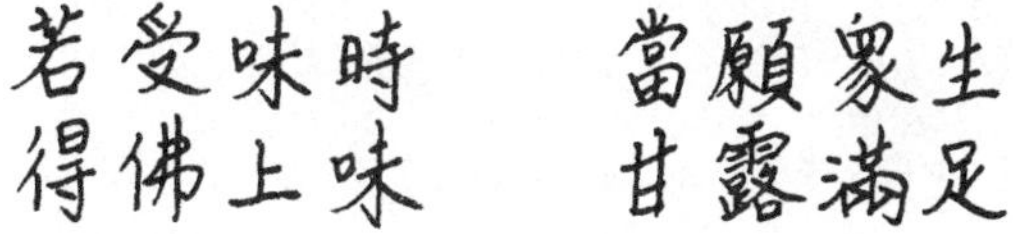

若受味時　　當願眾生
得佛上味　　甘露滿足

COMMENTARY:

WHEN I TASTE FLAVOR. Each person likes to eat a particular flavor: sour, sweet, bitter, hot, or salty. Each has his preference. That is why Universal Worthy Bodhisattva carried a lot of bottles with him when he was in charge of the kitchen--in order to be able to provide the flavors

that each person preferred. Even so, people com-
plained that he did not satisfactorily practice the
Bodhisattva conduct.

Therefore, when I taste flavor, *I VOW THAT
LIVING BEINGS WILL OBTAIN THE BUDDHA'S* superior
FLAVOR. One obtains the supreme flavor of Buddha's
Dhyana, or the joy of Dhyana. *AND BE SATISFIED
WITH SWEET DEW.* Sweet dew is a kind of medicine
that causes people not to die. You wish people to
obtain the flavor of sweet dew and always to be
filled with the sweet taste.

SUTRA:

AFTER I FINISH THE FOOD,
I VOW THAT LIVING BEINGS
WILL FINISH WHAT THEY SHOULD DO,
AND BE REPLETE WITH ALL BUDDHADHARMA.

飯食已訖　　當願眾生
所作皆辦　　具諸佛法

COMMENTARY:

Before, we talked about how, when one is eating
delicious or coarse food, one should engage
in the five contemplation. Now, we will talk about
how one should also contemplate after the meal.
It's not the case that you have nothing to do after
lunch. You have to make a vow after you finish
eating. *AFTER I FINISH THE FOOD.* After the meal
is done, *I VOW THAT LIVING BEINGS WILL FINISH WHAT
THEY SHOULD DO.* May they have success in all they
do, *AND BE REPLETE WITH ALL BUDDHADHARMAS.* You wish
that all living beings will accomplish what they
do, and be complete with all Buddhadharma. As it
is said,

*Those who practice giving are certain to be rewarded.
Those who give gladly will surely later be at ease.*

All those who make offerings to the Triple Jewel
will certainly attain the benefit and reward from the
offering. If you make the offering for the sake of

being eternally peaceful, joyful, and happy in the future, you'll certainly be successful. This is how, after eating, left-home people make transference for the people who have donated the meal.

SUTRA:

WHEN I SPEAK THE DHARMA,
I VOW THAT LIVING BEINGS
WILL ATTAIN LIMITLESS ELOQUENCE,
AND PERVASIVELY PROCLAIM THE ESSENTIAL
  DHARMA.

若説法時　　當願象生
得無盡辯　　廣宣法要

COMMENTARY:

WHEN I SPEAK THE DHARMA. When one is lecturing the Sutras and speaking the Dharma, one should also make a vow. *I VOW THAT LIVING BEINGS WILL ATTAIN LIMITLESS ELOQUENCE.* There are four kinds of unobstructed eloquence:

1. Unobstructed eloquence of phrasing.
2. Unobstructed eloquence of meaning.
3. Unobstructed eloquence of delight in
       speaking.
4. Unobstructed eloquence of Dharma.

AND PERVASIVELY PROCLAIM THE ESSENTIAL DHARMA. From less, one can speak more. From more, one can enter into less. More and less are non-dual. Understanding this, one is able to speak the essential Dharma. One explains the most important points of a Sutra.

SUTRA:

WHEN I COME OUT OF THE HOUSE,
I VOW THAT LIVING BEINGS
WILL DEEPLY ENTER INTO THE BUDDHA'S WISDOM,
AND TRANSCEND THE THREE REALMS FOREVER.

從舍出時　　當願象生
深入佛智　　永出三界

COMMENTARY:

Sometimes left-home people would step out of the house. On these occasions, you should not look around, or use a telescope to watch horse-races or dog-races, or simply enjoy the scenery. Don't be like this. what should you do instead? You should tie up your body and mind, and not let your eyes wander. You should make a vow when you encounter such a state. You *VOW THAT LIVING BEINGS WILL DEEPLY ENTER INTO THE BUDDHA'S WISDOM*. You wish that living beings can all quickly attain the profound, unsurpassed wisdom of the Buddha. *AND TRANSCEND THE THREE REALMS FOREVER*. The three realms are the desire realm, the form realm, and the formless realm. One should transcend the three realms, because, as it is said,

> *The three realms are not peaceful;*
> *They are like a burning house.*

Therefore, we should transcend the   three realms.

SUTRA:

> *WHEN I ENTER THE WATER,*
> *I VOW THAT LIVING BEINGS*
> *WILL ENTER ALL WISDOM,*
> *AND UNDERSTAND THE EQUALITY OF THE THREE*
> *PERIODS OF TIME.*

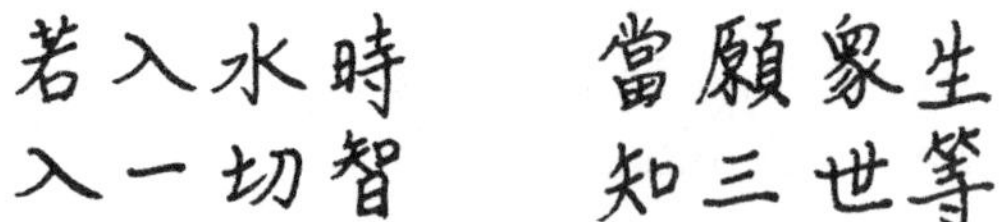

COMMENTARY:

WHEN I ENTER THE WATER. Sometimes you may go into the river to take a bath, or you may pass by a river. At this time, you also should make a vow. *I VOW THAT LIVING BEINGS WILL ENTER ALL WISDOM*, that they all attain the wisdom water. *AND UNDERSTAND THE EQUALITY OF THE THREE PERIODS OF TIME*. May they obtain the wisdom to understand past lives, the present life, and future lives.

SUTRA:

> *WHEN I BATHE MY BODY,*
> *I VOW THAT LIVING BEINGS*
> *WILL HAVE NO DEFILEMENTS IN THEIR BODIES*
>   *AND MINDS,*
> *AND WILL BE BRIGHT AND CLEAN INSIDE AND OUT.*

洗浴身體　　當願眾生
身心無垢　　內外光潔

COMMENTARY:

After you enter the water, you should bathe your body. When taking a bath one should not only clean up the defiling dust outside of the body, but also one should clean up the defiling dust in one's mind. *WHEN I BATHE MY BODY,* at this time, you should make a vow. *I VOW THAT LIVING BEINGS WILL HAVE NO DEFILEMENTS IN THEIR BODIES AND MINDS.* One should wash away the defiling dust from the outside of one's body. And the inside of one's body should also be cleansed of its poisons--greed, hatred, and stupidity. *AND WILL BE BRIGHT AND CLEAN INSIDE AND OUT.* When the inside and the outside of the body are free of defilement, then this is "to have no defilements in their bodies and minds, and be bright and clean inside and out."

SUTRA:

> *IN THE MIDST OF THE BLAZING AND POISONOUS*
>   *HEAT OF SUMMER,*
> *I VOW THAT LIVING BEINGS*
> *WILL RENOUNCE AND DEPART FROM ALL*
>   *AFFLICTIONS,*
> *AND COMPLETELY PUT AN END TO THEM.*

盛暑炎毒　　當願眾生
捨離眾惱　　一切皆盡

COMMENTARY:

IN THE MIDST OF THE BLAZING AND POISONOUS HEAT OF SUMMER. "Blazing" refers to when the weather is extremely hot. The "poisonous heat of summer" refers to a kind of heat that people cannot endure; it is like poison. At this time, you should not strike up false thinking; instead you ought to make a vow. *I VOW THAT LIVING BEINGS WILL RENOUNCE AND DEPART FROM ALL AFFLICTIONS, AND COMPLETELY PUT AN END TO THEM.* You should empty yourself of all afflictions and not even retain the tiniest bit.

SUTRA:

WHEN THE SUMMER IS OVER AND THE COOL SEASON
    BEGINS TO SET IN,
I VOW THAT LIVING BEINGS
WILL CERTIFY TO THE UNSURPASSED DHARMA,
AND BE ULTIMATELY CLEAN AND COOL.

暑退涼初　　當願眾生
證無上法　　究竟清涼

COMMENTARY:

The previous verse refers to when the weather is extremely hot. Now this verse refers to the time *WHEN THE SUMMER IS OVER*, and early fall has set in. At this time, you also should make a vow. *I VOW THAT LIVING BEINGS WILL CERTIFY TO THE UNSURPASSED DHARMA.* May they attain the unsurpassed Dharma, the pure and cool Dharma, *AND BE ULTIMATELY CLEAN AND COOL.* May they ultimately attain the happiness of being clear and cool--the joy of having no heat or afflictions.

SUTRA:

WHEN I RECITE SUTRAS,
I VOW THAT LIVING BEINGS
WILL ACCORD WITH WHAT THE BUDDHA SAYS, AND
UNITE WITH AND UPHOLD IT WITHOUT FORGETTING
    ANY.

諷誦經時　　當願眾生
順佛所説　　總持不忘

COMMENTARY:

WHEN I RECITE SUTRAS. This means when we read
and recite the Great Vehicle Sutras. If one reads
from the text, that is "reading." If one doesn't
have to read from the text, that is "reciting."
When we read and recite the Sutras, we also should
make a vow. *I VOW THAT LIVING BEINGS WILL ACCORD
WITH WHAT THE BUDDHA SAYS.* All living beings
should rely on the Buddha's teaching and follow the
Buddha's system. We should accord with the teachings and offer up our conduct. We should rely upon
the Buddhadharma to cultivate. Don't go against
the Way. Don't suppose that your wisdom is even
greater than the Buddha's, such thinking as "I
can also lecture the Sutra, I also can transmit the
teachings." We as Buddhist disciples absolutely
cannot have this type of arrogant attitude.
*AND UNITE WITH AND UPHOLD IT WITHOUT FORGETTING
ANY.* "Unite and uphold" means one always remembers
and maintains it, and does not forget. One remembers the Sutras and mantras. "Unite and uphold"
is also another term for *Dharani*. *Dharani* is Sanskrit,
and means "unite and uphold," to "unite all dharmas,
and uphold limitless meanings." Therefore, we
should remember all dharmas and not forget any.
If we can recite the Amitabha Sutra, Vajra Sutra,
or even the Dharma Flower Sutra, and Avatamsaka
Sutra, then we are able to unite with and uphold
them without forgetting any.

SUTRA:

>   WHEN I GET TO SEE THE BUDDHA,
>   I VOW THAT LIVING BEINGS
>   WILL ATTAIN UNOBSTRUCTED EYES,
>   AND BEHOLD ALL BUDDHAS.

若得見佛　　當願眾生
得無礙眼　　見一切佛

COMMENTARY:

WHEN I GET TO SEE THE BUDDHA. Sometimes when

we cultivate, we attain the Five Eyes or Six penetrations, so that we can see all the Buddhas. If you attain the Five Eyes, you can see all the Buddhas. Before you attain the Five Eyes, you can only see Buddhas who have shape and form, such as Buddha images carved out of wood or earth, or painted images. But no matter which kind of Buddha image you see with your flesh eyes, you still have to make a vow. *I VOW THAT LIVING BEINGS WILL ATTAIN UNOBSTRUCTED EYES.* Every living being can open the Five Eyes--the Buddha eye, the Dharma eye, the Wisdom eye, the Heavenly eye, and the Flesh eye. When you open the Five Eyes, you will attain unobstructed eyes. You can see all Buddhas without obstruction. Once you open your Five Eyes, you can see all the Buddhas of the three periods of time, to the exhaustion of empty space and the Dharma Realm. If you wish to see them, you should cultivate. If you cultivate, you will open the Five Eyes. If you don't cultivate, you will never get to have them. Some people who possess good roots also can open their Five Eyes, because in their past lives, their good roots were already very deep. Therefore, in this life they can see the Buddhas and Bodhisattvas as well as all the ghosts and spirits. So you shouldn't criticize those people who have ghostly eyes. Actually, it's not the case that they have good dispositions that they can see ghosts. But, is it the case that because we can't see ghosts that we don't possess good roots? No, we still have good roots. Even if you do have good roots, you still need to continue in your cultivation so as to nourish your good roots. If you don't plant good roots, you will never attain them. Somebody says, "I don't know if I have good roots or not." Why should you pay attention to whether or not you have good roots? If you don't have good roots, you should cultivate. Don't be lazy. But if you have good roots, you still need to be vigorous and step forward. This is most important! Don't produce a mind that retreats.

So, you vow that all living beings can *BEHOLD ALL BUDDHAS.* One can see all the Buddhas after one attains the eye of non-obstruction.

SUTRA:

WHEN I GAZE UPON THE BUDDHA,
I VOW THAT LIVING BEINGS
WILL ALL RESEMBLE UNIVERSAL WORTHY
    BODHISATTVA,
AND BECOME UPRIGHT, ADORNED, AND MAJESTIC.

諦觀佛時　　當願眾生
皆如普賢　　端正嚴好

COMMENTARY:

WHEN I GAZE UPON THE BUDDHA, that is, when
you are very attentive and wrapt in contemplating
the Buddha, you make a vow. I VOW THAT LIVING
BEINGS WILL ALL RESEMBLE UNIVERSAL WORTHY BODHI-
SATTVA. May all living beings become just like
Samantabhadra Bodhisattva, AND BECOME UPRIGHT,
ADORNED, AND MAJESTIC. One is like Samantabhadra
Bodhisattva who rides on a white elephant with six
tusks, and appears very adorned, fine, and replete
with awesome deportment.

SUTRA:

WHEN I SEE A STUPA,
I VOW THAT LIVING BEINGS
WILL BE AS RESPECTED AS THE STUPA,
AND RECEIVE OFFERINGS FROM GODS AND PEOPLE.

見佛塔時　　當願眾生
尊重如塔　　受天人供

COMMENTARY:

WHEN I SEE A STUPA. When one sees a stupa,
one should circumambulate it. No matter what the
circumstances, when a Buddhist sees a stupa, he
should bow to it, and circumambulate the stupa
three times. This is because the true bodies of
the Buddha, the Dharma, and the Sangha are stored
inside every stupa. The stupas contain the Buddha's
Sharira, as well as the Dharma Jewel, and the

Sangha Jewel. Therefore we have to circumambulate a stupa three times at the very least.

This makes me think of when I went to India to pay respect to the Buddha's Bodhi tree. There was also a stupa there. We bowed to it and circumambulated that stupa seven times. When I bowed, I contemplated myself as being a representative of all the Buddhists in Asia, all of the disciples who have taken refuge with me, and those who see me, or hear my name. I bowed to the Buddha's stupa three times on their behalf and wished that they might quickly accomplish the fruition of Buddhahood, and quickly attain irreversibility from Anuttarasamyak-sambodhi. I dedicated this vow on behalf of all people and offered up my resolve. I wasn't bowing to the stupa for my own benefit; rather I was representing all the living beings that I know as I made obeisance to the Great Sagely ground. At that time I made this kind of contemplation and transference to all people.

Therefore, when you see a stupa, you should *VOW THAT LIVING BEINGS WILL BE AS RESPECTED AS THE STUPA.* One respects all living beings just as one respects the Buddha's stupa. *AND RECEIVE OFFERINGS FROM GODS AND PEOPLE.* One vows that one will receive offerings from gods and people.

SUTRA:

> *WHEN I CONTEMPLATE A STUPA WITH RESPECTFUL*
> *   MIND,*
> *I VOW THAT LIVING BEINGS*
> *WILL BE GAZED UPON AND REVERED BY*
> *ALL GODS AND PEOPLE.*

敬心觀塔　　當願衆生
諸天及人　　所共瞻仰

COMMENTARY:

WHEN I CONTEMPLATE A STUPA, I should maintain a respectful mind. Therefore it says, contemplating the stupa *WITH RESPECTFUL MIND.* At this time, you also should make a vow. Left-home people shouldn't

strike up false thinking all the time. Instead
they should make vows on behalf of all living beings
throughout the Dharma Realm. Therefore, *I VOW THAT
LIVING BEINGS WILL BE GAZED UPON AND REVERED BY
ALL GODS AND PEOPLE.* Everybody gazes up at the
Buddha with deep respect.

SUTRA:

> *WHEN I MAKE OBEISANCE BEFORE A STUPA,*
> *I VOW THAT LIVING BEINGS*
> *WILL ATTAIN A SUMMIT THAT CANNOT BE SEEN*
> *BY GODS OR PEOPLE.*

頂禮於塔　　當願眾生
一切天人　　無能見頂

COMMENTARY:

WHEN I MAKE OBEISANCE BEFORE A STUPA. We who
are Buddhists should bow in reverence to the
Permanently-dwelling Triple Jewel of the ten directions enshrined in the stupa. We should bow to the
stupa and also make a vow. Therefore, *I VOW THAT
LIVING BEINGS WILL ATTAIN A SUMMIT THAT CANNOT BE
SEEN BY GODS OR PEOPLE.* The beings in the six
paths--gods, worldly people, and so forth--cannot
see the top of the stupa. Since it's an invisible
summit, there's no way they can see it. This refers
to the Buddha's invisible summit as described in
the <u>Shurangama</u> <u>Sutra</u>:

> *A hundred jewelled brilliant rays sprang from*
> *Shakyamuni Buddha's crown and a thousand-petalled*
> *precious lotus arose from amidst those rays. Upon*
> *the precious flower sat the Thus Come One's*
> *transformation. From its summit, a hundred brilliant*
> *rays spread forth to the ten directions.*

These hundred brilliant rays spreading forth to
the ten directions refers to the Dharma which is
composed of layer upon layer without exhaustion.
Within each brilliant ray, there are manifested as
many worlds as there are sands in ten Ganges Rivers.

And there are also that many Vajra Treasury Bodhisattvas who come to offer their protection.

We who study the Buddhadharma should know how to recite and uphold the Shurangama Mantra. Right before the Buddha proclaimed the Shurangama Mantra he emitted a hundred layers of lights. Within each glorious light there were revealed, throughout all of empty space, Dharma-protecting Vajra spirits as many as the sands of ten Ganges Rivers. The Sutra text says,

> *Each of them carried a mountain and held aloft a vajra. The Great Assembly gazed upward and felt fearful admiration. Seeking his kind protection, they single-mindedly listened. Then the transformation atop the invisible summit poured forth splendorous light and proclaimed this spiritual mantra.*

The Thus Come One's transformation atop the invisible summit poured forth splendorous light and proclaimed this spiritual mantra. The Shurangama Mantra was proclaimed by the Buddha's Dharma body. It is really wonderful beyond words. There's no way to describe its inconceivable state. As long as a single person can recite and uphold the Shurangama Mantra in this world, the Demon Kings will not appear. This Shurangama Mantra can subdue all the demon troops throughout the ten directions and the three periods of time. It is foremost in subduing demon armies.

So, "Invisible Summit" refers to the Buddha's invisible summit.

SUTRA:

> AS I CIRCUMAMBULATE A STUPA TO THE RIGHT,
> I VOW THAT LIVING BEINGS
> WILL NOT ENCOUNTER ADVERSITIES IN THEIR
>   PRACTICES,
> AND WILL ACCOMPLISH ALL WISDOM.

右繞於塔　　當願眾生
所行無逆　　成一切智

COMMENTARY:

AS I CIRCUMAMBULATE A STUPA TO THE RIGHT. One has to circumambulate a stupa by going around to its right. This is a gesture of reverence.

I VOW THAT LIVING BEINGS WILL NOT ENCOUNTER ADVERSITIES IN THEIR PRACTICES. Whatever they do is in accord with the Way. There's no adversity, which means one does not walk against the Way. One relies on the Buddhadharma to practice the Way. One does not go against the Buddhadharma. Adversity is stupidity. Compliance is wisdom.

AND ACCOMPLISH ALL WISDOM. May all living beings achieve and accomplish all the wisdom of all modes, and the wisdom of the wisdom of all modes.

SUTRA:

*WHEN I CIRCUMAMBULATE A STUPA THREE
    TIMES,
I VOW THAT LIVING BEINGS
WILL DILIGENTLY SEEK THE BUDDHA WAY,
WITHOUT THOUGHTS OF LAZINESS OR REST.*

繞塔三帀　　當願眾生
勤求佛道　　心無懈歇

COMMENTARY:

   WHEN I CIRCUMAMBULATE A STUPA THREE TIMES.
There is also a fixed number of times you circumambulate a stupa. You circumambulate it to the right
three times. Three times symbolizes one's tran-
scendence of the Triple Realm. It also means one
diligently cultivates precepts, samadhi, and wisdom,
and casts out greed, hatred, and stupidity. It
means one gets far away from the three evil paths.
If you bring forth the Bodhi resolve and seek the
unsurpassed Way, then you will not fall into the
three evil destinies. There's no a fixed way to
explain this. As long as you feel you can comply
with the situation, then there's no problem.
   Therefore, I VOW THAT LIVING BEINGS WILL DILI-
GENTLY SEEK THE BUDDHA WAY. While circumambulating
the stupa, one does not get lazy, but one diligently
seeks the Buddha path without thoughts of laziness
or rest. One doesn't give rise to a lazy mind, a
retreating mind. When we seek the Buddhadharma,
we should constantly be vigorous and step forward.
Don't retreat and go backward. Therefore, the
text says we should not have thoughts of laziness
and wanting to rest. To "rest" means that one
stops half way down the road (半途而廢). One
gives up one's mission half-way down the line and
retreats. When we bring forth the Bodhi mind we
should be courageous and vigorous. Don't stop or
hold back!

SUTRA:

   WHEN I PRAISE THE BUDDHA'S MERIT AND
      VIRTUE,
   I VOW THAT LIVING BEINGS
   WILL BE REPLETE WITH A HOST OF VIRTUES,
   AND WILL LAUD AND PRAISE WITHOUT END.

讚佛功德　　當願眾生
眾德悉具　　稱歎無盡

COMMENTARY:

   WHEN I PRAISE THE BUDDHA'S MERIT AND VIRTUE.

We recite and chant praises before the Buddha, to
laud and praise the Buddha's merit and virtue.
This is a basic practice within Buddhism, so you
shouldn't say that "chanting praises is the same
as singing a song," or "How does singing a song
help Buddhism?" You will increase your good roots
by praising the Buddha's merit and virtue. If you
don't praise the Buddha, your good roots will not
increase. If your good roots do not increase, then
your Bodhi resolve will not grow. If your Bodhi
resolve does not grow, you will not accomplish the
fruition of Bodhi. Therefore, we have to laud and
praise the Buddha's merit and virtue. If you
praise the Buddha's merit and virtue, you will
increase your own good roots. In America, I always
say,

> *Although going to the heavens is hard,*
> *   still it's not hard,*
> *But to teach and transform Westerners is most*
> *   difficult.*
> *Although penetrating the ground is hard,*
> *   still it's not hard,*
> *But to teach and transform Westerners is most*
> *   difficult.*

Why? This is not gossiping: I'm telling you the
truth. In America, there once were some Westerners
who didn't understand the importance of praising
the Buddha's merit and virtue. They would say,
"It's time to sing the song again!" For example,
during morning recitation, they would say, "Time
to sing a song again." During lunch offering
ceremony, they would say, "We have to sing songs
for half an hour before we eat, otherwise we can't
eat." If these Buddhists don't sing songs for
half an hour, then they don't get a meal in exchange.

Because we only eat one meal a day, we usually
perform the lunch offering at 10:30 a.m. We perform the lunch offering ceremony everyday, not just
on the first and fifteenth days of the lunar month.
In China, most monasteries used to perform the
lunch offering on the first and fifteenth days of
the lunar month, but in Gold Mountain Monastery,
we make the lunch offering everyday. Why do we do

this? First, it's because we eat one meal a day.
Since we have to eat, we have to first offer the
food to the Buddha. Second, it's because western
people don't understand how to play the Dharma
instruments before the altar. They are unfamiliar
with them. Some people say, "Those who tap, beat,
chant and recite are like stage players within
Buddhism." Well, even if they act as stage players,
still, left-home people should know how to chant.
If you are a stage player, and you don't know how
to chant, how can you be called a Buddhist disciple?
Therefore it is said,

> *Those who investigate Ch'an and meditation are*
>   *Buddha's disciples,*
> *But those who tap, beat, chant, and recite are*
>   *the Buddha's stage players.*

Anyway, you still should be a stage player. If
you don't know how to play Dharma instruments, how
can you qualify to be a Buddhist disciple? If you
don't understand such a superficial aspect, how
can you understand the deeper meaning of the
contents? Therefore we make offerings to the
Buddha. On the one hand, we make offerings to the
Buddha, and on the other hand we practice playing
the Dharma instruments, so we can get used to it
day by day. This is one explanation. But Western
people would say, "We sing the song in exchange
for food." All of you listen to this. Don't you
think those Westerners are really difficult to
cross over? They said they have to chant songs in
exchange for food, and that they can only get one
meal in exchange, not three! They would always
question me on the most trivial matters. Even
when they wanted to go to the toilet, they would
come and ask me, saying, "Teacher, is it O.K. for
me to go to the toilet and relieve myself?" See,
they'd bring up questions like these to ask me.
This doesn't show that they were obedient; it only
reveals their inability to handle things. That is
why I say teaching and transforming Westerners can
be bitter to the extreme. In China, although
there were some people with depraved character,
still I never heard them say, "We have to chant
songs in exchange for our meal." Well, what I

said was just an analogy, you don't have to believe
it. There's no truth in my speech. Everything is
false, but even if it is false, if you can find
the truth from it, then I have fulfilled my purpose.

Therefore when you laud and praise the Buddha's
merit and virtue, you should make a vow. *I VOW
THAT LIVING BEINGS WILL BE REPLETE WITH A HOST OF
VIRTUES.* A "host of virtues" is the Buddha's
myriad virtues. A "host" means many. "Myriad"
refers to a great number. The Buddha is adorned
with a myriad virtues. "To be replete with a
host of virtues" means the ten thousand virtues
are adorned. Because you laud and praise the
Buddha's myriad adornments, you will also be
replete with a host of virtues. That is, you will
obtain the adornment of a myriad virtues. How did
the Buddha become a Buddha? Well, although you
have studied the Buddhadharma for many years,
I believe you still don't understand. If you know,
you can speak up! Of course you know how the
Buddha became a Buddha. It's because he lauded
and praised the Buddhas' merit and virtue--therefore
he became a Buddha himself. If the Buddha scolded
living beings everyday-- "You are a ghost, you are
an animal, you are an ant,..."--if he had had
those kinds of thoughts, then he never would have
become a Buddha. But instead, he praised the
merit and virtue of all the Buddhas of the past.
Not only did he praise the Buddhas of the past, he
also praised the Buddhas of the present. Not only
did he praise the Buddhas of the present, he also
praised the Buddhas of the future. But, who are
the Buddhas of the future? Right now, all the
people in this lecture hall are the Buddhas of the
future. Not only the people inside this lecture
hall, but those who are outside of this lecture
hall, are all Buddhas of the future. Therefore,
those who bring forth the great Bodhi resolve to
become replete with great kindness and compassion,
cannot constantly criticize other people's mistakes.
I have said this before:

> *If you always look at others' faults,*
> *You haven't ended your own suffering.*
> *If you've already ended your own suffering,*
> *You will see everyone as a Buddha.*
> *All living beings are your parents of the past,*
>   *and the Buddhas of the future.*

Since all living beings are my parents of the past,
if I gossip about all living beings' faults, I am
just gossiping about my parents' faults. If I do
not respect living beings, I am not respecting the
Buddha. If we can think this way, then we will
have no difficulty in becoming replete with a host
of virtues. How did the Buddha come about? By
praising and lauding other Buddhas. The Ten Great
Kings of Vows of Universal Worthy Bodhisattva are
the best exemplars in this regard. The Ten Vows
are:

The first is to worship and respect all Buddhas.
The second is to praise the Thus Come Ones.
The third is to cultivate the giving of offerings.
*The fourth is to repent of and reform all karmic
    faults.*
*The fifth is to compliantly rejoice in merit and
    virtue.*
*The sixth is to request the turning of the Dharma
    wheel.*
*The seventh is to request that the Buddhas dwell
    in the world.*
The eighth is to always follow the Buddhas in study.
The ninth is to forever accord with living beings.
*The tenth is to universally transfer all merit and
    virtue.*

The merit and virtue of praising all Buddhas is
contained within these ten great Kings of Vows.
    Therefore, chanting praises before the Buddha
or bowing to the Buddha are conditions leading to
Buddhahood. They are the very foundation of
accomplishing Buddhahood. As for those who say,
"We sing a song in exchange for our meal," they
are those whom the Thus Come One called "people who
should be pitied."
    The text says, *AND WILL LAUD AND PRAISE WITHOUT
END*. This means that if you now praise the Buddha's
merit and virtue, then in the future, living beings
will also sing your praises without end. The
merit of praising the Buddha is perpetuated without
exhaustion.

SUTRA:

*WHEN I PRAISE THE BUDDHA'S MARKS AND
    CHARACTERISTICS,*

I VOW THAT LIVING BEINGS
WILL ACCOMPLISH THE BUDDHA'S BODY,
AND CERTIFY TO THE DHARMA OF NO MARK.

讚佛相好　　當願眾生
成就佛身　　證無相法

COMMENTARY:

WHEN I PRAISE THE BUDDHA'S MARKS AND CHARACTERISTICS. When we see a Buddha image, we contemplate the Buddha as being replete with thirty-two marks and eighty subtle characteristics. We should praise each mark and every characteristic. At this time, don't strike up another false thought. Instead you should make a vow. *I VOW THAT LIVING BEINGS WILL ACCOMPLISH THE BUDDHA'S BODY.* We also can accomplish the Buddha's thirty-two marks and eighty subtle characteristics, *AND CERTIFY TO THE DHARMA OF NO MARK.* Although we wish to attain such good marks and subtle characteristics, nonetheless we should not give rise to thoughts of attachment. First we should certify to true enlightenment, the true perfect Bodhi resolve, and then return to that which cannot be got at, because ultimately "there is no understanding and no attaining."

SUTRA:

WHEN I WASH MY FEET,
I VOW THAT LIVING BEINGS
WILL BE FULLY ENDOWED WITH COMPLETE
* SPIRITUAL POWER,*
AND BE WITHOUT ANY OBSTRUCTIONS WHEREVER
* THEY GO.*

若洗足時　　當願眾生
具神足力　　所行無礙

COMMENTARY:

Left home people always have to wash their

feet. Why? Because in India, and in South China,
the weather is hot. The Buddha always went around
with bare feet, and none of the Bhikshus wore shoes
or socks. Because they didn't wear shoes and socks,
their feet always got full of dirt and mud, so they
had to wash their feet every day. At the beginning
of the _Vajra Sutra_, it says,

> At that time, at mealtime, the World Honored One
> put on his robe, took up his bowl, and entered
> the great city of Shravasti to beg for food.
> After he had finished his sequential begging
> within the city, he returned, ate the food, put
> away his robe and bowl, washed his feet, arranged
> his seat, and sat down.

Therefore, washing the feet is a habit that left-
home people adopt. If you don't wash your feet,
your feet will dirty the Buddha hall, and that is
an act of disrespect to the Buddha. You should
not only wash your feet, but also wash your mind
and cleanse your thoughts. You have to bring forth
the Bodhi resolve while you wash your feet. You
should contemplate, "Did my mind produce any kind
of deviant thoughts? Is that a deviant or a proper
thought?" You have to purify your mind, return the
light and illuminate within, to see whether you
have given rise to sexual desire, or thoughts of
greed, hatred, or stupidity. Therefore, when you
are washing your feet, you should *VOW THAT LIVING
BEINGS WILL BE FULLY ENDOWED WITH COMPLETE SPIRITUAL
POWER, AND BE WITHOUT ANY OBSTRUCTIONS WHEREVER
THEY GO*. They can go wherever they wish.
   I suddenly thought of something. In San Francisco, I established an Institute for the Translation of Buddhist Texts for the purpose of translating Buddhist Sutras into English. We base our
translations upon original Sanskrit, Chinese texts,
so that we can make cross references
among the various manuscripts.
   As for the translation of Buddhist Sutras, we
know that several thousand years ago, Shakyamuni
Buddha spoke the Dharmas for forty-nine years in
over three hundred assemblies. But it wasn't until
the time of the T'ang Dynasty in China that the
Great Master Hsuan Chuang went to India to fetch the
Buddhist Sutras and brought them back to China,

during which time he withstood a myriad hardships
and bitter suffering.

     At that time, the Translation Institute in
China was composed of three thousand people, and
at no time were there fewer than eight or nine
hundred people at work. During that period, even
the King believed in Buddhism and became a Dharma
protector. But later on, people didn't want to
translate the Sutras from Chinese into foreign
languages. They only wanted to keep them in China,
and propagate them in a conservative method. They
didn't translate the Sutras into western languages.
For the next few years, some people may have been
aware of this limitation, but they did not take
any real action. The Chinese people could only see
their own country. They didn't see that there
were other countries beside their own. Therefore
Buddhist Sutras were not widely propagated. Some
contemporary high masters also considered this
issue, but they never took any real action. Forty
years ago, I suggested that young left-home people
should focus their attention on propagating the
Buddhadharma, and develop the requisite skills and
techniques to promote Buddhism in all countries.
In order to possess such communication skills, one
must have a command of foreign languages. More
than forty years ago, I encouraged young people to
study English and other foreign languages. At that
time, a few of them actually resolved to do this,
but nothing significant came out of it. In 1962
I came to America, resolved to train Westerners,
so that they could translate the Chinese Sutras
into English. But these causes and conditions did
not ripen for the next six to seven years. I "hid"
myself and lived in seclusion. Then, in 1968, the
conditions finally matured, and young Americans
started to arrive. That year five Westerners left
the home life. In 1969 I sent them to Taiwan to
receive the full Precepts. This was the first time
that there were Orthodox Bhikshus in the West.
Later, more and more people came to leave the home-
life. But it is not easy for those who wish to
leave the home-life with me. Now, is it the case
that I have to beg them to leave the home-life?
No, rather, it is very difficult for them to get
permission to leave home. These Americans have to

kneel before me and ask at least three times. They
would say, "I wish to leave home to become a
bhikshu." The first time I would say, "You had
better consider it carefully. Wait for awhile.
After you've thought it over carefully, then we
can talk about it some more."

Then they would think it over, say for three
to five months. If they didn't come back to talk
to me again, I'd know that they didn't really want
to leave home after all. But if they still came
back and said, "I have to leave home," I would
say, "You should think it over some more. See if
you really can endure this suffering, such as eating one meal a day at noon, and sleeping sitting
up."

Well, to sleep sitting up is not easy. Yesterday, I promised Dharma Master Chih Young that
I would talk a little about sleeping in the sitting
posture, so I'll go into it a bit now. There's no
special skill involved in sleeping sitting up.
You have to sit in an upright position. The best
is to sit in full lotus. It's not easy to sink
into a torpor when you sit in full lotus. This
sitting posture can subdue demons. It's also
called the Vajra Sitting position, because it is
very solid and durable. One does not easily fall
over or lean to one side. At that time, "the eyes
contemplate the nose. The nose contemplates the
mouth. And the mouth contemplates the mind." Your
tongue should touch the roof of your mouth, right
behind the front teeth. There is principle to
this. In China, there is a religion based on the
teachings of propriety. The adherents refrain
from smoking and drinking. They say, "Close your
mouth and hide your tongue. The tip of the tongue
touches the front part of the palate."

This teaching does not exclusively belong to
the teachings of Propriety; we also adopt the same
method in Buddhism. You can observe that when a
baby is born, the tip of its tongue naturally
touches the roof of its mouth. When your tongue
touches the roof of your mouth, it connects the
two main meridians (jen 任 and Tu 督), and regulates
your energy (*Ch'i*) and blood. If your blood and
breath are regulated, you will not sink into a
torpor. Moreover, you will not feel groggy in

meditation, and it'll be easy for you to enter
samadhi.   But you shouldn't be afraid of discomfort.
Don't be afraid that your legs will hurt.   Don't
be greedy to take it easy, saying, "I'd much rather
stretch out my legs and lie down.   That's much more
comfortable.   To sleep sitting up is not comfortable."   Of course, to sleep sitting up is not comfortable.   But if you look into the case histories
of all the Patriarchs of the past, you will find
that they were all brought to accomplishment
through discomfort.   If you're always greedy for
comfort, wanting to eat good food and sleep in a
relaxed manner, how will you be able to show your
sincerity in cultivation?   That is why, in India,
the Venerable Ribs (脇尊者) never once lay down
to sleep.   His ribs never touched the mat.   In
China, many cultivators also practice this method
of sleeping sitting up. vowing that their ribs
will never touch the mat.   And now, the seed of
Buddhism has begun in America.   Therefore I en-
courage the dhuta practices of eating one meal a
day at noon, and sleeping sitting up.

SUTRA:

> *WHEN IT'S TIME TO SLEEP AND REST,*
> *I VOW THAT LIVING BEINGS*
> *WILL OBTAIN PEACE AND SECURITY IN THEIR*
> *   BODIES,*
> *AND NOT BE MOVED OR CONFUSED IN THEIR*
> *   MINDS.*

以時寢息　　當願眾生
身得安隱　　心無動亂

COMMENTARY:

   WHEN IT'S TIME TO SLEEP AND REST, you have
to go to sleep.   You shouldn't be bowing before
the Buddha while other people are sleeping, or
sleeping when others are bowing.   Especially in
larger Way places among the great assembly, you
have to follow the rules and regulations of the
assembly.

    Therefore, you have to make a vow when you're about to go to sleep. *I VOW THAT LIVING BEINGS WILL OBTAIN PEACE AND SECURITY IN THEIR BODIES.* The body will attain peace and comfort. *AND NOT BE MOVED OR CONFUSED IN THEIR MINDS.* Don't strike up false thinking while lying on the bed, or sitting on the mat. You should not have false thinking. Once you have false thinking you will not be able to fall asleep. Some people complain that they suffer from insomnia. Well, it's because they think too much. There's no other reason. When people lie down on the bed, they reminisce about things of the past or trifling affairs which are as small as sesame seeds!

SUTRA:

> *WHEN I AWAKE FROM SLEEP,*
> *I VOW THAT LIVING BEINGS*
> *WILL ENLIGHTEN TO ALL WISDOM,*
> *AND HAVE A VISION THAT SPANS THE TEN*
>   *DIRECTIONS.*

睡眠始寤　　當願眾生
一切智覺　　周顧十方

COMMENTARY:

    The previous verse talked about the time when one goes to sleep and rests. Now this verse discusses the time one wakes up from sleep. Once there was a man called Cheng Wu Kung (鄭武公) who had a son called "one who was born during sleep (寤生)." Why was he given this name? When his mother gave birth to this son, she was just about to wake up from her sleep; therefore he was named "one who was born during sleep." His mother hadn't even opened up her eyes, and she didn't know how she gave birth to this baby. Therefore it is said,

> *Cheng Wu Kung married a wife from the Country of Shen, named Chiang Sze, who bore him (two sons), Chuang Kung and Kung Shu Tuan. Since Kung Hsu Tuan's birth alarmed his mother, she named him Wu Sheng-- "born during sleep."*

Cheng Wu Kung was very disgusted with this son. He thought this son was no good. His mother hadn't even awakened when he was born. Therefore, the father disliked this son.

When left-home people wake up they also should make a vow. *I VOW THAT LIVING BEINGS WILL EN-LIGHTEN TO ALL WISDOM, AND HAVE A VISION THAT SPANS THE TEN DIRECTIONS.* This means they should investigate everywhere, to the exhaustion of empty space and pervasively throughout the Dharma realm.

SUTRA:

DISCIPLES OF BUDDHA, IF ALL THE BODHISATTVAS FORMULATE THEIR THOUGHTS IN THESE WAYS, THEY WILL ATTAIN ALL SUPREME AND WONDERFUL MERIT AND VIRTUE. IN ALL WORLDS, THEY WILL NOT BE MOVED BY ALL THE GODS, DEMONS, BRAHMAS, SHRAMANAS, BRAHMANS,, GANDHARVAS, ASURAS AND SO FORTH. ALL THE SOUND HEARERS AND THOSE ENLIGHTENED TO CONDITIONS ALSO CANNOT MOVE THEM.

COMMENTARY:

Manjushri Bodhisattva calls out to Foremost Wisdom Bodhisattva, "Disciples of the Buddha! All of you disciples of the Buddha!" *DISCIPLES OF THE BUDDHA* includes all the Bodhisattvas at that time. *IF ALL* of you *BODHISATTVAS* who have wisdom *FORMU-LATE* your *THOUGHTS IN THESE WAYS,* and bring forth the vows as described above, if you maintain this kind of attitude, then you *WILL ATTAIN ALL SUPREME AND WONDERFUL MERIT AND VIRTUE.* You will attain all the most supreme, subtle, and inconceivable merit and virtue which will nourish the wisdom life of your Dharma body, and you will quickly attain irreversible Proper and Equal Enlightenment. "All supreme and wonderful merit and virtue" also means

> *One possesses virtue which is complete,*
> *And practices which are all encompassing.*

This just means accomplishing the fruition of Buddhahood. At this time, *IN ALL WORLDS, ALL THE GODS, DEMONS, BRAHMAS, SHARMANAS, BRAHMANS* (a reli-

gious sect in India which cultivates pure conduct),
GANDARVAS (musicians before the Jade Emperor),
ASURAS (those beings who lack upright features),
and *ALL THE SOUND HEARERS AND THOSE ENLIGHTENED TO
CONDITIONS*--those of the Two Vehicles--*ALSO CANNOT
MOVE* you. Your merit and virtue excels that of the
Sound Hearers and those who are enlightened to
conditions.

This time as I return to Taiwan to lecture
THE PURE CONDUCT CHAPTER, I feel very ashamed of
myself, because I don't have eloquence and also
lack knowledge. I haven't learned the teachings,
nor deeply entered the Treasury of Sutras. Therefore what I speak is very commonplace and ordinary.
I can only talk about principles that everybody
can understand, but I don't know how to expound
lofty theories or rhetoric. Actually, everyone can
lecture the Sutras.

Although my lectures are not very profound,
nonetheless, I have some deep Dharma affinities
with all of you. These affinities have not just
developed in one life, but through many lifetimes.
Therefore today it is fitting that we reap this
fruition of Dharma.   Those who came here to listen
to the lecture have great good roots. They came
here to be part of the influential assembly. For
those who have already brought forth the Bodhi
resolve, or who are just bringing forth the Bodhi
resolve right now, I wish that all of their Dharma
conditions will become deeper and deeper, day by
day. May their Bodhi resolve be greater day by
day. I have no other thing to offer all of you,
so I made another vow:

> *I vow that all of the present good knowing advisors,
> all the elders, and all the Dharma Masters, will
> quickly accomplish the Buddha Way.*

We who believe in Buddhism have no other wish but
the wish that we become Buddhas. I know that
everybody wishes to become a Buddha, and that no
one wants to fall into the three evil destinies.
Therefore I vow that all of you will quickly
accomplish the Buddha path!
Upasaka Ts'ao should always bring forth the
Bodhi resolve to protect and uphold the Triple

Jewel, so that the Buddha's wisdom life will not be
cut off, and the Proper Dharma will always abide
in the world. We wish the rulers of all countries
to also attain blessings, long life, and peace.
May the Bodhi of our companions and Dharma peers
grow each day; may they quickly accomplish the
Buddha path. This is my sincere hope. I hope that
all of you will recite the Great Compassion Mantra
twenty-one times on behalf of Wong Shau Ming, whom
we talked about yesterday, and that she will
recover as soon as possible. I don't have such
great power by myself. Of course, I hope she can
be cured, but I don't have great strength. Therefore I have to rely on all of you. Maybe in this
lecture hall there are transformation bodies of
Manjushri Bodhisattva, or perhaps Foremost Wisdom
Bodhisattva has already arrived. May they produce
the kindness and compassion to help Wong Shau Ming,
so that she may come out of her coma. This is
my small wish.

*****END OF CHAPTER ELEVEN--*PURE CONDUCT******

THE BUDDHIST TEXT TRANSLATION SOCIETY

CHAIRPERSON: The Venerable Tripitaka Master Hsüan Hua
                -Abbot of Gold Mountain Monastery,
                 Gold Wheel Temple, and Tathagata Monastery
                -Chancellor of Dharma Realm Buddhist
                 University
                -Professor of the Tripitaka and the Dhyanas

PRIMARY TRANSLATION COMMITTEE:

Chairpersons: Bhikshuni Heng Hsien
               Bhikshuni Heng Ch'ih

Members:

Bhikshu Heng Sure   Bhikshuni Heng Wen
Bhikshu Heng Kuan   Bhikshuni Heng Tao
Bhikshu Heng Shun   Bhikshuni Heng Jieh
Bhikshu Heng Tso   Bhikshuni Heng Ming
Bhikshu Heng Deng   Shramanerika Heng Tsai
Bhikshu Heng Kung   Shramanerika Heng Duan
Bhikshu Heng Wu   Shramanerika Heng Bin
Bhikshuni Heng Ch'ing   Shramanerika Heng Chia
Bhikshuni Heng Chü   Shramanerika Heng Liang
Bhikshuni Heng Chai   Upasaka Kuo Jung (R.B.) Epstein
Upasika Kuo Ts'an Nicholson Upasaka Kuo Li (Li-jen) Chou
Upasaka Kuo Chou Rounds   Upasika Kuo Choo Yiew

REVIEWING COMMITTEE:

Chairpersons: Bhikshu Heng Tso
               Upasaka Kuo Jung Epstein

Members:

Bhikshu Heng Sure   Bhikshuni Heng Chai
Bhikshu Heng Kuan   Bhikshuni Heng Wen
Bhikshu Heng Deng   Bhikshuni Heng Tao
Bhikshu Heng Gung   Shramanerika Heng Tsai
Bhikshu Heng Wu   Shramanerika Heng Duan
Bhikshuni Heng Hsien   Upasaka Kuo Jung Epstein
Bhikshuni Heng Ch'ih   Upasika Hsien Ping-ying
Upasika Kuo Ts'an Nicholson Upasaka Kuo Chou Rounds
Upasika Kuo Chin Vickers   Upasaka Chou Kuo Li
Upasika Phuong Kuo Wu

EDITING COMMITTEE:

Chairperson: Upasika Kuo Tsai Rounds
Advisor: Bhikshu Heng Kuan

Members:

Bhikshu Heng Sure
Bhikshu Heng Lai
Bhikshu Heng Shun
Bhikshu Heng Ch'au
Bhikshu Heng Tso
Bhikshu Heng Ch'i
Bhikshu Heng Wu
Bhikshuni Heng Hsien
Bhikshuni Heng Ch'ih
Bhikshuni Heng Ch'ing
Bhikshuni Heng Chü
Upasaka Kuo Jung Epstein
Upasaka Kuo Tsun (Randall
  Dinwiddie
Upasaka Kuo Chou Rounds
Upasika Kuo Ts'ung Dinwiddie
Upasika Kuo Lin (Nancy)
  Lethcoe

Bhikshuni Heng Chai
Bhikshuni Heng Wen
Bhikshuni Heng Tao
Bhikshuni Heng Jieh
Bhikshuni Heng Ming
Shramanera Heng Jau
Shramanerika Heng Tsai
Shramanerika Heng Duan
Shramanerika Heng Bin
Shramanerika Heng Chia
Shramanerika Heng Liang
Upasika Kuo Ts'an Nicholson
Upasaka Chou Kuo Li
Upasika Phuong Kuo Wu
Upasika Kuo Chin Vickers
Upasaka Kuo Lei Powers
Upasika Kuo Choo Yiew
Upasika Kuo Shun Nolan

CERTIFYING COMMITTEE:

Chairperson: Venerable Tripitaka Master Hsüan Hua

Members:
Bhikshu Heng Sure
Bhikshu Heng Kuan
Bhikshu Heng Tso
Bhikshuni Heng Hsien
Upasaka Wong Kuo Chün
Upasika Kuo Ts'an Nicholson

Bhikshuni Heng Ch'ih
Bhikshuni Heng Ch'ing
Bhikshuni Heng Wen
Bhikshuni Heng Tao

Upasaka Kuo Jung Epstein
Upasika Kuo Chin Vickers

CHINESE PUBLICATIONS COMMITTEE:

Chairperson: Upasaka Chou Kuo Li

Members:

Shramanerika Kuo Hua
Upasika Phuong Kuo Wu
Upasika Kuo Han Epstein

BTTS Publications

All the translation works by the Buddhist Text Translation Society are accompanied by an extensive inter-linear
commentary by the Venerable Tripitaka Master Hsuan Hua, unless otherwise noted. All works are available in softcover
only, also unless noted otherwise. ISBN Prefix: 0-917512

Sutras

Amitabha Sutra- Explains the causes and circumstances for
rebirth in the Land of Ultimate Bliss of Amitabha (Limitless
Light) Buddha. 30-6 , 204 pgs., $8. (Also Available in Span-
ish. $8.)

Dharani Sutra- This Sutra tells of the past events in the
life of the Bodhisattva of great compassion Avalokiteshvara
(Kuan Yin), and the various ways of practising the Great Compassion Mantra, and its many benefits. It is a fundamental
Secret School Method. 13-8, 352 pgs., $12.

Dharma Flower (Lotus) Sutra- In this Sutra which was spoken
in the last period of the Buddha's teaching, the Buddha pro-
claims the ultimate principles of the Dharma which unites
all previous teachings into one. When completed, the entire
Sutra will be from 15 to 20 volumes. The following are those
volumes which have been published to date:
> Volume I, Introductory Section. 16-2, 85 pgs., $3.95.
> Volume II, Introduction, Chapter One. 22-7, 324 pgs.,
> $7.95.
> Volume III, Expedient Methods, Chapter Two. 26-X,
>   183 pgs., $7.95.
> Volume IV, A Parable, Chapter Three. 62-6, 371 pgs.,
> $8.95.
> Volume V, Belief and Understanding, Chapter Four.
>   64-2, 200 pgs., $6.95.
> Volume VI, Medicinal Herbs, Chapter Five, and Confer-
>   ferring Predictions, Chapter Six. 65-0, 161 pgs.,
> $6.95.
> Volume VII, Parable of the Transformation City,
>   Chapter Seven. 250 pgs., $7.95. 67-7
> Volume VIII, Five Hundred Disciples Receive Predic-
>   tions, Chapter Eight, and Bestowing Predictions Upon
>   Those Studying and Beyond Study, Chapter Nine.
>   71-5, 160 pgs., $6.95.

Flower Adornment (Avatamsaka) Sutra, Verse Preface- A succinct
and eloquent verse commentary by T'ang Dynasty National Master Ch'ing Liang, who was the Master of seven emperors, which
gives a complete explanation of all the fundamental princi-

ples contained in the Sutra. This is the first English translation of this text. Bi-lingual edition, English and Chinese. 28-6, 244 pgs., $7.

Flower Adornment Sutra Prologue- A detailed explanation of Volume One, the First Door, the Causes and Conditions for the Arisal of the Teaching. 66-9, 252 pgs., $10.

Flower Adornment Sutra- Known as the king of kings of all Buddhist scriptures because of its great length (81 rolls containing more than 700,000 Chinese characters) and its profundity. It contains the most complete explanation of the Buddha's state and the Bodhisattva's quest for Awakening. When completed the entire Sutra-text with commentary is estimated to be from 75 to 100 volumes. The following are those volumes which have been published to date:
    Ten Grounds, Chapter 26, Part One. Contains the First Ground of Happiness, which focuses on the practice of giving. Bi-lingual edition, English and Chinese. 234 pgs., $7.
    Entering the Dharma Realm, Chapter 39. This chapter, which makes up one quarter of the entire Sutra, contains the spiritual journey of the Youth Good Wealth in his search for Ultimate Awakening.
        Part One. Describes the setting for the youth's quest, and his meeting with Manjushri Bodhisattva. 68-5, 280 pgs., $8.50.
        Part Two. In this volume Good Wealth meets his first ten teachers, who represent the positions of the Ten Dwellings. 70-7, 314 pgs., $8.50.
        Part Three. In this volume Good Wealth is taught by the ten teachers who correspond to the level of the Ten Conducts. 232 pgs., $8.50.

Heart Sutra and Verses Without a Stand- Each line in the text is accompanied by an eloquent verse by the Venerable Master Hsuan Hua, and his commentary contains an explanation of most of the fundamental Buddhist concepts. 27-8, 160 pgs., $7.50.

Shurangama Sutra- This Sutra gives the most detailed explanation of the Buddha's teachings concerning the mind. It includes an analysis of where the mind is located, an explanation of the origin of the cosmos, the specific workings of karma, a description of all the realms of existence and the fifty kinds of deviant samadhi-concentrations which can delude us in our search for Awakening.
    Volume One, The Venerable Ananda presents seven ideas on the location of the mind and the Buddha shows how each

one is incorrect, and then explains the roots of the false
and the true. 17-0, 289 pgs., $8.50.
        Volume Two. The Buddha explains individual and col-
lective karma, and reveals the true mind by showing ten different aspects of the seeing-nature. 25-1, 212 pgs., $8.50.
        Volume Three. The Buddha gives a clear description of
the qualities of all the sense-fields, their respective consciousnesses, and all of the internal and external elemental
forces of the universe. He explains how all are ultimately
unreal, neither existing through causes or arising spontaneously. 240 pgs., $8.50. 94-4
        Volume Four. In this volume the Buddha talks about
the formation of the world, the coming into being of sentient creatures, and the cycle of karmic retribution in
great detail. 200 pgs., $8.50. 95-2
        Volume Five. In this volume twenty-five sages explain
the method they used to transcend the realm of birth and
death. Of them, Manjushri Bodhisattva selects the method
used by the Bodhisattva Kuan Yin of "returning the hearing
to listen to the Self-nature" as the most appropriate for
people in our world system. 250 pgs., $8.50. 96-0

Sixth Patriarch Sutra- One of the foremost scriptures of
Ch'an (Zen) Buddhism, this text describes the life and teachings of the remarkable Patriarch of the T'ang Dynasty, Great
Master Hui Neng, who though unable to read or write, was enlightened to the true nature of all things. 33-2, 235 pgs.,
$10. Harcover, $15.

Sutra in 42 Sections- In this Sutra, which was the first to
be transported from India and translated into Chinese, the
Buddha gives the most essential instructions in cultivating
the Dharma, emphasizing the cardinal virtues of renunciation,
contentment, and patience. 15-4, 114 pgs., $4.

Sutra of the Past Vows of Earth Store Bodhisattva- This
Sutra tells how Earth Store Bodhisattva attained his position as one of the greatest Bodhisattvas, foremost in vows,
and also describes the workings of karma, how beings undergo
rebirth, and the various kinds of hells. This is the first
English translation. Hardcover only. 09-X, 235 pgs., $16.

Vajra Prajna Paramita (Diamond) Sutra- One of the most popular scriptures, the Vajra Sutra explains how the Bodhisattva
relies on the perfection of wisdom to teach and transform
beings. 02-2, 192 pgs., $8.

<u>Commentarial Literature</u>

Buddha Root Farm- A collection of lectures given during an Amitabha Buddha recitation session which explains the practice and philosophy of the Pure Land School. 11-1, 72 pgs., $4.

City of 10,000 Buddhas Recitation Handbood. Bi-lingual edition, Chinese-English. 175 pgs., $8.

Listen to Yourself, Think Everything Over- The first portion ofthis publication is instructions on how to practise the method of reciting the name of the Bodhisattva Kuan Yin. The last portion gives a very straightforward explanation of how to cultivate Ch'an meditation. All instructions were given during actual meditation sessions. 153 pgs., 24-3, $7.

Pure Land and Ch'an Dharma Talks- Instructions given during an Amitabha Buddha recitation and Ch'an meditation session. 08-1, 72 pgs., $4.

Shramanera Vinaya and Rules of Deportment- This text, by Great Master Lien Ch'ih of the Ming Dynasty, explains the moral code for novice monks. 04-9, 112 pgs., $4.

Shurangama Mantra Commentary- An ancient text explaining how to practise the foremost mantra in the Buddha's teaching, including a line-by-line analysis of the mantra. The first volume contains all the instructions on how to prepare before holding the mantra, and an explanation of the first portion of the mantra. 296 pgs., $8.50. (Bi-lingual, Chinese and English).

The Ten Dharma Realms Are Not Beyond a Single Thought- An eloquent poem on all the realms of being, which is accompanied by extensive commentarial material and drawings. 12-X, 72 pgs., $4.

<u>Biographical</u>

Records of the Life of the Venerable Master Hsuan Hua- The life and teachings of the Venerable Master from his birthplace in China to the present time in America.
     Volume One, covers the Ven. Master's life in China. 07-3, 96 pgs., $5. (Also available in Spanish. $8.)
     Volume Two, covers the events of the Master's life as he cultivated and taught in Hong Kong, containing many photos, poems, stores. 10-3, 229 pgs., $8.

Three Steps, One Bow- The daily journal of American Bhikshus
Heng Ju and Heng Yo, who in 1973-74, made a pilgrimage for
world peace from Gold Mountain Monastery in San Francisco
to Marblemount, Washington, bowing every third step.
18-9, 160 pgs., $5.95.

World Peace Gathering- A collection of instructional talks
on Buddhism commemorating the successful completion of the
bowing pilgrimage of Bhikshus Heng Ju and Heng Yo. 05-7,
128 pgs., $5.

With One Heart Bowing to the City of 10,000 Buddhas- The
moving journals of American Bhikshus Heng Sure and Heng
Ch'au, who made a "three steps, one bow" pilgrimage from
Gold Wheel Temple in Los Angeles to the City of 10,000 Buddhas, located 110 miles north of San Francisco, from May,
1977 to October, 1979.
      Volume One, May 6- June 30, 1977. 21-9, 180 pgs., $6.
      Volume Two, July 1- October 30, 1977. 23-5, 322 pgs.,
        $7.50.
      Volume Three, October 30- December 20, 1977. 154 pgs.,
        $6.
      Volume Four, December 17- January 21, 1978. 136 pgs.,
        $5.
      Volume Five, January 28- February 18, 1978. 127 pgs.,
        $5.

Open Your Eyes, Take a Look at the World- The journals of
Bhikshus Heng Sure and Heng Ch'au, and Bhikshuni Heng Tao,
written during the 1978 Asia-region visit by the Venerable
Master Hsuan Hua and other members of the Sino-American Buddhist Assn. 32-4, 347 pgs., $7.50.

Heng Ch'au's Journal- An account of the remarkable exper-
iences and changes undergone by Bhikshu Heng Ch'au, when he
first came in contact with Gold Mountain Monastery. 24 pgs.,
$1.95.

<u>Music, Novels, and Brochures</u>

Songs for Awakening- Words and music of over forty modern
American Buddhist songs, indexed according to title and first
line, with drawings, woodcuts, and photographs. The pictur-
esque 9" by 12" songbook makes a fine gift to introduce your
friends to Buddhism. 31-6, 112 pgs., $7.95.

Awakening- A 12" stereo record album of ten Buddhist songs
in Western style (all in English), ranging from pop to rock,

to folk and country. Subjects covered include: Bodhisattva
vows, the *I-Ching*, Ch'an meditation, Lao-tzu, the *Lotus
Sutra*, Abhidharma meditations, Amitabha Buddha and his Pure
Land, and more. The album includes a full lyric sheet, a
printed insert of Chinese translation, and linear notes
clarifying concepts and sources. $7. (Orders should be sent
to Wondrous Sound Music, City of 10,000 Buddhas, P.O. Box
217, Talmage, CA. 95481) Also available in casette tape.

City of 10,000 Buddhas Color Brochure- Over 30 color photos
of the scenic center for World Buddhism, along with many
poems and a brief description of its activities. 24 pgs.,
$2.

Celebresi's Journey- A novel by David Rounds describing
the events in a modern American's quest for enlightenment.
14-6, 178 pgs., $4.

Vajra Bodhi Sea- The monthly journal of orthodox Buddhism
published by the Sino-American Buddhist Association since
1970. Bi-lingual, with 24 pgs., each in Chinese and English
in an 8½" by 11" format. Single issues, $2., one year, $22,
and three years, $60. ISSN 0507-6986

<u>Postage and Handling</u>

United States: $1 for the first book and 40¢ for each addi-
tional book. All publications are sent via special fourth
class. Allow from 4 days to 2 weeks for delivery.

International: $1.25 for the first book and 75¢ for each
additional book. All publications are sent via "book rate."
We recommend that for orders of approx. 10 or more, an additional $3 per parcel of 10 books be sent for registration to
protect against loss. We are not responsible for parcels
lost in the mail.

All orders require pre-payment before they will be processed.

Send all orders to: Buddhist Text Translation Society
                      Gold Mountain Monastery
                      1731 Fifteenth St.
                      San Francisco, CA 94103, U.S.A.

The publishing and translation headquarters for the Buddhist
Text Translation Society is:

                 City of 10,000 Buddhas Box 217,
                 Talmage, CA 95481, U.S.A.

The Buddhist Text Translation Society

an affiliate of the Sino-American Buddhist Association

MARCH 1982

RECENT ADDITIONS:

BRAHMA NET SUTRA. The Buddha explains the ten major and forty-eight minor precepts of the Bodhisattva. Volume one contains the ten major precepts, and the first twenty minor precepts. First translation in the English language. Bi-lingual edition, English and Chinese. 79-0, 300 pgs., $10.00. The second volume which will complete this work will be available soon, and may be ordered in advance for $10.00.

DHARMA FLOWER SUTRA, VOL. 9, MASTERS OF THE DHARMA, CHAPTER 10, AND VISION OF THE JEWELED STUPA, CHAPTER 11. Chapter 10 explains the vast merit from upholding and propogating the Lotus Sutra, and in chapter 11, all of the many millions of·transformation bodies of Shakyamuni Buddha gather in one place so that those in the assembly could see Many Jewels Buddha who in the distant past had made a vow to appear wherever this Sutra is spoken. 85-5, 270 pgs., $9.00.

FLOWER ADORNMENT SUTRA:

> PROLGUE, VOL. 2. Explains the first part of the Second door, the Stores and Teachings In Which It Is Contained. 73-1, 280 pgs., $10.00
>
> TEN DWELLINGS, CHAPTER 15. Explains the state of the Ten Dwellings attained by the Bodhisattva. 77-4, 185 pgs., $8.00.
>
> BRAHMA CONDUCT, CHAPTER 16. Explains the meaning of the pure, Brahma practises cultivated by the Bodhisattva. 80-4, 65 pgs., $4.00.
>
> THE MERIT AND VIRTUE FROM FIRST BRINGING FORTH THE MIND, CHAPTER 17. Uses various analogies to describe the merit obtained the Bodhisattva when he first resolves his mind on becoming Enlightened, and explains his state at that time. 83-9, 200 pgs., $7.00.
>
> TEN GROUNDS, CHAPTER 26, PART 2. Covers the Bodhisattvas' Second Ground of Leaving Filth, Third Ground of Emitting Light, and the Fourth Ground of Blazing Wisdom. 74-X, 200 pgs., $8.00.
>
> ENTERING THE DHARMA REALM, CHAPTER 39, PART 4. In this volume Good Wealth meets the ten teachers who represent the Bodhisattvas on the level of the Ten Transferences. 77-4, 185 pgs., $8.00.

(OVER)

Sales & Distribution

GOLD MOUNTAIN MONASTERY
1731 Fifteen Street
San Francisco, CA 94103
U.S.A.

Tel: (415) 861-9672 or 621-5202

Translation & Publishing

CITY OF 10,000 BUDDHAS
Talmage, CA 95481
U.S.A.

Tel: (707) 462-0939

ENTERING THE DHARMA REALM, PART 5. In this volume Good
Wealth meets the six teachers who represent the first
Six Grounds. 81-2, 300 pgs., $9.00.

SHURANGAMA SUTRA, VOLUME 6. This volume includes the Buddha's
explanation of the four clear and unalterable instructions on
purity, how to establish a Bodhimandala, the wondrous functions
of the Shurangama Mantra, and the 12 categories of living beings.
200 pgs., $8.50.

SHURANGAMA MANTRA COMMENTARY, VOLUME 2. Contains an explanation
of lines number 30 to number 90 of the mantra. Bi-lingual, English and Chinese. 82-0, 200 pgs., $7.50.

WITH ONE HEART BOWING TO THE CITY OF 10,000 BUDDHAS, VOLUME 6.
Covers the period from Feb. 19, 1978 to April 2, 1978. 200 pgs.,
$6.00.

THE THREE CART PATRIARCH: A 12" stereo lp recorded by and for
children, based on the Monkey Tales of China, which features
stories, six sparkling musical productions, and many special
effects. $7.00 and $1.00 shipping in the U.S.A., and $2.00 for
international.

In addition to the City of 10,000 Buddhas, and Gold Mountain Mon-
astery, all the publications of the Buddhist Text Translation
Society are also available at Gold Wheel Temple, 1726 W. 8th St,
Los Angeles, CA 90017. Telephone: (213) 483-7497.

"With your own mind, you grasp at your own mind. What is not
illusion turns into illusion. If you don't grasp, there is no
non-illusion. If even non-illusion does not arise, how can
illusory things be established? This is called the Wonderful
Lotus Flower, the regal vajra gem of enlightenment."
(From the SHURANGAMA SUTRA)

中文佛書目錄

經典部分：

大方廣佛華嚴經疏序淺釋（漢英對照）美國萬佛城宣化上人講解，全一冊。定價美金七元。

大方廣佛華嚴經疏淺釋（平裝四冊）美國萬佛城宣化上人講解。

第一冊（第一門，教起因緣）定價美金五元。

第二冊（第二門，藏教所攝）定價美金五元。

第三冊（第三門，義理分齊。第四門，教所被機。第五門，教體淺深。第六門，宗趣通別）定價美金八元五角。

第四冊（第七門，部類品會。第八門，傳譯感通。第九門，總譯名題。第十門，別解文義）定價美金五元。

大方廣佛華嚴經淺釋（平裝八冊）美國萬佛城宣化上人講解。

第一冊（世主妙嚴品第一，卷一至卷二）定價美金七元。

第二冊（世主妙嚴品第一，卷三）定價美金五元。

第三冊（世主妙嚴品第一，卷四至卷五）定價美金七元。

第四冊（如來現相品第二。普賢三昧品第三。世界成就品第四）定價美金五元。

第五冊（華藏世界品第五。毘盧遮那品第六。如來名號品第七。四聖諦品第八）定價美金五元。

第六冊（光明覺品第九。菩薩問明品第十。淨行品第十一）定價美金七元。

第七冊（賢首品第十二。升須彌山頂品第十三。須彌頂山偈讚第十四。十住品第十五）定價美金七元。

第八冊（梵行品第十六。初發心功德品第十七。明法品第十八。升夜摩天品第十九。夜摩偈讚品第二十）定價美金五元。

大方廣佛華嚴經十地品淺釋（平裝三冊） 美國萬佛城宣化上人講解。

第一冊（第一歡喜地）（漢英對照） 定價美金七元。

第二冊（第二離垢地。第三發光地。第四燄慧地。第五難勝地） 定價美金五元。

第三冊（第六現前地。第七遠行地。第八不動地。第九善慧地。第十法雲地）定價美金六元

千手千眼大悲心陀羅尼經（全一冊） 定價美金六元。

般若波羅蜜多心經非台頌解（全一冊） 美國萬佛城宣化上人講解 定價美金五元。

楞嚴咒疏句偈解（漢英對照）（第一冊） 美國萬佛城宣化上人講解 定價美金八元五角。

梵網經講錄（漢英對照）（上冊） 慧僧法師述 定價美金十元。

梵網經講錄（漢英對照）（下冊）．定價美金八元

地藏菩薩本願經淺釋 定價美金六元五角

　　佛書部分：

永嘉大師證道歌詮釋（全一冊） 美國萬佛城宣化上人講解 定價美金二元五角。

緇門崇行錄 蓮池大師著 弘一大師集（贈閱）

宣化上人偈讚闡釋錄（全一冊） 定價美金五元

宣化禪師事蹟（全一冊） 定價美金四元。

放眼觀世界（亞洲弘法記）（全一冊） 定價美金七元五角

修行者的消息（三步一拜兩行者一心頂禮萬佛城之來鴻） 定價美金七元

佛教精進者的日記 （平裝上冊） 定價美金六元。

萬佛城聯語集（一）　定價美金四元

水鏡回天錄（全一冊）美國萬佛城宣化上人著　定價美金五元

沙彌律儀要略解（全一冊）美國萬佛城宣化上人講解　定價美金五元

楞嚴咒疏句偈解（漢英對照）（第二冊）　定價美金七元五角

宣化上人語錄　定價美金五元

即將出版：

大方廣佛華嚴經淺釋（十定品至入法界品）

大佛頂首楞嚴經淺釋

佛教精進者的日記（下冊）

總流通處：

中美佛教總會萬佛城
The Sino-American Buddhist Association, INC
Headquarters: City of Ten Thousand Buddhas, POBox 217, Talmage, CA 95481, USA.
Tel: (707) 462-0939

三藩市分會金山聖寺
San Francisco Branch: Gold Mountain Monastery
1731 15th Street, San Francisco, CA 94163
Tel: (415) 626-4204, 861-9672

三藩市國際譯經學院
The International Institute for the Translation of Buddhist Texts
3636 Washington Street, San Francisco, CA 94118
Tel: (415) 921-9570

洛杉磯分會金輪寺
Los Angeles Branch: Gold Wheel Temple
1728 W 6th St., Los Angeles.
CA 90017
Tel: (213) 483-7497

DHARMA PROTECTOR WEI T'O BODHISATTVA

南無護法韋馱尊天菩薩